The Selling of
the Babe

ALSO BY GLENN STOUT

Fenway 1912

Young Woman and the Sea

Nine Months at Ground Zero

The Selling of
the Babe

**The Deal That Changed Baseball
and Created a Legend**

GLENN STOUT

Thomas Dunne Books
St. Martin's Press
New York

THOMAS DUNNE BOOKS.
An imprint of St. Martin's Press.

THE SELLING OF THE BABE. Copyright © 2016 by Glenn Stout. All rights
reserved. Printed in the United States of America. For information, address
St. Martin's Press, 175 Fifth Avenue, New York, N.Y. 10010.

Title page: Babe Ruth with the Red Sox at Fenway Park, 1919.
George Grantham Bain Collection, Library of Congress
Prints and Photographs Division.

www.thomasdunnebooks.com
www.stmartins.com

The Library of Congress Cataloging-in-Publication Data is
available upon request.

ISBN 978-1-250-06431-8 (hardcover)
ISBN 978-1-4668-7000-0 (e-book)

Our books may be purchased in bulk for promotional, educational, or business
use. Please contact your local bookseller or the Macmillan Corporate and
Premium Sales Department at (800) 221-7945, extension 5442, or by
e-mail at MacmillanSpecialMarkets@macmillan.com.

First Edition: March 2016

10 9 8 7 6 5 4 3 2 1

Contents

The Selling of the Babe

Introduction

Babe Ruth is arguably the biggest figure in baseball history, the
one player who, since he first stepped on a major league diamond just over
one hundred years ago, has cast a deep and still lengthening shadow over
all things baseball, both its most cherished icon and one of its most transformative figures.

Nothing has ever damaged or cheapened his legacy. Somehow, the more
we learn about Ruth, even of his colorful and occasionally unsavory personal history, he is never diminished. Even those who have since challenged
his records or even broken them fail to touch him. In comparison, their
deeds seem smaller, while Ruth's achievements, given his era, become even
more impressive. He did not just break records—he created records where
none existed before, for feats never imagined, for doing what no one thought
possible.

In a very real way, Ruth took a two-dimensional game, baseball, and gave it
two additional dimensions, first by lifting it from the ground and launching
it into the air, and secondly by giving baseball its history, by creating space
in the game for history to live apart from the present, and for a limitless
future to seem possible. He is the figure who took baseball from its distant, daguerreotyped past and made it into the game we still see on the
field today. As much as any other figure in the game, he is both a pioneer
and an enduring presence.

Yet at the same time, Ruth is also elusive. Perhaps no other personality
in sports has been so exalted, mythologized, and obscured by history. Ruth's
public persona, certainly by the time he made it to New York in 1920, and
even for several years prior to that, has always been presented through a
filter, a ghostwritten sieve that sought to smooth his rough edges, cloud his

true behavior, and simplify his biography. There are thousands upon thousands of words credited to Ruth's lips, but to paraphrase Yogi Berra, Ruth himself never said most of the things he said, and to pretend otherwise is to present a false portrait. His ghostwriters did his talking for him, his various autobiographies and columns under his own name written by others without any input on his part. Fortunately, in regard to Ruth, it is not so much what he said that intrigues us, but what he did, and how he did what he did, that is most captivating. This book focuses on the latter, rather than trying to parse through Ruth's "statements," to determine which are his and which are the words of others. How George Ruth became "the Babe" is the essential question we try to answer.

But there is one thing that, even today, has towered over Ruth himself, something he himself created that nevertheless has cast a shadow over him, one so deep and so dark that at times it is barely even possible to discern the mighty Babe—or at least impossible to seem him clearly. Even Ruth is subservient to something more: the home run. Baseball's biggest hit, perhaps sports' most dramatic and instantaneous event, as first propagated by Ruth, became the most significant outcome in the game. Almost every other American sport has adopted the home run as a descriptive metaphor, "going for the home run," as both the ultimate risk and the ultimate reward.

Yet the home run wasn't always there, at least not in the way it was when unveiled by Ruth. Although the home run has been a possibility since the very beginning of the game, for decades it was a rare and almost accidental occurrence, a happy accident no one would dare actually try to accomplish. Outfield fences were meant to keep crowds off the field, not to keep the baseball in, for the notion of hitting a ball over the outfield fence was, in most instances, absurd, the fences too distant and the ball too soft.

And then came Ruth, the catalyst during a unique time and set of conditions, when baseball was moribund and war was changing America faster than any time before or since. Without warning, suddenly and unexpectedly, the home run became baseball's most exciting and defining moment, disruptive, inspiring a profound change in the way the game was played and viewed and written about, dramatically impacting players and fans, leaving no one untouched. Even today, young boys still dream of being Ruth, and his story still touches them in a way no other ballplayer's does.

No one was more affected by the home run than Ruth himself. He was like a new species overrunning the environment and remaking the land-scape. The home run at once both created him and defined him, making it almost impossible to extract Ruth from it, to view him separately, to see him clearly before that moment, even at a time when the home run had yet to determine the course of his life, or the course of baseball. The home run has rendered the earlier figure of Ruth almost invisible, so overwhelming that it has distorted his biography ever since.

Nowhere is this more true than during the transition, during those few brief months from the beginning of the 1918 season through 1920, when Ruth evolved from George Herman Ruth, a pitcher of considerable ability for the Boston Red Sox, to the Babe, the Yankees' mighty Bambino, a leg-endary and almost mythic Colossus of the game, the greatest home run hitter of all time, which according to a new definition, also made him the greatest player of all time. This makeover was so thorough, so complete, that it has been almost impossible to see Ruth in any other context, to sepa-rate the man and the player before the home run from what the home run turned him into: the Babe, the unbridled King of Swat. Previous bio-graphers have usually become so enthralled with the results of this trans-formation, so blinded by the white heat of the home run, that the precise details of the change have almost been entirely overlooked. The sale of Ruth from Boston to New York is almost inevitably viewed with the kind of hindsight reality does not provide, leaving Ruth's evolution during this time period, essential to understanding the dynamics of the sale, virtually unexamined.

That is what this book does. By examining the selling of the Babe as both a historic event in real time and as a historical metaphor at this moment of change, when Ruth and the home run—together—changed everything, *The Selling of the Babe* explains why and how this happened, and why and how the figure of the Babe came to be. In these pages we learn what became of George Herman Ruth, precisely why he was sold by the Red Sox to the Yankees, and how an entirely new game, built around the home run, with Babe Ruth as the catalyst, was sold to the American public.

It remains the most important transaction in the history of the game, touching everything, even today.

Prologue:
September 11, 1918

In the eighth inning of the sixth and final game of the 1918 World Series between the Boston Red Sox and the Chicago Cubs, with the Red Sox nursing a 2–1 lead and only six outs away from their fourth world championship in seven seasons, the Cubs' Turner Barber cracked a short line drive to left.

Boston's left fielder, playing shallow, tore in. As the ball sank toward a base hit, he did not hesitate. Instead of playing it safe, he lunged, left his feet, and stretched out for the ball. Bare inches from the turf, he gathered it in two hands, landed heavily, then tumbled, somersaulting over the rough ground, the worn, gray ball still tight in his glove.

Barber, visions of heroic headlines evaporating, kicked the dirt and turned toward the Cubs dugout. The crowd at Fenway Park shot to its feet, all 15,238 souls roaring and cheering, slapping each other's backs and holding their heads in wonder. He had done it AGAIN. The outfielder rose, threw the ball softly back in to the shortstop, then, grimacing, did not bask in the applause or tip his cap, but twisted his head back and forth and rolled his shoulders as he slowly walked back to his position.

The delay only increased their ardor. For a full three minutes, the crowd cheered as the outfielder tried to shake off the effects of his tumble, bending to clutch his knees and trying to stretch out his neck and upper back. He continued to flex and bend in between pitches as Boston hurler Carl Mays set down the next hitter, but he could not continue and would not risk remaining in the game and maybe costing his team a win, and perhaps even the World Series. He was not that kind of player.

He waved toward the bench and when the umpire held up his hand and called time, started trotting in. The crowd noticed and with each step more of them stood and applauded again, this time with the respect and admiration accorded to a hero. He had been the unabashed star of the Series, his timely hitting—moving runners along, then taking an extra base—sparking several Boston rallies and his glove squelching several Cub comebacks. His selfless removal of himself from the game underscored his contribution; this was a team victory, and here was a man who thought only of his team, and not of himself.

As he approached the Boston bench and manager Ed Barrow rose to greet him, he gave a brief nod to his replacement. Then George Whiteman entered the dugout to the cautious but warm embrace of his fellow Red Sox.

As Whiteman sat heavily on the bench and Boston's trainer attended to him, a teammate, almost unnoticed, grabbed his glove and bounded up the dugout steps to take his place, running heavily out to left field.

George Herman Ruth had already pitched, and won, two games in the Series, but apart from a few innings as a defensive replacement, had not appeared in the lineup of the other three Series contests, something that had surprised observers at first but also something that Whiteman's spectacular play throughout the Series rendered moot. For much of the year, with rosters reduced due to the American entry into the Great War, Ruth, out of necessity, had sometimes played outfield, usually Fenway Park's short left field, where the earthen embankment known as Duffy's Cliff and the wall behind it kept spectators from peering in from atop the garage across the street and left the emergency, part-time outfielder little room to cover. As manager Ed Barrow went with the hot hand, Ruth had more or less split time in left with Whiteman, a thirty-five-year-old career minor leaguer playing his first full year in the major leagues. For much of the season, Ruth had hit far better than anyone expected—in stretches, he seemed like one of the best hitters in the league, and led all baseball with 11 home runs. But he had only hit well in spurts, and over the final weeks of the season he had struggled, particularly against left-handed pitching, leading Barrow to decide to stick with the right-handed bat of Whiteman in the Series against Chicago's predominantly left-handed pitching staff.

It was an act of genius. No one realized it yet, but the 1918 World Series was the last quiet gasp of the Dead Ball Era, the lowest-scoring World Series in history, as both teams tried to scratch out runs through a combination of seeing-eye ground balls, short flares, bunts, stolen bases, and hit-and-run plays, punctuated by the rare long hit that rolled between out-fielders to the distant fence. The baseball itself, the dead ball, made even deader by the use of inferior wool wrapping and horsehide due to the war, made scoring a premium. Only 19 runners would cross the plate in the six-game Series, neither team scoring more than three runs in any one game, and every man on either team who took the mound during the Series pitched well. It would prove to be the last World Series in history in which no one on either team struck a home run.

The lack of scoring, combined with the distraction of the war and some political misplays by the men who ran baseball, left fans less than enthusiastic. Attendance in the Series had been poor, and on this day, Fenway Park was barely half full for what would prove to be the finale, and the last world championship the Red Sox would win in eighty-six long and frustrating years.

Only George Whiteman had made it seem worthwhile. As veteran baseball writer Paul Shannon wrote in the *Boston Post*, "In nearly every run the Red Sox scored in the six games, Whiteman, the little Texan veteran, has figured mightily." Fans identified with the stocky minor leaguer finally getting his chance to play, the ultimate Everyman underdog, only receiving the opportunity because the real heroes were buried in the mud of a trench somewhere in France. After the Series, Whiteman's face would grace the cover of *Baseball Magazine*, which asked the question "Hero of the Series?????" In his ghostwritten account of the Series, Ty Cobb, the game's greatest star, would answer that he was.

Ruth? Oh, he played well, too, when he played. Pitching a shutout in Game 1 and then collecting a second victory in Game 4, albeit with relief help after he took the mound with his finger swollen to nearly twice its size due to some mysterious altercation on the train from Chicago to Boston, one that put his fist into contact with either a solid steel wall, a window, or the jaw of another passenger. Although he still set a new record for consecutive scoreless innings pitched in the World Series at 29, one that would grow in stature over the years, it went almost unnoticed at the time.

As George Whiteman left the field that gray afternoon, the spotlight shone only on him, the unabashed star of the Series. Hell, hardly anyone even noticed that Ruth had entered the game. He was upstaged, a bit player in Red Sox owner Harry Frazee's latest baseball production, standing in for the star as the curtain fell.

It would be the last time.

Whiteman's catch left the Cubs with the knowledge this was not their year and they went out quickly. Boston followed, and in the bottom of the ninth, Mays, the submariner and Boston's best pitcher in 1918, retired Max Flack on a foul. Then Charlie Hollocher lofted an easy fly to Ruth for the second out. For many fans, it was the first time they noticed he was even in the game.

The crowd stood to witness the final out as Ruth stood before Duffy's Cliff and watched the Cub's Leslie Mann bounce a lazy grounder to second base. Forty-year-old Dave Shean, another wartime fill-in, fielded the ball cleanly and flipped to first. Stuffy McInnis, foot on the bag, caught the ball with both hands and the Series was over, Boston winning four games to the Cubs' two.

Another quick cheer rose from the stands, and a few strands of confetti and torn newspapers floated through the air. As the Sox ran in, the other Boston players trotted from the dugout to congratulate each other, but as celebrations went, particularly in Boston, it was muted, more handshakes and hurrahs than screams of joy and dancing in the street.

Although the Red Sox won the World Series, the endless war in Europe, an emerging outbreak of Spanish influenza, an abortive player strike that delayed Game 5 and caused fans to heckle the players with calls of "Bolsheveki!" combined with chesslike play had kept the crowd down and interest in the Series low. Even the Royal Rooters, Boston's famous group of rabid fans that had followed professional baseball in Boston for nearly three decades, failed to make their usual appearance. After the final out, there was not so much a celebration as a collective sigh of relief that the most trying season in memory was finally over.

About the only player already looking forward to the 1919 season was Ruth. He raced in from left, clutching his mitt in his gigantic hands, ready for a party whether his teammates wanted one or not. While the 1918 season had been something of a disaster for most of baseball (and, despite their victory, even for the Red Sox), Ruth had a great time anyway. Hell, he almost always did.

He might have been a forgotten man at the end of the 1918 season, upstaged by a minor leaguer who would never play another inning of major league baseball. But never again. Over the next two years, the twenty-three-year-old pitcher many newspapers still referred to as George would thoroughly transform himself, the fortunes of two teams, and, most importantly, the game of baseball itself, ushering the sport into the modern era. Ruth, whom the papers had started calling by his nickname, "Babe," often still placing it in quotation marks, would become THE BABE, the greatest name in the game and the most dominant figure in American sports.

He sprinted to the infield as if he already knew it, as if it was already Opening Day, as if he already could see what lay head.

He couldn't wait.

1

George Herman Ruth

"I saw a man transformed from a human being into something pretty close to a god."
—*Red Sox outfielder Harry Hooper*

When George Ruth arrived at Boston's South Station to catch a train to spring training in Hot Springs, Arkansas, on March 9, 1918, he carried two large bags, a set of left-handed golf clubs, and a smile that covered most of his cartoonish face from ear to ear. After spending much of the winter with his wife, Helen, at their farm in Sudbury, Massachusetts (called "Home Plate"), the notion of a month in Hot Springs almost made the long wait worthwhile. Oh, he looked forward to playing ball again, and a little golf and soaking in the steaming natural mineral baths, but it was every-thing else in Hot Springs that he really relished: the whores and the card games, the booze and the dance halls and the food. "Spring training" itself would consist of a little more than some long hikes and a few hours of fool-ing around on a ballfield each day—hell, the players didn't even get paid to do that. That left plenty of time for everything else, which was one of the reasons ball clubs tended to go to places like Hot Springs or Tampa or other resort and vacation towns for spring training. They needed the nice weather, sure, but they also needed to entice the players to show up on time and stay reasonably happy while they were there. You couldn't play baseball all the time.

Ruth had plenty of reasons to smile, anyway. By the end of the 1917 season, at age twenty-two, he was arguably the best pitcher in baseball. And if he was not, he was close to the top of a very short list, one that included the Senators' Walter Johnson, Grover Cleveland "Pete" Alexander of the Phillies, and perhaps one or two others—White Sox knuckleballer Eddie Cicotte, or perhaps the Indians' Stan Coveleski. But there is no question that Ruth was the best young pitcher in baseball, and it wasn't even close.

In a little more than three full seasons in the major leagues he had already won 67 games—18 in 1915, when the existence of the Federal League diluted major league talent, making it an ideal time for a young pitcher like Ruth to break in and, significantly, learn to pitch against diminished competition, 23 in 1916, and another 24 in 1917. Moreover, he had helped Boston win the world championships in 1915 and 1916, collecting a legendary 14-inning, 2–1 victory in the 1916 World Series, giving up a first inning inside-the-park home run and thereafter tossing a shutout. And even though the Red Sox had missed out on the pennant by nine games in 1917, finishing second behind the White Sox, after three full big league seasons Ruth's performance finally earned him a big contract—$5,000, a $3,000 raise over what he had made in 1917. He would start collecting it as soon as the season started.

The young boys who gathered at South Station to catch a glimpse of Ruth before he left and their fathers who trudged to work every morning and passed around the newspapers during lunch break knew all that. But that wasn't what made Ruth interesting.

What did was everything that didn't make the papers and what wasn't told through statistics. He just wasn't like other players; he was an evolutionary leap. At six-two and more than 200 pounds, he was a giant at a time when the average American infantryman in the Great War stood only five-six or five-seven and weighed barely 140 pounds—for the time, Ruth was the equivalent of a man six-six or six-seven today, and strong beyond measure. Players any larger than Ruth, such as former Boston catcher Larry McLean, six-five, or the Browns' six-six Dick Davenport, were routinely referred to as "giants," and few clubs counted more than a player or two much above six feet. Although ballplayers tended to be bigger than the average American, Ruth still stood out. He was not only tall, but both rangy and barrel-chested, with massive forearms and thick wrists. One writer noted, "he bends things of metal in his hand as if they were switches and has a hand grip that crushes."

He was hard not to notice, drawing attention even when he wasn't trying to do so. Neighborhood boys shagging flies when Ruth took batting practice in Fenway Park before the games saw someone swinging a bat like no one else. He didn't push at the ball like most other hitters. They swung as if afraid of missing, their hands held apart for better bat control, and took a controlled, level swing, parallel to the ground, designed simply to make contact and slap ground balls or line drives between fielders. Ruth *attacked* the ball, swinging a baseball bat almost like a lumberjack wielding an ax, but loose and free with a pronounced uppercut, gripping it at the end, wrapping it around his neck before he swung, and then just *unloading*, swinging as hard as he could, the momentum of his swing causing him to twist and spin into the ground, almost toppling over.

And that was when he missed. When he connected—and in batting practice, he did far more often than he ever did during the games—the ball soared through the air and over the boys' heads deep into the outfield, sometimes even into the right field bleachers. While the fence in right at Fenway was only a bit more than 300 feet down the line, the bleachers, in what would now be termed the power alleys, were nearly 400 feet away. When it did, the crack of the bat was soon followed by the sound of the ball striking the pine benches, echoing through the park like two rifles shot in rapid succession. Moreover, Ruth actually tried to hit the ball over the fence, not stepping into the ball as much as leaning away and pulling his arms and hand through the strike zone so he didn't just make contact with a pitch, but so it hit the bat in a specific place, down toward the end. When it did, when he timed if just right . . . well, the ball took off and there was no other feeling like it in the world. For both Ruth and his fans, it was almost orgasmic.

He didn't even use the same bat as other players. Most favored maple or hickory cudgels that weighed up to 40 ounces or so, thick in the handle, with barely any taper toward a heavy barrel. Ruth's bat was even heavier in weight, usually 44 ounces or 46, and in practice sometimes more than 50. But over time he began to shave and sand the handle down like the fungo bats coaches used to hit fly balls in practice. His hands made it seem even thinner, and he whipped the bat through the strike zone in a blur.

As he took batting practice, Ruth's coaches and teammates just shook their heads and rolled their eyes. You couldn't hit like that; everybody knew it. But since Ruth was a pitcher—and something of an incorrigible pitcher at that—they let him be. They had all learned that it was often easier to let Ruth do what he wanted than to hover over him like a schoolmarm. When he didn't get his way, he'd mope and moan around the ballpark and be a bother to everyone. It was easier just to let him have his fun. Besides, if they needed him to drop a bunt or hit behind the runner, he could do that when asked. There was no harm in letting him fool around, and every once in a while, even in a game, he'd connect with one, and even if it didn't clear the fence, it often carried so high into the sky it almost disappeared. The fans seemed to like that, and you could hear the gasps of wonder well up from the stands.

No one yet realized it, but Ruth's swing was revolutionary. The uppercut not only put the ball into the air, but as hard as Ruth swung, into the air for a long, long way. Moreover, the angle of his swing nearly matched the downward drop of the pitch toward the plate, meaning that Ruth's bat stayed in the hitting zone for a longer time than that of other hitters. That's just common sense, but baseball tradition and common sense have long been at odds as much as the game's history has been to its myths.

Yet even more drew the boys to Ruth. His personality was as compelling as his performance. He didn't keep them distant like the other players, spit tobacco on their shoes, brush them off, or lecture them like a teacher or a cop on the corner. His persona was as oversized as his physical dimensions. He laughed and joked and used language they didn't dare use around their own parents. He tossed them baseballs and nickels and took them out for ice cream and roughed their heads and let them follow him down the street. He seemed to enjoy all the things boys enjoyed as much as they did.

He was no less fascinating to their parents—fathers and mothers. In the neighborhoods near the ballpark, the Fenway, Governor's Square (now Kenmore), the South End, and Roxbury, Ruth was a familiar face—and so were the bottoms of his feet after he had too much to drink. His exploits were already legendary.

Although he had the Sudbury farm, during the regular season Ruth rarely hung his hat there. When he first arrived in Boston, he stayed in a hotel, but he soon moved to an apartment and by 1918 was living at 680 Commonwealth Avenue, the current location of Boston University's Warren Towers, a short walk from Fenway Park. Years later, his Yankees teammate Ping Bodie remarked, "I don't room with him. I room with his suitcase." Well, that was already true in Boston and the speaker could have been Ruth's young wife, Helen, the teenaged South Boston waitress Ruth met and married soon after making his first appearance in a Red Sox uniform in 1914 (a woman his teammates later speculated might have been Ruth's first sexual experience—at least the first he didn't pay for). Yet it wasn't long before Ruth discovered the privileges of being a professional athlete: not only were the drinks and meals free, so were the women. And even Puritan Boston offered more than its share of that. After all, Boston was a port of call and the "girls of Boston" were mentioned in more than one sea shanty.

The nearby South End already had a reputation as one of the most liquid neighborhoods in the country, with a bar on virtually every corner. The neighborhood popping up around the ballpark, the Fenway, already had a well-deserved reputation as a red-light district, one that lasted into the 1980s—Batavia Street became so notorious the city later renamed it the more sedate Symphony Road. Although many of Boston's larger cultural institutions, such as the Opera House and the Museum of Fine Arts, were only a few blocks away on Huntington Avenue, it was always tempting to take a turn off Massachusetts Avenue and stray into the darker thorough-fares, where in many local establishments the line between bar and brothel was notoriously thin. Ruth not only crossed that line but also tripped over it and virtually passed out on it on a regular basis. Bill Carrigan, Ruth's first manager in Boston, even found it necessary to pay Ruth on a per diem basis, or else he'd run out of money only a few days after cashing his check. Finding Ruth after a bender—usually sleeping it off somewhere, often in the back alley behind a brothel, his pockets turned inside out—became something of a pastime for his teammates. Stories of Ruth's nighttime es-capades were well known among Boston working men . . . and some of their wives.

Every woman he saw was as tempting a challenge as a fastball over the heart of the plate, and Ruth's advances were often as crude and direct as his approach at the plate. Married or single, beautiful or plain, it mattered little to him. Plenty accepted his advances, finding his unpolished approach almost irresistible. Besides, after the United States entered World War I on April 6, 1917, an awful lot of young husbands had boarded troopships for France, leaving an awful lot of young wives in need of companionship and eager for a night of fun. With the average yearly household income of less than $1,000, Ruth's wallet, combined with his celebrity, made him immensely popular. While Johnny was fighting the Hun, Ruth kept the home fires a blushing, randy red.

Regardless, with Ruth, almost everyone looked the other way. The basics of his biography were well known and it was hard to feel anything but sympathy toward him. Born in Baltimore to George Ruth, an American saloonkeeper of German Catholic heritage, and his sickly wife, Kate, George Jr. was born on February 6, 1895, one of eight children. But in those poverty-stricken times, all but two of the eight children, George and his sister, Katherine, died as infants.

Almost abandoned from the start by his father, who worked long hours, and mother, who was in near constant mourning and ill health, Ruth ran the streets around the Baltimore waterfront as a boy and rarely went to school. Eventually he was sent to St. Mary's Industrial School for Boys, a church-sponsored institution for orphans, incorrigibles, boys abandoned, and those whose parents were just too poor or too overwhelmed to care for them. After first entering St. Mary's in 1902, Ruth spent much of the next twelve years under the watchful eyes and forceful hand of the Xaverian Brothers who ran the institution, learning to be a shirtmaker and playing sports in whatever free time he had. He was particularly impressed by Brother Matthias and Brother Hermann, both of whom took a particular interest in him and both of whom enthralled the boy with their prowess at hitting a baseball. Matthias, in particular, made a lasting impression by hitting one-handed fungoes far over their heads.

The game saved Ruth. Bigger than the other boys, and better coordinated, he excelled as a pitcher, making his mark first pitching against other area schools and institutions. He eventually caught the eye of Jack Dunn, owner and manager of the minor league Baltimore Orioles, who more or less purchased his emancipation in 1914 at age nineteen (Ruth and everyone else thought he was only eighteen at the time) and took him from St. Mary's directly into professional baseball, where he split time between Baltimore and Providence in the International League and won 22 games in his first professional season, even making a few appearances in the majors for Boston.

Ruth's crude talent was undeniable, as was his naïveté of the ways of the adult world. He still acted like the hard-to-handle boy and spent his first-ever paycheck on every boy's dream, a bicycle. A year later, in 1915, despite lacking the education, social graces, and the manners of his fellow ballplayers, Ruth's talent brought him to the major leagues for good. By the end of his rookie year he was well on his way to becoming a star, and someone who had already learned the greatest lesson of his life—talent on the field forgave many sins and allowed him to indulge in behaviors that got regular fellows in trouble.

It was almost impossible not to like him. In turn, he could be funny, crude, rude, and tempestuous, but he was so unware, so guileless, so clueless that he was doing anything wrong that it was hard to assign him any blame. He just did what he wanted, impulsively, whether it was take a bite from another fellow's sandwich, use his roommate's toothbrush, or let out an enormous belch. And, let's face it, most of those who kept his company not only admired his talent but, if not his personal hygiene, his freewheeling, carefree attitude. Ruth lived for today—well, at least for the next ten minutes, and rarely gave the rest of it a thought. He did the things everyone else wanted to do but were stopped by either their conscience or their breeding.

An anonymous sportswriter in the *Boston Post* likely had all that in mind when he wrote before the start of spring training that "Ruth's power as a turnstile clicker is well-known. . . . The Baltimore boy is a trifle temperamental. He does things in a 'different' manner from most ballplayers, He has a walk all his own. He has a way of talking all his own. When he comes to bat the outfielders drop back to the far barriers . . . he is the type over which the small boy and the tired businessman go wild."

Yet by the start of the 1918 season, Ruth was still something of a local phenomenon, easily Boston's most popular player, but not yet a baseball figure on par with guys like the Tiger's Ty Cobb, the Indians' Tris Speaker, or the White Sox' Joe Jackson. Unless your name was Walter Johnson, the Washington Senators pitcher whose fastball made him stand out, or Christy Mathewson, the New York Giants star nearing the tail end of his career, pitchers, playing only every four or five days, generally didn't fill the seats. That was about to change—sort of.

Ruth was the only active player to embark from Boston that morning, joined by a few club officials and a contingent of Boston sportswriters and newspaper cartoonists nearly as eager to flee their families as he was. The train had barely left South Station before Ruth was already in his element. He discovered that he shared the train with a group of soldiers from Camp Devens, free on a weekend pass, and the party got under way.

At nearly every stop, it increased. Red Sox principal owner Harry Frazee and his new manager, Ed Barrow, chugged up the Hudson from New York and joined the train in Albany, and as the entourage wound its way westward through Buffalo and Akron for St. Louis, where it turned south, at every stop they were joined by more recruits and more soldiers, most ready to have a good time.

Ruth loved it. To him, even after several big league seasons, a train ride was still a grand adventure. The card games and cigar smoking went on almost nonstop, punctuated by repeated trips to the dining car and a steady stream of new passengers in awe of traveling in the company of Ruth and a growing group of ballplayers, guys whose names they'd seen in the papers. By the time the train reached Hot Springs just after noon on March 11, Ruth, in a sense, was already in midseason form, having entertained the press, shared more than a flask or two with his fans, and dropped a bundle at the card table with his teammates. Already, Barrow found it wise to impose a 10-cent limit on card games between players, just to keep the conflict down.

That was a real worry. Ruth loved to gamble but didn't really seem to get the concept that he was supposed to win. According to Harry Hooper, during an earlier spring visit to Hot Springs, Ruth had gambled away the bulk of his season's pay in only a few weeks.

Yet Barrow had other reasons to be concerned. Not only did the new manager need to get to know the players on his new team, they needed to get to know each other and he needed a refresher course himself in running a ball club, something he had not done at the major league level in more than a decade. After winning a world championship in 1916 and finishing in second place in 1917, by the spring of 1918 the Red Sox were an entirely different team.

That wasn't entirely of their own making. The United States entered the Great War on April 6, 1917, woefully unprepared militarily. Government officials naively believed that upon a declaration of war patriotic young Americans would storm military recruiting offices to sign up, and set a target of a million recruits. Six weeks later, after only 73,000 volunteers had signed up, President Woodrow Wilson accepted the recommendation from Secretary of War Newton Baker to put forward a bill authorizing a draft for men between the ages of twenty-one and thirty-one.

It didn't become law until May 18, and even then, those affected had another three weeks to register. When they did, it still took the nation's military months to get up to speed—early recruits drilled using sticks as often as guns and the American military was still primarily a horse-driven operation. Initially, the draft affected only those young men who were unmarried and with no dependents. As such, the war barely affected major league baseball in 1917. As a married man, Ruth was exempt, and a scant few players were stirred by patriotism to enlist. Only a handful lost any significant time to the service—a great many more found it convenient to take a bride. The White Sox boat-raced Boston by nine games in 1917 to take the American League pennant, and then swamped the Giants in six games to become world champs. But not all was smooth sailing in the baseball world.

The war made most of the men who owned major league teams nervous. In 1914 and 1915 baseball had a faced a challenge from a new league, the Federal League, which raided it of players and in some cities went head-to-head with existing franchises. Although the league failed, for two seasons fans had three leagues to choose from, and in many cities, multiple teams, which had simultaneously hurt attendance and caused salaries to escalate as teams outbid one another for the best talent, leaving teams hurting. And while many observers expected the war to end within a few months of America's entry—Boston owner Harry Frazee claimed to have placed a four-figure bet on just that—the Axis powers dug in and by the 1917 World Series it was clear the United States was in for a protracted period of involvement. Although attendance was nominally up for the year, and salaries were down, most clubs were still recovering from the financial hit of the clash with the Federal League, had little cash to spare, and the war left them edgy. According to *New York Sun* sportswriter Joe Vila, writing in *The Sporting News*, only six of seventeen teams made money in 1917. Fortunately, the Red Sox were among them.

Still, no one was quite sure how the war would affect the game in 1918. At the time, under the National Agreement between the two leagues that determined how baseball was governed, the game was ruled by a three-member National Commission that included the president of each league, and a chairman. In 1918, the commission consisted of John Tener, former professional ballplayer, banker, and governor of Pennsylvania, August Herr-mann, the chairman and president of the Cincinnati Reds, and Ban John-son, the founder and president of the American League.

In theory, the three-man commission ruled by consensus, or lacking that, a majority, but in most matters only one vote and one opinion counted: Ban Johnson's. After studying law and working for a newspaper, the young Johnson was a savvy businessman, acute organizer, and ambitious. In 1893 he had been president of a minor league, the Midwest-based Western League. In 1899, when the National League, the only existing major league at the time, decided to drop a few franchises, Johnson made his move, trans-ferring several teams into what had previously been National League towns, renaming his circuit the American League, and undercutting ticket prices.

The new league was a financial success, and one year later Johnson de-clared that it, too, was a major league and began raiding National League franchises. The AL proved to be so successful that the NL was eventually forced to make Johnson a partner, operating under the National Agree-ment, which installed the three-man National Commission as the sport's ruling body. A strong personality, Johnson slowly took command, becom-ing the most powerful person in the game. And although he had started out as something of a reformer, setting up his American League as a cleaner and more wholesome version of baseball than that played in the National League, as his wealth and power increased, so did his increasingly pomp-ous, hard-drinking management style.

By 1918, Johnson considered the game his, and as a member of the National Commission he had the means to act on his impulses. Increas-ingly, he acted with impunity, playing favorites among the owners, bullying those who tried to resist him, telling everyone what to do and how to do it as power corrupted his rule. Those who referred to him as a czar and a despot were close to the mark.

After the federal government instituted the draft, Johnson, as unable to see past his own self-interest as he was to see his shoes due to his massive belly, put in a request to the War Department that each team be allowed to exempt eighteen players from service. The proposal got him laughed out of Washington as hopelessly out of touch and put ballplayers everywhere under the bull's-eye of local draft boards. All the request did was make an already uncertain situation even more tenuous, and cause the public to view ballplayers as slackers desperate to avoid serving their country. It was a public relations disaster, one that would eventually put the whole season at risk.

Of all the club owners in the game, perhaps none was as affected as fifty-five-year-old Philadelphia A's owner and manager Connie Mack. Mack, who had already been in the game for more than thirty years, including nearly twenty as a magnate, had already weathered several financial storms. Now he saw war and decided to hunker down in his own trenches, try to save as much money as possible, and wait it out. He had already sold off many of his players during the Federal League war and decided he would sit out this one, too. Most fellow owners came to the same conclusion.

Not Harry Frazee. The Boston owner did things his way.

Who was Harry Frazee? Even today, it depends on who you ask and how much they've cared to examine the question. For years, Frazee was considered the unqualified villain in the sale of Ruth, a man sportswriter Fred Lieb dubbed an "evil genie," and charged with raping the Red Sox even as Lieb asked for free tickets to the plays Frazee produced. In baseball history, the theatrical portion of Frazee's biography was widely dismissed as inconsequential and consistently ignored. Yet in the world of musical theater, where his ownership of the Red Sox was seen as an interesting yet rather insignificant sidelight, Frazee was considered something of a forgotten genius, a visionary and a pioneer.

Neither characterization is wholly accurate, wholly false, or complete. To separate Frazee the theatrical entrepreneur from Frazee the baseball magnate is to fail to view him in his full dimension and complexity, and to lose sight of a human being in favor of a historical caricature.

To put it mildly, Harry Frazee was nothing like most of the other men who owned baseball teams. They were black-and-white, with all the person-ality of a tinted tin portrait. Frazee was all garish color and traveled with his own orchestra making up the sound track. In more modern terms, he was as brash as Bill Veeck, as outspoken as Mark Cuban, and as independent as Al Davis. And Ban Johnson hated him.

Everything the other owners were, who almost without fail were long-time baseball men who had been in the game for years, moneyed friends of Johnson, or both, Frazee was not. Johnson represented baseball's con-servative hierarchy that sought to preserve their little fiefdom with as little interference as possible; it was a dirty little secret for instance, that John-son owned part of several American League clubs, and that he often arranged "trades" between teams that weren't necessarily equitable, but helped both his bank account and those owners he favored. It smacked of "syndicate baseball," the holding of a financial interest in multiple clubs by a single individual. In the 1890s that had caused National League fans, rightfully, to question the integrity of the game. This was little different. In a sense, over time the American League became Johnson's own private fantasy league. In the end, he always won and everyone involved knew enough not to complain very hard about the arrangement.

From the start, Frazee was a threat, not in terms of trying to seize John-son's power for himself, but in exposing it. A native of Peoria, Illinois, Frazee, born in 1880, got his start sweeping up a theater as a boy, learning the business from the bottom up a self-made man in every way possible. Like every other boy at the time, he also played some baseball on his school team, where he was a teammate with Harry Bay, later an outfielder with Cincinnati and Cleveland.

At age sixteen, he left home, determined to find his place in the world, and became the business manager of the Peoria Theatre, which meant he probably did everything there was to do but sing and dance. When a show came through town and the advance agent backed out, Frazee took over, going on the road ahead of the production, booking theaters, drumming up publicity, and meeting everybody who was anybody in the theater world all across the Midwest.

He was only nineteen when he got his start in baseball. The Western Association, a minor league, disbanded in midseason. Frazee treated the Peoria ball club like a play, taking them on a barnstorming tour to little towns where Peoria meant the big city, and made money. He also learned a valuable lesson: baseball and the theater were not all that different. You sold tickets, you put on a show every day, and the real money wasn't on the field, but in the front office. No matter how much the players earned, the guys who owned the team usually made more.

He stumbled upon a show called *Mahoney's Wedding* and talked a few investors, including Harry Bay, into providing some seed funds and then took it on the road, putting on a professional play in places that had never seen the likes of one before. He reportedly earned Bay a 1,000 percent profit and suddenly had no lack of suitors wanting to back his next venture. Over the next few years he kept striking gold again and again, eventually moving from the small towns to Chicago, where he built the Cort Theatre, enabling him to make money not just with his own shows, but with somebody else's.

By 1910, Chicago had grown too small for him and he took on New York. He was just as successful there as he was in Chicago, embraced by the elite, and in 1912 gracing the cover of the *New York Clipper*, a theatrical and sporting newspaper, already so well known the paper didn't see the need to identify his photograph with a caption. No wonder, he'd been printing money with a string of hits, then taking them on tour and making even more. He wisely branched out, spreading his risk, opening all sorts of other businesses, buying real estate, building the Longacre Theatre, investing in the stock market, and rubbing shoulders with an ever increasing roster of A-list celebrities, friends, or acquaintances with every notable actor in the country, like Frank Morgan, Nora Bayes, and every playwright, producers like the Shuberts, and composers like the Gershwin brothers. Nearly every day his mailbox bulged with another new play, and letters from young men of means—and young women—pleading for a job, for a way to learn the theater business, or for a break as an actor. He learned that power and money made him attractive, that access to young actresses opened a lot of doors and lot of wallets. He soon had an empire that stretched from New York to Chicago, making million-dollar real estate transactions and always parlaying what he had just done into what he wanted to do next, using some of his own money and a lot of somebody else's.

He was no dummy. The theater was a cash business and Frazee took full advantage of that. The Harry H. Frazee Collection held by the University of Texas consists of more than eighty boxes of material, mostly consisting of plays, sheet music, and a hodgepodge of financial records, some personal but primarily theatrical, literally tens of thousands of documents. It is clearly an incomplete picture of his finances, for it contains very little corporate data and includes only a smattering of baseball-related material, most confined to a single box. Short of a full forensic accounting, which would take an expert months, it is dangerous to extrapolate with certainty much of anything from the collection apart from the complexity of his financial arrangements, but it does include some intriguing items. For example, if one is to take Frazee's personal federal tax worksheets at face value, over a twenty-year period Frazee personally earned any income at all only twice, in 1925 and 1926—when *No, No, Nanette* was the biggest hit the theater had ever seen. Similarly, if one is to believe the existing records, of the dozens of shows he produced, only *Nanette* was profitable. Yet at the same time, most of Frazee's shows ran for hundreds of performances and he lived the high life each and every day for nearly three decades. How?

Like a lot of rich people, like Ban Johnson, like Yankees owner Jacob Ruppert and a lot of other men in baseball and business, Frazee buried his wealth in corporations, trusts, and assorted other properties. It mattered little if the money was in his name as long as he had access to it. For people like Frazee, debt is actually a good thing. As part of the deal to get Congress to support a national income tax in 1913, the Revenue Act included two very important elements to secure the support of the wealthy and influential: it made corporate tax rates much lower than individual rates, allowing the wealthy to disguise their wealth in corporate holdings, and it made interest payments deductible. This was not done so much to help out the little guy buying a bungalow but the big guy buying everything else. To men like Harry Frazee, money was a river that ran past. Whenever he needed any, he just reached in and fished some out. The whole time, he usually controlled the flow of the stream.

For Frazee, life was both a party and a performance. He lived high, usually with a drink in his hand, but he had a brilliant sense of what the public wanted before anyone else knew it. Although mischaracterized for years by a series of bumbling sportswriters as a minor figure in the theater, as the lyricist Irving Caesar later described him, "Frazee never drew a sober breath in his life, but he was a hell of a producer. He made more sense drunk than most people do sober." He viewed baseball as "essentially show business"—as "entertainment"—the ballpark a stage, and the players as actors, and every game a performance.

In a sense, he and Babe Ruth had a lot in common—they didn't just break the mold of what a person could be, they smashed it to bits. Neither man knew it yet but they were both revolutionaries in a sport that was distrustful of change. And in the spring of 1918, both men were about to undergo the greatest transition of their lives, both on the precipice of everlasting fame as something other than what they had been before. Neither would have existed without the other. For now, however, neither man was looking much past the upcoming season.

It is something of an accident that Frazee even owned the Red Sox in the first place. Ban Johnson ran major league baseball like a private club and Frazee, who many thought was Jewish due to his strong ties to both the theater and New York, simply wasn't part of the in crowd. But two years earlier, just before the start of the 1916 season, then Red Sox owner Joseph Lannin, a hotel man, flush with confidence after winning a world title in 1915 and in the wake of the collapse of the Federal League, decided to cash out. Besides, his major investor, Charles Somers, was out of money and Lannin never really had the cash to buy the team in the first place.

Ban Johnson sensed weakness. When star outfielder Tris Speaker balked at signing a reduced contract and held out, the league founder pulled the trigger on Lannin. Johnson cut a deal with the Indians—which Johnson owned a part of—to trade Speaker for pitcher Sad Sam Jones, infielder Fred Thomas, and, most notably, $50,000, the biggest transaction in baseball at the time, but still a bargain for Speaker. Only then did he tell Lannin, and the club owner had little choice but to accept the deal—he didn't have the money to say no. Although the Red Sox, buoyed by the performance of a host of younger players, including Ruth, won another pennant and a world championship for Lannin in 1916, owning the Red Sox had been nothing but a headache. He was losing money and saw war in America's future. Claiming he was "too much a fan" to put up with the game's hardball politics, he decided to get out. Johnson himself pondered buying the Red Sox, or at least having a straw man buy it for him and cut him in.

There is an old adage in Boston that the city's three favorite pastimes are sports, politics, and revenge. Now Lannin, having experienced the other two, decided it was time for revenge.

Up to this point, Johnson's fingerprints were on every sale of an American League team—he usually picked the buyer, sometimes set the price, ordered the seller to the table, and often provided the financing through one of a series of financial angels, all of whom owed Johnson their loyalty when it came to deciding league matters. The result was a lucrative little fiefdom.

This time, however, Johnson miscalculated. Lannin was still stinging over the Speaker deal and when he decided to sell the Red Sox, he cut Johnson out. He ignored entreaties from people like Joe Kennedy, the grandson of infamous Boston politician Honey Fitz, and found his own buyer—Harry Frazee.

Frazee had been angling for a ball club since at least 1909, when he first inquired into buying the Red Sox, and in subsequent years had made noise about buying Boston's National League team, the Braves, as well as the Cubs and Giants, but baseball's cliquish power structure put Frazee off. They didn't trust him—that he was "too New York" was a slur—and it didn't help when he paired with boxer Jim Corbett and began managing the boxer Kid Chocolate, and put the money up for the famous bout between Jess Willard and black champion Jack Johnson in 1915. Why, he even employed *black actors*. In a lily-white sport, Frazee was a wild card.

He convinced an associate, Hugh Ward, to kick in some funds and offered Lannin $675,000 for the Red Sox, far more than anyone else. That was enough to get Lannin out of debt and walk away with a profit—particularly the way the deal was structured. Lannin was so eager to sell, he took only half the money up front—Frazee could pay the balance on the installment plan.

The deal was done before Johnson even heard about it. He was livid at being cut out and kept in the dark, and almost from the start did everything he could to muck things up, particularly when Frazee started making wild offers for talent, trying to tempt the Senators into selling Walter Johnson for a reported $60,000. At a time when every owner in the game was cutting salaries, offers like that made playing hardball at contract time more difficult.

But without Johnson's assistance, Lannin and Frazee hadn't made the smartest deal, either. Although at the time the sale was announced it was presumed to include Fenway Park, that wasn't the case—the Taylor family, who under General Charles H. Taylor and his son John owned the *Boston Globe* and had built Fenway and before selling the team to Lannin, retained stock in the ballpark and even some voting shares in the club. An already complicated deal was, in reality, even more complicated, and the convoluted ownership structure of the team would wreak havoc on the franchise for most of a decade. Determining exactly who owned what without the assistance of an army of lawyers would eventually prove almost impossible.

That didn't bother Johnson. Aptly described by Charles Somers as someone who "never forgets an enemy," when Frazee purchased the Red Sox he became enemy number one to Ban Johnson. After Johnson initially tried to convince Lannin to back out of the deal, saying, "Lannin will be given every opportunity to reconsider," Johnson now sat back biding his time, trying to work Frazee into a corner and taking advantage of his money when he could.

Frazee had showed up at baseball's Winter Meetings in late 1917 eager to spend and anxious to let everyone else know it. Where the other owners saw fear and anxiety, Frazee saw opportunity. He alone was optimistic about the upcoming season.

To survive in the theater, you had to have that attitude. You had to believe every show was destined to be a hit and tell people that, even when you knew better. Besides, the public was fickle. He knew that more than one surefire smash had closed after only a few shows, and a fair share of dogs somehow found an audience and ran for months. Today's hot actor was yesterday's old news, and an ingenue could be thrust into a starring role and become a sensation.

No one in the theater lacked nerve. But baseball was different. In that world Frazee's aggressively optimistic temperament made every other team appear as if it were in retreat.

After winning the pennant and the World Series in 1913, a pennant in 1914, and then fighting off the Federal League, the A's Connie Mack was left with one of the highest payrolls in baseball. Nevertheless, his club finished last in the following three seasons and in 1917 he lost more than $60,000. At the winter meetings, Mack was looking to sell and Frazee, smarting over finishing second in his first year as owner and bullish on baseball's ability to thrive despite the war, was in the mood to spend.

Johnson, more or less directing league affairs like a puppet master, steered Frazee to Mack. Johnson was already plotting Frazee's removal and getting Mack some of the Boston owner's money first was part of the plan.

Frazee couldn't resist and the two eventually made two deals. The Red Sox added outfielders Amos Strunk, catcher Wally Schang, pitcher Joe Bush, and infielder Stuffy McInnis, players who could have made the starting lineup for any team in baseball, while Mack received $60,000. After the Yankees howled that the deal was lopsided, Boston sent over a couple more players, most notably longtime third baseman Larry Gardner. Cumulatively, the deal was richer, by far, than the Speaker sale a year before, easily the biggest in the history of the game, something Frazee underscored in a telegram to the Boston papers that called the deal "the heaviest financial deal ever consummated at one time in the history of baseball." Advanced baseball statistics underscore Frazee's haul. In terms of WAR (wins above replacement), Frazee added nearly 10 wins to his ball club in 1918—and had he been able to keep Gardner, the haul would have been even better. On those terms, purely as a transfer of talent, the deal was roughly on par in terms of total value with the Ruth sale still to come. It gave Mack the cash to survive the season and made the Red Sox the most powerful team in baseball.

On paper anyway. That was the challenge they faced in Hot Springs, to turn the paper tiger into a potent force, a team that pulled together. And that wasn't going to be easy.

Frazee had already lost his manager in 1917, Jack Barry, to the Navy, and in the off-season one more thing became certain—it was unclear precisely who would be available to play in 1918, or for how long. The war was dragging on, and as it did it drew more and more players into the fray—Boston lost outfielder Duffy Lewis and pitcher Ernie Shore, among others. In order to compete, teams had to fill their rosters with unproven talent, the infirm, or players otherwise past their prime. By mid-December, no fewer than eleven Red Sox players had been lost to the war—the most of any team in baseball.

That's where Ed Barrow came in. The International League president and onetime manager of the Tigers had been in baseball for more than two decades and knew virtually everyone—Frazee had been an acquaintance for years. Barrow was one of several baseball figures Frazee regularly consulted to keep his finger on baseball's pulse while he jockeyed to buy a team. Well, now he had one, but he didn't have a manager, and he still needed more players. After efforts to get Barry released from military duty failed— Frazee wasn't shy about asking for special treatment, either, as long as he benefited personally—Barrow, fully aware that the job was open, dropped in on Frazee at his office.

"Well, Ed," said Frazee, "I guess it's about time I begin looking around for a manager." Barrow feigned indifference, as did Frazee, before finally blurting out, "I've just selected you as a manager of the 1918 Red Sox. Want the job?" Barrow was delighted to accept. He needed the job, knew Frazee was in a mood to spend, and no one in the game had a better idea about who might be available to play in 1918 than he did, and in his new position he acted as both manager on the field and general manager, responsible for trades and signing players. However, this being baseball circa 1918, there was also more at play. A year before, Barrow had tried to duplicate Johnson's ploy and reorganize the International League into a third major league, the Union League, a move that, according to some reports, initially had Johnson's support. He even promised Barrow the presidency of the Red Sox if he could force Frazee to sell. Barrow tried to put together a deal with some International League backers—but then he'd been left hanging. Joseph Lannin, after selling the Sox, had since made amends with Johnson. He owned the International League's Buffalo franchise and took offense at the league president working the back room. He led a move to cut Barrow's salary by two thirds, which caused Barrow to resign.

Barrow wasn't finished—he was tough, a disciplinarian who wasn't above playing the revenge game, either—Frazee called him "Simon Legree," after the greedy slave owner in *Uncle Tom's Cabin*. By joining forces with Frazee, Barrow was looking forward to the chance to prove Lannin and Johnson wrong. One of his first acts was to skim the International League of some veteran talent, signing outfielder George Whiteman, a longtime minor league star who hit .340, mostly for Toronto in 1917.

The end result, however, was that as the train chugged from Boston to Little Rock, picking up the stray player along the way, by the time they all arrived in Arkansas, Barrow still wasn't quite sure what kind of team he had. If everyone showed up and could play out the season, they looked to be the class of the league. But even with the addition of Mack's best remaining players, the war was still certain to leave some holes, and besides, with so many new recruits, half the players had never met one another before. Barrow wouldn't really know what kind of team he had until they dumped the equipment bags out on the ground at Whittington Park.

Spring training began on March 12 with a gingerly played practice. The only regulars among the starting eight in attendance were outfielder Harry Hooper and Everett Scott. Ruth was the only frontline pitcher and he was not yet in shape to pitch. As a result, after the players limbered up, the Red Sox, a major league team in name only as the rest included a dozen or more raw recruits and handful of aging has-beens, barely had enough players to hold a full scrimmage.

It was probably the best thing that ever happened.

2

This Means War

*"I'd be the laughingstock of baseball if I turned the best lefthander
in the game into an outfielder."*
    —Ed Barrow

Of the vast impact Gavrilo Princip's assassination of Archduke Franz
Ferdinand of Austria, presumptive heir to the Austro-Hungarian throne,
and his wife, Sophie, Duchess of Hohenberg, would have on the history of
the world, the bearing on the game of baseball would be no less profound.
Although in later years Harry Hooper, Ed Barrow, and a handful of others
would scramble to take credit for the decision to move Ruth off the pitcher's
mound and into the batter's box, credit should rightly go to Princip. For
had it not been for the war, Ruth would be remembered today for his
prowess as a pitcher, and nothing else.

Spring training was a rather loose affair in 1918—the three-mile-or-so
walk to and from the hotel was considered part of the players' training,
and apart from some extra throwing, pitchers were treated little different
from the other members of the roster. Everyone more or less went through
the same drills, "playing" their way into shape through batting practice,
shagging flies, taking infield, and intra-squad games. Barrow, who hadn't
managed a big league team team since Detroit in 1904, kept the boys on
the field a long time, but was hardly an organizational genius. Frazee

brought in veteran infielder Johnny Evers—known as "the Crab" for both the way he scooted abound the diamond and for his sour disposition—into camp to help Barrow out. His managerial skills, never particularly profound, were rusty.

There was nothing strange about a pitcher taking a turn at another position, especially during the first days of spring training before the games got under way. During spring training in 1916, while Tris Speaker was a holdout, Ruth had played a little outfield, but his fly catching had reminded no one of the Gray Eagle. But in 1918, due to a shortage of talent, there was a little more opportunity than usual.

Ruth, who today would likely be diagnosed as ADHD and drugged into somnambulism, was just as hard to contain on the field as he was off it. He loved to play, and he never forgot that play was supposed to be fun. It was a holdover from his time as a boy at St. Mary's Industrial School for Boys. Although Ruth credited the school and the Xaverian Brothers with changing his life, make no mistake—it was no finishing school. His time there was heavily regulated and the only relief from the drudgery of the regimented lifestyle of church, study, and work was playing sports. For Ruth, this meant baseball. Only on the ballfield was he both valued and free to be himself. He took full advantage of the opportunity.

No one ever said Ruth didn't work hard on the diamond, and in the spring of 1918 he was particularly irrepressible, dashing back and forth between activities with the enthusiasm of a young boy let loose in the backyard. He could only throw so much, and if there was room for an extra man to shag some flies, take some ground balls in the infield, or, in particular, take a few extra cracks at the plate, Ruth was ready and jumped right in.

Usually, by the time the squad was in good enough shape to play exhibition games, the regulars took over and once the games began pitchers such as Ruth waited their turn. But there was nothing usual about the spring of 1918.

For one, in the early days of March it was hot in Hot Springs, and humid. The temperature touched 90 degrees, leaving some out-of-shape players panting in pools of sweat and leading Barrow to warn some slackers, who would douse their heads and then claim fatigue, that he was on to their "water bucket camouflage." Nevertheless, the heat gave Ruth more opportunity to play. In the early days of the spring, Barrow was already scrambling to fill every position. As Barrow struggled to make up for the loss of Gardner, catcher Sam Agnew was pressed into duty at third, as was first baseman Stuffy McInnis.

So during those first few practices, by necessity as much as anything else, Ruth played a little first base, which also gave him some incentive to turn in before dawn. Barrow already had him rooming with coach Dan Howley for just that reason—later, he'd be paired with Johnny Evers. But as the exhibition season began on March 17 when the Sox played the first of a series of exhibitions with the National League Brooklyn Robins at Whittington Park Ruth took the field for that initial contest, not on the mound, but at first base.

That was newsworthy in itself—in the *Globe*, Ed Martin called him "'Hal Chase' Ruth" after the slick-fielding first sacker considered the best in the game. But what Ruth did at the plate attracted even more attention.

He hit two home runs, one to left center and the other to right, where it cleared a fence that served as a barricade between the park and an alligator farm, and where, Martin noted, "It kicked up no end of commotion among the alligators." The headline in the newspaper the next day referred to Boston's "Great Bombardment," and the *Boston Post* reported that even the Brooklyn players had stood and cheered the hit into the gator pen.

It was a great achievement—but also not quite as impressive as it first appeared. The two pitchers Ruth faced that day, Harry Heightman and Norman Plitt, were barely major leaguers and hadn't been throwing a week. It was also the start of spring training and balls were nearly new and still relatively tight, as lively as the dead ball would ever be. Ruth's performance was impressive but hardly unheard of.

Significantly, every report of the game also left out one very important fact. Although it was about 360 feet to the fence in left field and more than 400 to center, down the right field line it was only 260 to the alligator farm. Although the field had once been spacious, due to floods it had been reconfigured several years earlier and the dimensions made much more cozy. Had the game been played anywhere else, such as Majestic Park, the other spring training park in Hot Springs and Boston's home there in both 1917 and 1919, Ruth may not have even hit a home run at all, and had he not, well, what would have happened if Princip had been a bad shot?

The reporters weren't being too cute: press was important. The Red Sox planned to barnstorm their way back north, and anything that could drum up publicity mattered. The alligators were good copy, and most reports made sure to mention the farm. Crowds were important and word traveled fast. While not quite the attraction of the local casino, seeing Ruth scatter a group of gators with a baseball was a draw, even if it was little more than a routine fly. The crowds at Boston's morning workouts began to increase and attendance at the exhibitions between the Sox and Brooklyn were almost on par with turnout at the racetrack. Ruth was the primary reason.

He loved the attention and played to the crowd every chance he had. When he took batting practice, he made no pretense of trying to do anything but hit the ball as high and far as possible—as a pitcher, he didn't have to. Years later, the Tigers' Ty Cobb noted that this was a huge advantage for Ruth, saying, "He could experiment at the plate. He didn't have to get a piece of the ball. . . . No one cares if a pitcher strikes out or looks bad at bat, so Ruth could take that full swing." And that's exactly what he did, and had been doing since reaching the big leagues, often using an oversized bat that weighed as much as ten or twelve ounces more than the bats many other players usually used.

The result in four big league seasons so far had been 68 strikeouts in 361 major league at bats, something that made the game's wise old heads shake their heads. Striking out nearly 20 percent of the time was unacceptable—for anybody, regardless of the result the other 80 percent of the time. Nevertheless, in the spring of 1918, Boston's fledgling pitching corps complied and grooved the ball for Ruth as the writers breathlessly noted his accomplishment and whether he made contact or not. They also noted that most of the veteran players made sure to wait and take their batting practice off the new recruits instead of Mays, Ruth, or the other front liners who trickled in every day.

On March 20, Ruth managed to scatter the gators four more times during batting practice. Each one meant a lost baseball, leading Harry Frazee to mutter, "This is getting painful," a reference to the cost of a replacement ball. Burt Whitman of the *Boston Herald* took to referring to Ruth as "the Colossus," and a cartoon in the *Boston Post* showed Ruth pestering Barrow to play in the field, but that was as much a reference to his enthusiasm as his batting prowess. (Note: the *Boston Herald* and

Boston Journal merged in 1917 and were known in 1918 as the *Boston Herald and Journal,* becoming simply the *Boston Herald* in 1918. To avoid confusion I refer to it as the *Boston Herald.*)

Word of Ruth's performances continued to spread. The home runs might have been cheap, but nevertheless they were home runs, and no one else in camp was hitting them so frequently. Ruth had filled out and was now man-strong, topping 200 pounds. When the Sox and Brooklyn traveled to Little Rock for an exhibition only to have it be rained out, Ruth entertained the big crowd of soldiers by taking batting practice and swinging for the fences, dropping four or five balls over the barrier just for fun. According to one hyperbolic report, the balls landed thirty feet farther away than "the right field pavilion at the Polo Grounds," a good poke if not a very specific one, as the stands were only 258 feet from home down the line but much deeper where the pavilion ended. The soldiers looked at Ruth just as he had once looked up to Brother Matthias, his mentor at St. Mary's, when he was hitting home runs one-handed.

The next day, 2,000 fans turned up for another exhibition at Whittington Park. With first baseman Dick Hoblitzell finally in camp and needing work, and both Carl Mays and Ruth scheduled to pitch, Barrow knew good business and stuck Ruth in right field to start the game. He didn't disappoint. In the third inning, pitcher Al Mamaux grooved one. Barrow had already told his men to swing and swing hard against the Brooklyn scrub and Ruth did, once again hammering the ball over the fence in right. If press reports are to be believed, this time the blast cleared not only the gators but both a street and a duck pond. Astounded witnesses called the drive the longest they'd ever seen at Whittington Park, some claiming the ball traveled 500 feet, something normally possible with the dead ball only if one included a considerable roll.

Still, his performance was more a novelty than anything else. There were no serious calls for Ruth to change position. It wasn't as if he was unstoppable. Only the home runs stood out. The Robins veteran Rube Marquard, known for his fastball, kept him quiet in one exhibition, striking him out three times. Ruth only connected off his replacement, and even that drive was reported to be wind-aided. By the end of the month there were finally enough players in camp to play intra-squad games between the "Regulars" and the "Yannigans," which kept Ruth on the field, but in exhibitions against

Brooklyn Ruth resumed his mound duties, and as the pitchers got into shape, his home run swing began to prove less effective.

By the time the Sox broke camp in early April and began to wend their way north, playing exhibitions in Dallas, New Orleans, Chattanooga, and elsewhere, Ruth's early spring performance was already becoming something of an afterthought. It was akin to that of the prospect who gets off to a hot start only to be forgotten as soon as the pitchers start throwing curves.

Barrow was beginning to settle on a lineup and there was little question that Ruth was back where he belonged—pitching. His performance at the plate was certainly valuable when he came through, but nothing the Sox felt they could depend on or cause them to flout tradition.

But it was nice to have a pitcher who could hit a little. Smoky Joe Wood, the Boston fireballer who won 34 games in 1912 before a sore arm drove him to the outfield, had always been a good hitter, and more than one sportswriter had chided the usually weak-hitting Washington Senators for not making better use of Walter Johnson's bat. In most years, he was one of their better hitters. But then as now, conventional baseball wisdom held it was far too taxing to pitch every fourth or fifth day and still play regularly between starts. No major leaguer has ever done so on more than a temporary basis, and only a scant few, such as Red Lucas, have even been used regularly as pinch hitter.

Yet one more factor made it somewhat difficult for the Red Sox or anyone else to see what they might have in Ruth. While today all manner of analytic tools and formulas measure not only batting average, but also power and a player's total value, none of these were available in 1918. When observers spoke of Ruth's hitting, they primarily meant only his batting average, not home runs and strikeouts. Even such a commonplace statistic as slugging percentage, which measures power by dividing total bases by at bats, was unknown. Most baseball men considered taking a base on balls almost a sign of weakness and sacrifice bunts and stolen bases were valued all out of proportion to their true contribution to the scoring of runs and the winning of ballgames.

In combination, all this rendered Ruth's gifts as a hitter partially invisible, obscuring the value of his doubles and triples and walks, while giving too much prominence to his strikeouts. And in the context of the era, even the home run was viewed with suspicion, such an irregularity that it was considered pure folly to hope for one, much less to expect a player to hit one on command, even in batting practice. A home run then was the baseball equivalent of a Hail Mary pass in football today; a wonderful surprise when it happens, but hardly worth counting on.

The only observers who wished for that were members of the press. They were beginning to realize that Ruth's home runs sold papers. A column by the *Herald*'s Bob Dunbar, a fictional scribe whose byline was ghostwritten by younger staffers and generally included the kind of hometown pap that others would not allow to see in print under their own name, noted that fans were "disappointed when they don't read that big Babe hit a home run."

The Red Sox worked their way back toward Boston, generally thumping Brooklyn with ease, taking their preseason series seven games to five. Once the weather turned cold, forcing the cancellation of a game in Chattanooga due to snow, they returned to Boston five days before the start of the regular season, more or less set on their lineup.

Frazee's acquisitions had come through, as Stuffy McInnis took over at third for Gardner, Amos Strunk patrolled center field, Wally Schang earned the starting nod behind the plate, and George Whiteman, the thirty-three-year-old minor leaguer Barrow nabbed from the International League, took over in left. Holdovers remained in Harry Hooper in right field and Everett Scott at shortstop, while veteran Dave Shean, acquired in a trade late in the spring after it became clear Johnny Evers now only acted like a crab instead of moved like one, played second, with Dick Hoblitzell winning the first baseman's job. Pitchers Dutch Leonard and Carl Mays joined newcomer Joe Bush as part of the club's strength: the pitching staff. And at the center of it all, still Boston's number one pitcher, was the same man who had occupied that spot the year before, Babe Ruth.

The club got in a day's work out at Harvard, giving Ruth a taste of the Ivy League, and one day before the season started, Barrow told the *Boston Herald,* "There is every reason to believe the Red Sox will be in the hunt." As opposed to other clubs that had been forced to use what Barrow referred to as "emergency players," he felt his club was made up of "high class material," and offered that he expected the greatest challenge to come

from the defending champion White Sox. Of his own team, he took particular note of his infield, and called his pitching staff of Mays, Leonard, and
Bush, anchored by Ruth, "the best quartet in the league."

For the record, Ruth collected nine hits in 21 exhibition game at bats
that spring, including four home runs, most of it against subpar pitching in
a ballpark with a short porch in right field. He had been very entertaining,
but as yet there was no hint that Ruth would ever play even a single inning
anywhere else but on the mound.

3

1918

"He was like a damn animal. He had that instinct. They know when it's going to rain, things like that. Nature! That was Ruth."
—*Philadelphia A's pitcher Rube Bressler*

Just as he had the previous two seasons, when the umpire yelled "Play ball" on Opening Day, standing in the center of the diamond, grinding the ball into his hip with his enormous left hand was Babe Ruth. On the field, all seemed right with the Red Sox, but if there was reason to worry, one only had to look in the stands.

It was pathetic. Despite Frazee's off-season deals, barely 7,000 paying customers braved the chill April air for the start of the 1918 season, nearly 3,000 fewer than the year before. To pump up the crowd, Frazee even let a couple of thousand servicemen in for free. Yet despite the bunting that hung from the front of the grandstand and the roof, Fenway Park, only seven years old, was already looking shabby. The wall in left field and just about every other open space was covered with a motley collection of signage, much of it faded and peeling. The bulk of the crowd huddled in the concrete and steel grandstand and the covered right field pavilion, where a knot of several hundred gamblers turned out for every game and held sway, openly plying their trade like stockbrokers working the floor of the exchange. The rest of the park—the bleachers in center field and the stands in right and along the third base line hurriedly constructed for the 1912 World Series—were nearly empty. Constructed entirely of wood, after almost seven years the raw pine was splintered and warped from the summer sun and the winter ice. Only the poor and the brave—and those who could afford a new pair of pants—braved the ballpark's outer reaches and then only when a big crowd gave them no other choice.

In retrospect, Frazee had made a grave error when buying the Red Sox in not acquiring the ballpark. The Taylors gladly took Frazee's rent checks but were loath to perform any but the most cosmetic maintenance. The ballpark as first built in 1912, not to mention the jury-rigged, expanded ballpark with extra seats cobbled together for the that year's World Series, was nothing like the gussied-up, faux antiqued Fenway Park that exists today. It was spare and utilitarian. Within a few more years, portions of the wood stands would periodically be cordoned off, condemned as unsafe. In the meantime, it gave fans one more reason not to come out to the ballpark.

America was changing. For decades, America had turned its back on Europe and as it now awoke and looked around, it was beginning to realize the world was rapidly evolving. As men went to war, women went to work in their stead and began to act and think independently. In recent years, the spread of electricity and the affordability of the automobile had ushered in the greatest transformation in American society to date. Everything America had ever been suddenly seemed old and out of date.

That included the game of baseball. The recent failure of the Federal League underscored the trouble in the game. Baseball had thrived for years as the national pastime primarily because there was no alternative, really— nothing other than vaudeville and the theater to occupy workers' few spare moments. But the spread of electricity offered new outlets—the nickelodeon, recorded music, and nightclubs and dance halls. In less than a decade, the number of minor leagues had tumbled from more than fifty to only ten by 1918. Major league attendance had peaked at more than seven million in 1909 and then dropped steadily to barely half that. The game's long-term survival was hardly assured. Twenty years before, bicycle racing had been nearly as popular as baseball. Now, almost every city of any size sported an empty or abandoned velodrome. In a few years, the ballpark risked a similar fate.

The game was boring. No one would say it aloud, but that was the truth.

The men who ran the game had been brought up with baseball in the 1880s and 1890s and still thought it should be played that way it had been then. "Scientific," inside baseball ruled and managers such as Connie Mack and the Giants' John McGraw were considered stars as much as any player, brilliant tacticians who controlled their men as if chess pieces, squeezing out runs through a combination of bunts, scratch base hits, stolen bases, and sacrifices.

Unfortunately, that mixture was becoming ever more predictable, and more rare. At its highest level, such as in the World Series, the style of play made every pitch, like the move of every pawn, replete with meaning and significance. But for the rest of the year, players and managers alike too often simply went through the motions as if they couldn't wait to get off the field. In one spring training game in 1918, the Red Sox and Brooklyn Robins (later the Dodgers) played seven full innings in only thirty minutes. It was only an exhibition, but still . . . More often the only people who really enjoyed the contests were die-hard insiders and the men who whiled away their afternoons making "do they or don't they" bets in stands, arcane wagers based on the intricacies of the game, like whether the next hit would be in the air or on the ground, regardless of the score.

Since 1901 the total number of runs scored per game had dropped by nearly four and was showing no signs of increasing as improvements in gloves (they were bigger), field conditions (they caused fewer errors), and pitching approach combined to make it ever more difficult to score runs. Now almost every pitcher either threw a spitball or scuffed the ball in some way to make it move and dart erratically, all of which made runs more precious.

What had *not* changed much was the ball itself. It was made much the same way as it had been made forty years before when it was still allowable to "soak" a runner, or put him out by hitting him with a thrown ball.

The first baseballs had been handmade, generally four pieces of leather stitched together over a tightly wound ball of yarn, known as a "lemon-peel" due to the configuration of the stitching, but by the 1850s organized teams tried to agree on a uniform size and method of manufacture. Still, it wasn't until the 1870s that a true standard was set by the National League of Professional Baseball Clubs, calling for a ball "formed by yarn wound around a small core . . . covered with two strips of white horsehide or cowhide, tightly stitched together. It shall weigh not less than five nor more than 5.25 ounces avoirdupois and measure not less than nine nor more than 9.25 inches in circumference." Manufacturers adopted the popular figure-8 style of stitching and the modern ball, constructed from a simple round rubber center wrapped in wool yarn and covered with stitched horsehide more or less, was born. It was tough, resilient, and almost impossible to hit more than a couple hundred feet, becoming softer and more lopsided with each use, and the game and its strategy evolved in line with the ball. Baseball was played primarily within only a couple hundred feet of home plate.

In 1911 a rubber-covered cork center was introduced that caused a brief uptick in runs, but that was quickly offset as pitchers adapted—using the spitball and scuffing the cover to make it move—and penurious club owners kept the same ball in play throughout the game, turning softer—and deader—by the inning. The game wasn't marked so much by the crack of the bat on the ball as a dull thud. Batters tried to place hits between fielders as if shooting pool with a moving target, taking a choppy, short, level swing designed as much to avoid the embarrassment of a miss as it was for the glory of a base hit.

Although the modern game was only about twenty years old, it was already living in the past. Ever since Ban Johnson created the American League and major league baseball took on its now familiar two-league structure in 1903, the same few names had dominated the sport—batting stars like Detroit's Ty Cobb, Pittsburgh shortstop Honus Wagner, Napoleon Lajoie of Cleveland, the White Sox' Joe Jackson, Eddie Collins of the A's, and the Yankees' and A's Home Run Baker, and the pitchers such as Walter Johnson and Christy Mathewson. But by 1918, Cobb was entering his 14th season in the major leagues. Lajoie, Wagner, and Mathewson had recently retired, and the few remaining stars, like Jackson and Collins and Tris Speaker, lacked the charisma and appeal of their predecessors.

The game needed a star. The last thing it needed was a war. In the end, it got both. In the long run, the carnage that overspread Europe was the best thing that ever happened to the game.

For Babe Ruth, Opening Day on April 15, 1918, began just as it usually did for him. He arrived early and, as was his custom, probably helped the young vendors bag peanuts while scooping up great handfuls and leaving a hefty tip before taking the mound. Ruth spent nearly as much time with the people who worked at the park as he did the players—he didn't see much of a difference, and in fact, that was how he met Johnny Igoe, a man who was becoming his best friend and advisor. Igoe, who now ran a drugstore, had started out at Fenway Park as a peanut vendor.

Once he took the mound, the Philadelphia A's found hitting Ruth about as productive as taking swings at peanut shells. After the usual pregame honorifics, which included the Red Sox marching out onto the field, raising the flag, and making appeals to the public to purchase Liberty Bonds to support the war, Ruth took the mound. He threw a scoreless first inning before giving up a run in the second when he botched a pick-off throw, and the Red Sox took a 2–1 lead in the bottom of the inning, Ruth knocking in run number two with a hard single past A's first baseman George Burns.

Ruth pitched the rest of the game as if he didn't have a care in the world and Boston cruised to an easy 7–1 victory, one that barely stirred the crowd, which the *Globe* described as behaving "with a sort of conservation of appreciation apparent." In other words, they sat on their hands bored out of their minds.

If Ruth hadn't a care in the world, Harry Frazee had nothing but worry to contend with. Although he had acted boldly during the off-season, as had, to a lesser degree, owner Charles Comiskey of the White Sox, the rest of his brethren, in particular AL president Ban Johnson, were cowering before an uncertain future. In short, they were mucking everything up.

The previous December, when Frazee was acting boldly, baseball had announced it would proceed regardless of the war and play a full 154-game schedule. But they had since backtracked, cutting the season back to a scheduled 140 games. To someone like Frazee, who had acted with confidence, the loss of fourteen playing dates—seven at home—hurt. Players were paid by the season, not by the game, and he had budgeted accordingly. Had he known that was going to take place, he may not have been quite so audacious. Now he was stuck.

And he was also stuck with the repressive presence of both Boston's Puritan past and its more Catholic present. At the time, weekday games started at 3:00 p.m. to accommodate professional men who could scoot out of the office early. Factory workers didn't have that luxury. They could generally only attend games on holidays and weekends, and in Boston, that meant Saturday: so-called blue laws were in place, and Sunday baseball was banned. That cost the Red Sox ten or twelve lucrative home dates a year. Only a few years before, that hadn't been a problem. Sunday baseball had once been banned almost everywhere, but that was changing—it was legal now in several American League cities and would be legal in New York in 1919, helping the Yankees to turn their first profit under co-owner Jacob Ruppert and his financial partner, Tillinghast L'Hommedieu Huston, more often known as Cap Huston. Already, Frazee's Broadway shows had to shutter on Sundays (one of the reasons he was so eager to take his shows on the road to smaller cities with looser restrictions), but on Broadway at least, everyone had to play by the same rules.

He must have found it galling that the competition was allowed to profit when he was not. Indeed the inability to play baseball on Sunday would hamstring Boston's major league franchises for more than another decade. Whereas the A's, for instance, might pull in a crowd of 40,000 or 50,000 over a weekend, usually ten times what they would draw on weekdays, Frazee, at best, could count on only one large crowd, on Saturday. Increasingly, this left the Red Sox at a severe disadvantage, one that soon would become even more pronounced. They courted the Church and politicians with free tickets and season passes, but didn't get much for their generosity

To no one's surprise, the Red Sox got off to a quick start in 1918, opening the season with six straight wins at home including three against the Yankees before finally falling in the last game of their four-game series. Ruth picked up win number two on April 19, defeating Hank Thormahlen 9–5, and chipping in a single and an RBI, but the crowds remained disappointing—and the team was forced to play a doubleheader after a rainout the previous day. In his next start, Ruth picked up another hit, but fell 3–0 to the A's. For the first time all year, he had a complaint; he said his arm was sore.

Still, everything seemed to be going more or less according to plan as the Red Sox finished the month 11–2, with a three-game lead in the pennant race. About the only player not performing to expectations was first baseman Dick Hoblitzell. Batting cleanup, the ten-year veteran and team captain opened the season 1-for-25. Even worse, he'd been declared eligible for the draft, which may well have weighed on his performance. A notice to report could come at any time.

But the big news came from Frazee. On April 30 the papers announced that Frazee had been offered upward of $100,000 for Ruth, whom the *Boston Herald* described as a "colossal southpaw pitcher and hitter most extraordinaire." Frazee was clearly titillated by the offer, which a few days later he claimed was actually $150,000, saying, "I might as well sell the franchise and the whole club as Ruth." But there is no solid evidence that the offer, which the press speculated came from either the White Sox or the Yankees, was genuine or just idle talk, even though it later became fashionable among the baseball magnates for nearly all of them to claim to have seen the future and been the first to put in a bid for Ruth.

Frazee knew the power of publicity and may well have been trying to seed a cloud and see if he could make it rain—it was becoming clear the war wasn't about to end anytime soon, and he might have been pondering cutting and running. Besides, the Red Sox would soon play in New York. Pumping up a crowd there, where the Polo Grounds seated 38,000, was simply good business. Even the visitor's share of a full house—or close to it—would make Frazee more than a crowd a quarter of that size in Fenway Park.

If there was an offer, the White Sox and Yankees were the two teams most likely to afford to make such a generous bid, and in 1918, Frazee's most likely trading partners. Charley Comiskey, the longtime owner of the White Sox, was flush with cash and generally known to be interested anytime a valuable player was made available. Although he paid his players like serfs, he didn't mind paying big money for them. That's how the game was played.

The New York Yankees were the most intriguing destination. Although Ban Johnson, eager to cut the legs out from the Giants' stranglehold on the lucrative New York market, had long promised to help make the Yankees contenders, he had never followed through. Their original owners, William Devery and Frank Farrell, two grotesquely corrupt members of New York's Tammany Hall political machine, cared about little more than fleecing their own ball club. Although beer baron Ruppert and Huston purchased the team after the 1914 season and stabilized the franchise, the team's on-field performance had barely improved. They remained a stepchild of the Giants, and even paid their National League counterparts $60,000 rent each year to use the Polo Grounds. The club had abandoned their original field, Hilltop Park, in 1913 after the Giants rebuilt the Polo Grounds after a fire. The move was intended as a stopgap measure until the Yankees could build their own concrete and steel park—fire was making the original wooden parks impossible to insure—but Ruppert and Huston hadn't been able to afford to do that yet. And although Johnson wasn't fond of the Giants, Ruppert, like Frazee, had proven difficult to control, so Johnson was again balking at giving the Yankees significant help.

But Jacob Ruppert was impatient and, unlike his predecessors, a real businessman and savvy politician. The dominant man in the Yankees partnership, Ruppert, whose family had been brewing beer in America for almost a hundred years, was a New Yorker and firmly ensconced in the upper crust of New York's manufacturing society. He had served in the National Guard, reaching the rank of colonel, and dabbled effectively enough in the politics of Tammany Hall to serve several terms in Congress. The longtime baseball fan had tried to buy both the Giants and Cubs before partnering with Huston, a former United States Army engineer and captain, and buying the Yankees for $480,000 in 1915. At the time, Johnson pledged to help his ball club, a promise Ruppert expected him to make good.

Yet when Johnson had steered Frazee to Connie Mack in the off-season and Frazee came away with the guts of Mack's ball club, Ruppert complained: he would have loved to make a bid. Two years before, Ruppert had felt put out when Tris Speaker was sold to Cleveland before he knew about it. Now Johnson tried to pacify him and helped engineer a deal that delivered once valuable second baseman Del Pratt to New York, now temporarily considered damaged goods after being charged with throwing games. He then helped arrange a trade that delivered outfielder Francesco Stephano Pezzolo—better known as Ping Bodie—from the A's to the Yankees. It didn't match Frazee's haul, but it helped keep the Yankees competitive and keep Ruppert quiet.

That was becoming more important by the day. Ruppert, who essentially took over the club when Huston went overseas in the service, understood New York. Despite his affected German accent, he was New York to the core—he knew the Italian American Bodie would be an instant draw among New York's growing class of Italian immigrants. And he also understood that with Prohibition in the air, this was no time for a beer baron to be buying only barley. Looking ahead, he realized that in another year or two baseball might be his only business. Thus far he'd already lost nearly a quarter of the club's purchase price, as a poor record and the onerous rent he paid the Giants made it hard to make money.

Ruppert needed the Yankees not only to win, but also to win the New York box office from the Giants. To do that, he needed a star, and Ruth was the best young star out there, an intriguing player who could help on both the mound and elsewhere—a particularly precious commodity in 1918.

He'd been paying attention, and entering the 1918 season, although Ruth had hit only 9 career home runs, four of them had been against the Yankees, three in the Polo Grounds, where the right field porch was perfect for Ruth's pull-hitting, all-or-nothing, swing-from-the-heels stroke. It was a small sample size, to be sure, but so dramatic that everyone had already noticed. In Fenway Park, with its distant right field fence that, except for directly down the line, was 370 or more feet from home, Ruth's drives, while impressive, resulted in outs, proverbial home runs in an elevator shaft. In New York . . . well, he made you wonder what he would do if given the opportunity. The Polo Grounds simply fit Ruth as a hitter in a way that Fenway Park never did. For his career, Ruth would amass a slugging percentage of .583 in Fenway Park—the worst, by far, of any park in which he played more than 10 games. In the Polo Grounds, he would slug .828. Although Yankee Stadium would also be kind to Ruth, no place would prove kinder than the Polo Grounds. Besides, New York fans, with little else to root for, had taken to Ruth. It probably didn't hurt that the young pitcher was of German extraction, either. At the time, German Americans were New York's dominant immigrant ethnic group.

Moreover, from the first time he played there, Ruth and New York seemed to fit each other. Fans responded to him in a way in New York they never quite did in Boston, and Ruth thrived under the attention. In Boston, he was like a big gawky kid in a store full of glassware, always bumping into something. There was too much scrutiny, too much tsk-tsking. In Boston, being famous was like being under a microscope and made Ruth feel claustrophobic; everybody knew his business. It was truly a small town, parochial in all the worst ways. In New York, fame brought anonymity and freedom . . . not to mention an endless supply of women even more eager to ignore social strictures.

If Ruppert had made an offer for Ruth, his performance at the Polo Grounds on May 3, 4, and 6 would have left the brewer salivating like a drunk watching the day's kegs roll in. After the Sox dropped the first game of the series 3–2, Ruth took the mound on Saturday opposite Allen Russell. The Yankees toyed with Ruth, who was becoming more rotund by the year—the phrase "the buxom Babe" was used by more than one cheeky sportswriter—by deciding to bunt early and often down the third base line to see if Ruth and McInnis, new to the position, could handle it. They couldn't, at least at first. Ruth made two errors and New York got an early 4–0 lead.

The Red Sox could barely touch Yankees spitballer Russell—Ruth struck out on three pitches his first time up, but in the seventh he came to bat with two out and a man on first. This time he hit the dry side of the ball, lifting a line drive down the right field line that made the second deck, but foul by inches. According to W. J. Macbeth of the *New York Tribune*, the knock put "the fear of the Lord" into the Yankees.

As he returned to the plate, the ever-confident Ruth reportedly turned to umpire Billy Evans and called his shot with godlike authority, telling him "I'll hit this one right back, Bill." Then he did, smacking Russell's next pitch higher, farther, and fair. Despite cracking a ninth-inning double, Ruth still lost the game 5–4, but afterward the talk was not of the score, but of Ruth and his bat. The headline in the *New York Times* was emblematic, reading "Babe Ruth Is Hero, Wields Vicious Cudgel," with the final score relegated to a subhead.

The Great War was making it tough on everyone and everything, newspapers included. Competition was keen. Readers were both desperate for war news, loath to receive it, and eager to forget it once they'd read it. Ruth and his exploits provided a momentary escape—who cared who won the game—did anything happen that made it possible to ignore the war?

The conflict was beginning to impact daily life in ways that no one could foresee as the government gobbled up resources needed to supply the troops and the industries that supported them. There were shortages of almost everything, and the government espoused programs like "gasless Sundays" to save resources and even the most basic goods—meat, coal, and other fuels—were in short supply. Baseball was not immune.

As American troops entered into actual combat, their supply needs changed as the military quickly discovered that some items and materials that worked during training exercises were almost useless in the trenches of France. The company that eventually became known for "Wolverine" brand boot developed a new tanning process for horsehide just before the start of the war that made horsehide the leather of choice for high-top boots, just as it was already the preferred option for most military jackets and gloves. As a result, in May of 1918 the U.S. government, through the War Industries Board, commandeered the nation's supply of horsehide. Similarly, once American men took to the field, they rapidly discovered that wool, which retains warmth even when wet, was the best choice for almost everything, and high-quality wool yarn was similarly appropriated for military use, both in manufacturing and by millions of American women who were enlisted to knit a wide variety of garments for Allied troops. The wool shortage was so acute that President Woodrow Wilson set an example by allowing sheep to graze on the White House lawn, and ball clubs replaced popular "Ladies Day" promotions with "Knitting Days," allowing women with a ball of yarn and knitting needles into the ballpark free. The only raw material used by baseball that wasn't in short supply during the 1918 season was lumber.

Like everyone else, baseball paid a price. At the time, sporting goods manufacturer A. J. Reach was the leading manufacturer of recreational baseballs and supplied the balls to both major leagues (although the NL balls were stamped with the name of the Spalding Company). Almost overnight, the quality of materials available to the company dropped dramatically, and they produced baseballs made from lower quality leather and wool, which as any knitter can tell you, can vary widely in strength and resilience.

The impact was unnoticeable at first, as both the company and most major league clubs retained a healthy supply of the old balls, but as the 1918 season progressed, the consumers began to notice that the balls, now wound with inferior yarn and covered with lower quality horsehide, were even deader than before and wore out much faster. Reach responded by changing the setting of the machines they used to wind the yarn, winding it tighter. It helped some, but it took more than a full season before the old supply of subpar baseballs was used up. As a result, in 1918 teams began the season using the normal dead ball, but as the season progressed inferior balls that were even deader came into play. And over the course of the 1918 season, from beginning to end, there was a slow drop in power for both Babe Ruth and the Red Sox. The impact of that would extend in the 1919 season as well, in reverse fashion. Over the course of the year, as materials improved and the Reach company neglected to change back the setting on their winding machines, the ball became ever more lively and would help lead to an increase in power and offense to levels never before seen.

Of course, in early May of 1918 neither the Red Sox, Harry Frazee, Jacob Ruppert, Babe Ruth, nor anyone else in baseball knew anything about that. But they would soon learn that Ruth just might be a singular talent.

During the Saturday loss to the Yankees, Dick Hoblitzell reportedly injured either his hand or a finger, or aggravated a previous injury. At any rate, the next day, Sunday, as the Red Sox played an exhibition in Clifton, New Jersey, due to the blue laws still in effect in New York, Hoblitzell got a rest and Barrow let everyone play just about anywhere they wanted. Little used pitcher Weldon Wyckoff played the outfield and veteran shortstop Heinie Wagner, nominally an active player but as much a coach as anything else, started the game at first base. Halfway through, Ruth took over for Wagner at first, flying out and whiffing against a semipro pitcher.

When Hoblitzell showed up at the ballpark the next day, May 6, he was still unable to play. That solved one problem for Barrow, because thus far in the 1918 season, whether it was because he was hurt or distracted by his impending call-up to the military, Hobby was hitting .080, with only four singles in 50 at bats.

But replacing him still left Barrow in something of a quandary. Stuffy McInnis was one of the best first basemen in the league, but Barrow had decided to play him at third and wasn't eager to make a change. Besides, who then would play third? The logical choice was second baseman Dave Shean, but that would leave a gap there. And Heinie Wagner, who had once played a little third base, had a bad arm and could no longer throw.

So with little fanfare, Barrow, after likely talking things over with Harry Hooper and Wagner, made the next most logical decision. Ruth had played first during the spring, and had filled in one day before in the exhibition, so he might as well step in at first base now. Besides, another bat in the lineup, particularly Ruth's, especially in the Polo Grounds, was useful. So on May 6, 1918, three years to the day after he'd cracked the first home run of his career, also in the Polo Grounds, Ruth stepped onto a major league diamond for the first time as something other than a pitcher or a pinch hitter, which he had done for the Red Sox only a handful of times.

It was intended to be a temporary measure, a stopgap until Hoblitzell came around or Barrow came up with another solution. There was no indication at the time that the move was permanent, or that it was the result of some great revelation or grand design—those claims, by Barrow, Hooper, and others, would come years later. For now, all it meant was that Hoblitzell was hurt, Ruth was left-handed, and someone had to play first, so it might as well be the Babe. He hit sixth.

Once again, Ruth won the headlines even though the Red Sox lost the game. The one in the *Globe* read "Ruth Starts Rally, but Red Sox Lose."

Ruth's noise came in the fourth after Wally Schang—usually a catcher, he was pressed into service in left field—doubled. Stuffy McInnis, up next, did what he was supposed to according to the widely accepted baseball strategy of the time and tried to move the runner to third with a bunt—it mattered not who was up next, be it Babe Ruth or Ty Cobb. It backfired, as he bunted straight back to the pitcher, George Mogridge. He put out Schang at third, leaving McInnis at first.

Ruth did not try to move the runner along. Neither did he simply try to make contact. He tried to hit the hell out of the ball. And he did.

The bat met the ball square and Ruth lifted a drive to right, not straight down the line but 40 or 50 feet fair and leaving the park, not where the fence was only 258 feet away, but where it was closer to 330, near where the second deck ended. The ball crashed into the low-hanging second deck, which was only a few feet farther back than the fence, the front facade only about 40 feet above the field of play. There, according to Macbeth in the *New York Tribune*, it "knocked the back out of the seat."

In regard to Ruth's home runs in the Polo Grounds, it's important to remember that during his time there the second deck in right did not completely enclose the field of play, but stopped at a point estimated to be

somewhere around 340 and 350 feet from home. That's significant, because at the end of the second deck the right field wall angled steeply toward center, and a ball that would otherwise reach the second deck, but
struck another 30 or 40 feet more toward center field, would fall 60 or 70
feet shy of leaving the ballpark. In almost every instance, a ball hit into the
right field bleachers past the grandstand was a longer drive than one into
the upper deck.

Wherever it hit, it counted, and Ruth's drive gave Boston a brief lead. But
Carl Mays quickly gave the runs right back and plenty more. He was pulled
in the fifth and Boston fell 10–3, the only remaining excitement coming in
the sixth, when Ruth pulled the ball over the roof of the grandstand, sending the crowd to its feet before they watched the fly ball curve foul, a drive
that probably traveled less than his earlier home run, but appeared more
impressive. Such was hitting at the Polo Grounds—a ball hit 260 feet but
pulled hard down the line could fall for a home run, and a much more solid
blast of 400 feet, pulled but not pulled hard, could fall short of the fence.
Little wonder that as Ruth grew and matured as a hitter, he became ever
more adept at pulling the ball. You got more mileage that way.

Sitting together in a box just off the field were Harry Frazee and Jacob
Ruppert. The two men already knew each other from league business and
both kept offices in New York and held the same opinion of Ban Johnson.
If the earlier rumor of an offer for Ruth was true, it was likely discussed,
and if Frazee had simply been floating the notion, on this day Ruth's performance gave him the opportunity to bring it up again.

At any rate, Ruth was certainly the object of conversation, for as Paul
Shannon of the *Boston Post* noted, "Babe Ruth remains the hitting idol of
the Polo Grounds."

After the game, the Red Sox and Ruth took a train to Washington and
the next day faced off against the Senators' ace, Walter Johnson. The Red
Sox, having dropped three straight, were in a tailspin and Ruth started at
first base for the third game in a row. So far he'd been good for histrionics,
but not for wins.

It would be so again. In the sixth inning, he drove one of Johnson's fastballs over the wall in right field. Taking advantage of wartime hyperbole,
the *Boston Herald* reported "it sailed on and on over the wall, messing up
a war garden and scaring a mongrel pup half to death." It did not, how-

ever, scare Johnson much, who collected three hits of his own and knocked in two runs while beating the Sox 7–2. Boston was now officially in a slump, losers for four in a row despite Ruth, their quick start to the season all but squandered.

An interesting and somewhat inexplicable pattern was beginning to take shape, one particularly noticed in Boston: in terms of wins and losses, Ruth's home runs did not often seem to matter. Indeed from 1915 through 1919, while playing on three pennant winners, a second-place club that won 90 games, and a 1919 team that finished five games below .500, Boston's record in games during which Ruth hit a home run is only 26–21 and 20–18 in 1918 and 1919. In each case, the club's record was slightly worse than in those games in which he did not hit a home run. While the statistical difference is virtually insignificant, in terms of perception it was not. Just as Ted Williams earned a reputation he did not fully deserve as a selfish hitter who did not come through in the clutch, over time Ruth would battle a similar opinion in Boston. Even some of his own teammates believed he was a poor clutch hitter.

But there was another factor at work, too. Although Ruth added value as a hitter, at the same time, over the course of the 1918 and 1919 seasons, his value as a pitcher diminished. It was almost as if he were two players at once; a hitter coming into his own and making an ever-larger impact, and a once great pitcher slowly fading away. The overlap between the two was small. In terms of WAR, the contemporary statistic that measures a player's value in wins versus an average replacement player (wins above replacement), Ruth's value as a pitcher in 1916 and 1917 was 8.7 and 6.5 wins above average respectively, but only 2.3 and 0.8 in 1918 and 1919. As a hitter, the numbers are nearly reversed—in 1916 and 1917 he was worth 1.7 and 2.1 wins, but in 1918 and 1919 his value skyrocketed to 5.1 and 9.4 wins per year. Cumulatively, his most valuable year with the Red Sox was 1916 when he was primarily a pitcher with a combined WAR of 10.4—a mark he would better only six times in his 16 seasons as primarily a hitter.

Consider this: Had Ruth been able to retain his prowess as a pitcher, he may well have proven to be more valuable on the mound while making only the occasional appearance in the field as a hitter. Had he been able to do both at once—pitch and play more or less regularly as a hitter, even for just a few years—his value would have been astronomical, likely approaching a

WAR of 20 or more each season, his impact on the game incalculable (the single season record for WAR is Ruth's 14.1 in 1923, the only time in baseball history a player has topped 13).

As it was, in terms of WAR alone, Ruth essentially became as valuable to the Yankees as a hitter in the 1920s as Walter Johnson was as a pitcher to the Senators in the teens. Yet as remarkable as that was, had he been able to both hit and pitch at a high level simultaneously, even for just a few years, the results would have been extraordinary. Instead, one kind of greatness was simply substituted for another. Already in 1918, he wasn't quite the dominant pitcher he'd been in the past, his record a scuffling 3–3, his strikeout total down significantly. Although Ruth had always said that he felt "at home" on the mound, his performance was starting to say something else. He was pitching in some hard luck, but he also had lost some games that he used to win, and due to rosters decimated by the war he wasn't exactly facing top-notch competition.

For now, after hitting three home runs in three games, observers were just trying to place the feat in perspective. Only one other major league player had ever done so before. Oddly enough, it was a pitcher, the Yankees' Ray Caldwell, who on June 10, 11, and 12 in 1915 hit home runs in three straight games—as a pinch hitter. In fact, Caldwell was considered such a good hitter that in 1918 he'd play 41 games in the New York outfield and hit .291.

For the time being, Barrow left Ruth in the lineup. He continued to hit, although with less power than during his streak, and played an adequate first base. The Red Sox, however, continued to stumble, dropping their sixth in a row on May 9 as Ruth took the mound for the first time since April 29, squaring off against Johnson.

It a sense, it was Ruth's most amazing game of the season. Hoblitzell returned to the lineup to play first, but Barrow installed Ruth in the fourth position in the batting order, a rarity for the pitcher. He came through, too, tripling in his first at bat and then following up with a single and two doubles.

But Walter Johnson was just as good, if not better, and the two teams went into extra innings tied. Ruth nearly won it with his fifth hit of the day, another double to right field, but the one-man team took that to heart and he was thrown out trying to steal third. Ruth then gave up the winning run as the Red Sox lost 5–4 and tumbled out of first place.

Now people were starting to talk. On the one hand, since joining the starting lineup, Ruth was hitting .563. For the last week, he had been the best hitter in the league and the talk of all baseball. On the other hand, there was that nasty little six-game losing streak, over which time the Red Sox pitching staff, save for Ruth, had virtually collapsed.

No one quite knew what to think. Some thought that putting Ruth into the lineup every day threw the club off kilter, making some players jealous and causing others to look over their shoulders, while increasing the burden on Boston's already faltering pitching staff. In the *Globe*, Mel Webb offered that "putting a pitcher in as an everyday man, no matter how much he likes it or how he may hit, is not the sign of strength for a club that aspires to be a real contender." Well, the Yankees were doing it with Caldwell, too, and how could you take a guy out of the lineup who was now batting .500? Still, it was confounding—*The Sporting News* compared it to "college or school baseball" where the pitcher is often the best player in the team, yet admitted, "Ruth is the large rumble in the Red Sox family."

The Red Sox returned to Boston, and now Barrow had another idea. Hoblitzell was back, and back at first base, but Barrow still wanted Ruth's bat in the lineup. As a lefty, there was only one place to put him. Harry Hooper was a fixture in right, hitting .361, and since arriving from Philadelphia, Amos Strunk had been a revelation in center and was batting .319. The only place that remained was left field.

So far, at least at the plate, George Whiteman had demonstrated why he'd spent a decade in the minor leagues. Although a fine fielder, even against the subpar pitching of 1918 he was struggling. With right-hander Dave Davenport scheduled to pitch for St. Louis, Barrow stuck Ruth in left field and hoped for the best. Backed by Duffy's Cliff and the left field wall, even if Ruth screwed up there was little damage he could cause in the field. Besides, one big hit could make the difference in a game.

Unfortunately, none did. Ruth went hitless, but Boston won 4–1, as Ruth had an uneventful day in left, fielding only three soft singles. Ruth seemed a bit lost afterward, complaining, "It's lonesome out there," and "hard to keep awake. There's nothing to do." But there was still some unease over

Ruth's role. Writing in the *Boston American*, Nick Flatley still viewed him as a pitcher, "There is a world of speculation as to what regular playing will do to the $150,000 Babe Ruth arm," he wrote, concerned that outfield throws could cause harm. And in the *Boston Record*, Harry Casey called Ruth "the most valuable player in either the American or National League" but offered the opinion, seconded by Stuffy McInnis, that all Ruth had to do to really make good was change his swing and start chopping at the ball like everyone else. "If Babe ever learns to chop them," said McInnis, "he will set a new record for hitting."

Ruth was back at first base the next day. The Red Sox lost again, but snuck back into first place with a record of 13–10 when the White Sox defeated the Indians. With the season nearly a month old, the pennant was up for grabs with all eight teams within three and a half games of one another.

That's what made what happened next so infuriating to so many club owners, all of whom, even poor old Connie Mack, were beginning to think that in this crazy season, his club just might have a chance. Although crowds were down, there was parity. When spring turned to summer, well, a hot ball club and a tight pennant race just might bring out the fans and make it possible to make a little money after all.

On May 16, word leaked out that Provost Marshal General Enoch Crowder, responsible for administering 1917's Selective Service Act, and acting under the orders of Secretary of War Newton Baker, would execute a "work or fight" order. That meant anyone with a high draft classification who had heretofore escaped the draft had either to enlist or find a job in the war industries. Certain "essential" occupations were exempt—but baseball was not among them.

The logic behind the ruling was obvious—the draft had been a disaster. Although every American man between the age of twenty-one and thirty was supposed to register—some 23 million—three and half million or so never bothered and another three million registered and then treated their draft notice like so much tissue paper and never reported. Draftees were an administrative nightmare to track and enforce enlistment—everything was on paper records and it was nearly impossible to communicate, making service astonishingly easy to avoid; the IRS, created in 1913, was having a similar problem enforcing tax laws. Cheating was massive and pervasive, as was draft dodging. When those who had registered and were exempt due to the fact they were married or had other dependents were included, the draft was coming up way short of American military needs. The "work or fight" order essentially ended the exemptions for healthy draftees—except for those with "essential" work status.

For the next week, baseball stomped its feet and whined, openly wondering what this meant and publicly pleading with the authorities to somehow find a way to make ballplayers "essential" war workers. But the chances of that happening were slim—Ban Johnson's earlier politicking to make major leaguers exempt from the draft had not been forgotten, either by the public or the government, and whining about the war tax levied on ticket sales hadn't helped matters.

Yet when the details of the ruling were made public a week later on May 23, baseball was given something of a temporary reprieve. The War Department anticipated resistance to the order and released a statement that read "No ruling as to whether baseball players . . . come under the regulations regarding idlers or nonessential pursuits will be made until a specific case has been appealed." In other words, give it try, baseball. Test the ruling if you want, but if you fail, be prepared for the consequences.

Every owner in the game realized that if the players were considered nonessential that meant the end of the season. Of all the Boston players, only Heinie Wagner, due to his age, was clearly exempt. Frazee was politic, saying, "Certainly we want to win the war, even if we have to close the ballparks or destroy them . . . [but] I do not believe the Government proposes to unnecessarily disturb vested interests in legitimate business." In other words—of course we want to beat back the Hun, but not at our expense. Frazee was doubly affected by the ruling, which also threatened to shut down the theater, which currently was exempt due to the role it played in the nation's morale. Although he had no plays in production, he owned a number of theaters and no plays meant no rent, just as no baseball meant no ticket sales and no way to pay off mortgages and notes.

Most other club owners made similar statements—but not Ban Johnson. He was prepared to protect what remained of his own personal investments in several clubs, put the whole game in mothballs, and go down without a fight. He suggested not only shutting down baseball, but "all forms of amusements, ball parks, theaters etc." The men who owned baseball did not appreciate their fearful leader throwing up the white flag. Frazee, in particular, lost whatever slim affection he might have held for Johnson and now considered him both a fool and an adversary, a position soon adopted by several of his colleagues, most notably Charles Comiskey and Jacob Ruppert. Their wary relationship began to crumble. A slow erosion of Johnson's unmatched power would soon begin.

And what of Babe Ruth, the emerging crown prince of baseball and suddenly the name on every fan's lips? Well, he was lucky to be alive.

He stayed in the Boston lineup, where he returned to left field, collecting a few hits, hitting no home runs but giving Barrow a heart attack for his erratic outfield play. His strong arm was a force in left and he was okay tracking fly balls, but on several occasions he crashed into the unforgiving wood fence in front of the stands in foul territory, leading the *Herald* to comment, "It is a wonder he did not muss up the entire stand by the force of his impact." But that is not what brought Ruth nearly to the verdict of St. Peter.

May 19 was a Sunday, and in Boston that meant no baseball on the first real warm day of the year. Ruth, who'd been bothered by a sore throat for a few days, took his wife to Revere Beach, just north of the city, where he cavorted with another 150,000 or so Bostonians along the boardwalk and in the surf, likely quaffing beer and clams the entire time. By the time he got home, his throat was throbbing and his temperature raging, reportedly 104. Scheduled to pitch the next day, he showed up at the ballpark looking like death.

He was clearly too sick to play. The club trainer reportedly took Ruth to a nearby drugstore, where he picked up some silver nitrate, a caustic compound commonly used in the days before antibiotics as an antiseptic. The trainer liberally swabbed Ruth's throat and intended to send him home, but Ruth had a bad reaction. His throat began to swell and as he choked and gagged he was rushed to the Massachusetts Eye and Ear infirmary.

Those who saw Ruth carried into the infirmary thought the worst, and rumors swirled around Boston that he had died. Fortunately, a specialist, Dr. George Tobey, was able to reduce the swelling. He ordered Ruth to stay in the hospital and rest until his fever was under control. The newspapers—after some first reported his demise—now wrote that Ruth was suffering from an acute case of tonsillitis.

That may have been true, but it also may have been something more. It hadn't earned the name yet, but Ruth may well have contracted a case of the most deadly pandemic the world has ever seen, the so-called Spanish flu. The sore throat and rapid, high fever were classic early symptoms.

The malady, which likely first appeared in Austria in the spring of 1917, made it to the United States in Haskell County, Kansas, in January of 1918. This first wave of the disease reached the East Coast in March, and in the spring there were sporadic outbreaks throughout the Northeast. The government partially suppressed news so as not to cause panic during wartime.

And there was reason to panic. In a three-year period approximately one third of the human population became infected, killing 10 to 20 percent of everyone who contracted the flu—perhaps as many as 100 million people worldwide, 6 percent of the human race. The first wave was less virulent and tended to be most dangerous to the very young, the old, and those with weaker immune systems. At the start of the season, nearly a dozen members of the Cleveland Indians were sick, and soon thereafter most of Detroit's pitchers became ill. Younger and healthier subjects, like Babe Ruth and other ballplayers, were usually able to fight off the disease and, significantly, gain some immunity. During the summer, it appeared as if the epidemic had passed. It was a good thing, because the second wave of the disease, a mutation that swept over the United States in the fall, proved to be much deadlier, and for reasons still not fully understood, most dangerous to healthy young adults like Ruth.

Ruth stayed in the hospital for the next five days, until the following Sunday, much of it with his neck wrapped in ice and Helen by his side, as the swelling went down and his fever finally broke. Ruth was tickled when Dick Hoblitzell and Bill Carrigan sent him flowers; no one had ever sent him flowers before. He got a huge kick out of it and showed them off every time anyone entered his room.

He went to the ballpark the day after his release as the Red Sox hosted Chicago, and after playing .500 ball with Ruth in the hospital, as he sat on the bench still recovering they ripped off four straight wins. But the signs were not good. On Memorial Day, a doubleheader versus Washington drew only 11,000 fans, Ruth returning to the lineup in game two as a pinch hitter. The uncertainty over whether the season would continue played havoc with attendance. A year earlier, the Sox had drawn twice that on

Labor Day. It wasn't just that interest was down; simply being able to go to the ballpark was akin to a public acknowledgment that you probably weren't doing your share to support the war. They might as well have posted a sign outside that read "Welcome Slackers and Draft Dodgers."

Ruth didn't make it back into the regular lineup until June 2, when he took a turn on the mound in Detroit. He was wild, and lost 4–3, but he launched a home run to right field that allegedly landed on Trumbull Avenue, described as both "the hardest hit ball of the year" in Detroit and a feat never accomplished before. Even Cobb, the greatest hitter in the game, had never done it. As the Red Sox then split the four-game series with the last-place Tigers, Ruth played the rest of the series in center, as Barrow was afraid he would run into the fence in left.

But the only fence that mattered to Ruth was in right field, as he duplicated his home run three more times, setting a new record with home runs in four straight contests, including one in a no-hitter tossed by Dutch Leonard. Barrow now admitted "it's almost impossible to keep him out of the game," and fans throughout baseball, already thrilled with Ruth, now became enthralled.

With the pennant race and the season entirely up in the air, what Ruth did became more important than who beat who and what place that gained in the standings. For perhaps the first time in baseball history, fans, en masse, were not so much rooting for a team, and following the score, but rooting for an individual player, and following his every action. In Europe, the Allies were bogged down in the trenches, the war proceeding inch by bloody inch. In comparison, Ruth was the precise opposite, all kinetic action and excitement.

Even Ruth was getting into the act. Dick Hoblitzell's number had finally come up and he was on the precipice of joining the service, so Barrow moved Stuffy McInnis back to first base and installed Fred Thomas at third. Ruth wasn't happy about that. Playing outfield was boring, and he didn't give a damn what was best for the team. He wanted to play first and complained, "I get sleepy out there in the field."

But there may have been something else at play as well. Ruth's home run explosion in Detroit, giving him seven for the year in only 23 games, may have also marked a turning point in the season, because from that point forward, not only did Ruth's home run production drop, but so did that of the entire league. Of the 95 home runs hit in the American League in 1918, 59 came during the first half of the season, when most teams presumably were still using baseballs manufactured before the war effort commandeered wool and horsehide. By midseason, these inferior baseballs, wound with lower quality wool and covered with hides that would have been discarded before the war, were coming into use, a subpar and less resilient product that rapidly turned soft. Although hitting, in general, was not much affected, home run hitting was. After averaging a home run every three games so far in 1918, Ruth would hit only four more over the remainder of the season.

Day by day, which team won and which team lost seemed to matter less and less. While baseball hemmed and hawed and waited around for Washington to make a decision, some players began looking around at other options. There was already a tradition of industrial semipro baseball in many places in the United States, and more than a few players earned more money playing semipro ball than they ever could have in professional baseball, with the added benefit of being able to live in one place and have a cushy job in the postseason. The captains of industry who operated the nation's largest industrial plants liked nothing better than to beat the competition, so at some levels these teams were semipro in name only. Most ballplayers never saw the assembly line.

With the "work or fight" order pending, there was a sudden buildup in industrial production, particularly in the steel, textile, and shipbuilding industries. Eager to avoid the war, and afraid that if they waited much longer they might be drafted, major leaguers began to entertain offers from "essential" industries that also just happened to sponsor a potent baseball team. The White Sox star outfielder Joe Jackson was already threatening to quit and Red Sox pitcher Dutch Leonard was mulling an offer from the Fore River shipyard in nearby Quincy, Massachusetts. Lacking any real leadership at the top from Ban Johnson, the season was taking on the character of a sinking ship. It was every man for himself and not enough lifeboats.

Ruth was not an exception, and he led the way in the "what's in it for me?" brigade. The Red Sox needed him on the mound—particularly if they lost Leonard or anyone else. Yet after pitching in relief and losing to Cleveland 14–7 on June 7, walking the only two batters he faced, Ruth let Barrow know he didn't want to pitch anymore.

He didn't make a big announcement, and Barrow didn't push back very hard, but Ruth now balked every time Barrow brought it up, first telling the manager that pitching and playing in the field made him too tired. The press didn't make much of it, either. With the Red Sox on the road, there wasn't even a Boston beat writer with the team.

The next day Ruth struck out to end the game, stranding the tying run as he swung for the fences. When Barrow pushed him again about pitching when his turn came up next, Ruth suddenly complained of a sore arm. When that raised eyebrows it suddenly morphed into a sore wrist, one that he decided to treat by wrapping with a leather strop just to make sure everyone noticed, a malady that miraculously disappeared as soon as he lifted a bat or had to make a throw in the outfield.

It didn't sit well with either Barrow or many of his teammates. They recognized that as much as they liked his bat, it was even more valuable when paired with his arm, and if Ruth couldn't pitch, and Leonard went to "work" in a shipyard, they would not only have a short pitching staff, but one without any reliable left-handers, leaving them exposed.

It was uncanny, almost even comical, but the uncertainty of the season left Ruth feeling immune. He received little criticism in the Boston press. The fans' preoccupation with whether or not Ruth hit a home run sold newspapers, and in that pre-radio era, when the only way to know what took place at the ballpark was either to attend the game in person or cobble together a full accounting from several papers, Ruth moved newsprint.

It almost didn't matter if he hit a home run or not. Either one paper or another described damn near every swing in excruciating detail. There may never have been a player in baseball history whose pop-ups, fly-outs, foul drives, and grunting misses attracted more press, or apparently never committed an inconsequential act on the field. The newspapers had created a mythic Colossus and now they had to keep feeding the public appetite for it.

Over the next few weeks, Ruth got his way, playing left field, first base, and even center, hitting relatively well but not quite to his earlier standard, his home runs much less frequent as the deader ball came into play. The

Red Sox stumbled along, playing barely .500 baseball, clinging to a narrow lead of a game or two as New York, Chicago, and Cleveland remained in pursuit, with no team able to get any traction.

The pennant was Boston's for the taking, but the team could not overcome the twin loss of Ruth and Leonard, who last pitched on June 20 and then joined the Fore River team. After a slow start, he'd been Boston's best pitcher over the last month, giving up only a single earned run in his final 32 innings. His departure from Boston's rotation left it in shambles. After Mays, Joe Bush and Sad Sam Jones, Barrow was left flipping coins. Frazee picked up players when he could and even tried to entice former star Ray Collins, now retired, off his Vermont farm, but as more and more players left for jobs or joined the service, everyone was looking for help.

Then Ruth made a bad situation even worse. During the brief home stand, he crashed his car into a telephone pole and although he escaped unscathed, it was his fourth or fifth car accident in the past few years and was almost certainly alcohol related. The Red Sox then went into New York and dropped three of four to the Yankees, although Ruth, as was his custom in the Polo Grounds, managed to crack a home run—significantly, in the first inning, before the ball got soft—one the *Boston Herald* described as a "tornadic thump" that caromed off the concrete facade of the upper deck in right field. Although good ole Bob Dunbar, the *Herald's* faux byline, offered, "Babe can hit telegraph poles as hard as he hits the horsehide. We love him just the same," Barrow didn't share the sentiment.

He didn't just want Ruth to pitch—he needed him to, even after he cracked another home run, his 11th of the year, off Walter Johnson in Washington.

Everyone seemed caught up in the hype—at least everyone with a typewriter. Dispatches to soldiers in Europe supplied only the scores—unless Ruth hit a home run. And there was all sorts of wild speculation, or at least speculation that seemed wild at the time. One writer in the *Boston American* calculated that if Ruth remained in the lineup "his collection of four-play slams at the end of the campaign would be forty-four."

Everything came to a head on July 2. After Barrow and Ruth argued about Ruth taking the mound again and Ruth refused, he came to bat in the sixth inning with the Red Sox trailing the Senators 3–0. Washington's Harry Harper was having no trouble as the Red Sox hitters seemed to be going through the motions, and Barrow ordered Ruth to take the first pitch—maybe they could start to tire Harper out, or get a good pitch to hit.

But that was not Ruth. He was already fuming over the way he'd been pitched to recently, as pitchers were beginning to figure out the best way to retire him was to let his aggressiveness work against him. It had worked, too, as over the last month his batting average had tumbled from over .400 to just over .300. He was becoming an "all or nothing" hitter, something the savvy gamblers in the stands—and the pitchers—were starting to realize. Ruth ignored Barrow, swung at the first pitch to fall behind, then took a couple more wild swings and walked back to the bench.

Barrow let him have it. His patience was gone. "That was a bum play," he told Ruth, and Ruth responded by telling Barrow if he called him a bum again, he'd get a punch in the nose, although Ruth likely used a few additional adjectives. Barrow snapped back "That will cost you $500," and Ruth stormed out of the dugout, changed into his street clothes, and after sitting in the stands for a bit left the park, showing up several hours later at his father's saloon in Baltimore, still hot. After the game, Barrow told the press Ruth left the game because of stomach trouble, but no one was fooled for long. Ruth had become a headache.

He had options. As his fame increased so, too, had his opportunities to make money on the side. Johnny Igoe, also a member of the Royal Rooters, Boston's famous group of Red Sox fans made up of equal parts of politicians, gamblers, and businessmen (most of whom were all three), had gained Ruth's confidence in money matters and acted as sort of a de facto agent. He was always alerting him to opportunities to earn a little extra. If Dutch Leonard had found it more lucrative to play shipyard ball than stay in the major leagues, what was Ruth worth?

Barrow didn't know it, but Ruth had already been approached by representatives of a shipyard in Chester, Pennsylvania, just south of Philadelphia. He knew enough to send a wire to their manager, Frank Miller, asking what he could get. The shipyard immediately dispatched a representative to Baltimore to work something out. The July 4th holiday was coming up, and if Ruth appeared, a big crowd was guaranteed. The Red Sox would be playing the A's in a doubleheader in Philadelphia at the same time, but with Ruth onboard, the shipyard just might outdraw the major leaguers. While Ruth, technically, could only be paid a shipyard worker's wage, there

is little question that some kind of side arrangement was in the works—
Ruth was always eager to accept offers of cash. While much would be made
of his joyous behavior during public appearances, much of the time those
appearances were not quite as spontaneous as they appeared but rather
were accompanied by a fat envelope of hundred-dollar bills. It was easy to
smile then.

Everything was up in the air. Reporters tracked Ruth down in Baltimore
while Barrow sent a representative, likely veteran Heinie Wagner, to Baltimore to talk sense to his star. In the meantime, the shipyard began to
advertise Ruth's appearance—they planned to have him pitch—and
Frazee, never one to take a breach of contract lightly, threatened legal
action against the shipyard. After all, he did have Ruth under contract.

Over the next twenty-four hours, all parties tried to stake out their position. Ruth's feeling were hurt and he complained that when he didn't take
the first pitch, Barrow had called it a "bum play. . . . I thought he called
me a bum and I threatened to punch him," admitting "I couldn't control
myself," and complaining that the Red Sox had been mistreating him for
weeks and intimating that a boost in salary might make him feel better.

Frazee for his part, was ready to sue the shipyard "for heavy damages,"
and added, "I think I will win." Barrow, for his part, stayed mostly silent,
and when he did speak tried not to escalate the confrontation. "He's not
here," he said of Ruth, "that's all I know."

The Boston papers, while not making a public statement, were not happy,
and directed their disaffection at Ruth. Paul Shannon of the *Post*, probably the leading baseball writer in the city, was blunt: "Not a single player
on the team is in sympathy with him. The Red Sox first and last are disgusted with the actions of a man whom they say had his head inflated with
too much advertising and his effectiveness impaired by too much babying."
To a man, they realized that whatever Ruth gave them at the plate was
undercut by what they lost by not having him on the mound, and right
now they needed pitching. Besides, the circumstances of the war were
tough on everyone. Ruth wasn't special—at least not that special, not yet.
What was special was his utter lack of concern for anyone but himself.

There is a long history of ballplayers, even star ballplayers, jumping a
team in midseason, usually over a contract issue or some disagreement over
discipline, but few instances were more crass or self-centered than Ruth's

threat to join the shipyard. While Ruth, personally, would hardly pay a price for the indiscretion, his behavior, like Joe Jackson's earlier threat to play shipyard ball, reinforced the notion among the public that most ballplayers were selfish slackers. During a season in which interest was rapidly dwindling, his actions hardly helped. And as much as they detested his behavior, even his own teammates found it difficult to be angry with Ruth directly; he was so self-focused and unaware it was almost comical. They were just part of the ongoing parade of his life—nameless and almost faceless. All you could do was shake your head half in disgust and half in wonder that he could possibly be so oblivious. *The Sporting News* later summed it up nicely, describing Ruth as "only a big boy [who] views things through youthful lens, and is utterly reckless of consequence."

But by the time the news reached Boston on July 4th and the headlines were screaming about his departure, Ruth was already back in the fold. He wasn't keen on pitching and had already returned to the team with a promise that things would be worked out.

Barrow gave him the silent treatment, as did many of his teammates, who in this instance were finally beginning to hold him accountable, and Ruth sat in game one of the doubleheader, a sloppy 11–9 win over the desultory A's. Ruth nearly walked out again, but between contests he and Barrow had it out and the manager told him bluntly that if he wanted to play he'd have to follow the rules and stop putting himself above the team.

Ruth had heard similar admonitions after indiscretions at St. Mary's and reacted the way he always did, with boyish petulance and a trembling promise to do better. Installed in center field for game two, he knocked in the tying run but made a weak throw to the plate on a sacrifice fly in the 11th, and the A's won 2–1.

The next day Ruth pitched for the first time in almost a month. He won 4–3 in 10 innings despite coughing up a lead in the ninth. "I like to pitch," Ruth later told *Baseball Magazine*'s F. C. Lane, claiming his only objection was that "pitching keeps you out of so many games," although he wondered how many seasons he could do double duty. He would play the rest of the year—somewhere, usually in left field or first base—and eventually take a turn in the regular rotation, and after reminding everyone that "my wing was a little off," Ruth's complaints about a sore arm or wrist soon faded.

Over the next few weeks Barrow leaned heavily on Mays, Bush, and Jones and the Red Sox surged, playing their best ball of the year, and Ruth even chipped in with a five-inning shutout. It probably helped that a little over a week later Harry Frazee agreed to adjust Ruth's contract, adding a $1,000 bonus with another $1,000 due if Boston won the pennant. But day by day, what was happening on the field seemed to matter less and less and it seemed more likely there would be no pennant to win in 1918.

Ban Johnson's bombastic bullying as he tried to convince the powers that be that baseball was essential to the nation's morale was not only getting nowhere but, like Ruth jumping his team on the precipice of a national holiday, was having the opposite of the intended effect. In late June the National Commission sent Crowder a statement making a purely economic argument, claiming the "work or fight" order "will absolutely crush a business that has more than $8,000,000 capital invested," and Johnson himself doubled down, whining that baseball had already suffered enough and had paid $300,000 in extra war tax. It was one thing to argue that baseball served a purpose keeping up morale during wartime—it was another to cry poverty. The impression that baseball was concerned only with its own well-being was reinforced.

On July 19, following an appeal in regard to Washington's Eddie Ainsmith, who had been drafted and appealed the ruling that playing ball was not considered "essential" to the war effort, Secretary of War Newton Baker, trumping a few local draft board decisions, definitively ruled that "the work-or-fight regulations include baseball." He could not have been any clearer.

And Ban Johnson could not fall on his sword fast enough. Although nothing in the ruling ordered the major leagues to cease operations, and Baker even inferred that the game could continue, albeit by the "use of persons not available for essential war service," Johnson declared that the season was over "except for cremation ceremonies." He ordered an end to the season after the games of Sunday, July 21, saying, "We accept the ruling without protest."

Except Johnson wasn't a king, and his use of the royal "we" was meaningless. He was just one of three members of the National Commission, one leg of a stool that also included chairman August Herrmann and National League president John Tener, both of whom served at the behest of the club owners. And they were none too eager to end the season, particularly Harry Frazee, whose team had opened up a six-game lead in the pennant race—a World Series financial windfall still offered the promise that he might turn a profit, or at least not lose as much money as it appeared. Besides, if they shut down the season, the club owners worried they'd still be liable to fulfill player contracts, leases, and other financial obligations. Ending the season was akin to going bankrupt without the promise of release from debt.

And while Johnson was clumsy in his relationship with politicians, Frazee was slick. His archives are littered with requests from the rich, the famous, and the powerful asking for tickets and other favors, including some from sportswriters who later claimed to detest him. Front-row tickets or an introduction to a certain young actress bought a lot of goodwill—at least for a while. Frazee called Johnson's order "not right and not necessary" and he led a brigade of owners to Washington to plead their case.

This time they ditched the economic argument and wrapped the game in patriotic fervor. In the theater, the show went on, regardless of the war, because Frazee and other theater owners had argued successfully that putting on a play was akin to volunteering to wrap bandages. Led by Frazee and other renegade owners, like Pittsburgh's Barney Dreyfuss, the only Jewish owner in the game, baseball now made a similar appeal. Rather than ask that players be made exempt and classified as "unessential" to the war effort, they simply asked that the order be delayed until the end of the season so the American Pastime could fulfill its duty. Frazee even floated the notion of taking the two pennant-winning teams overseas and playing the World Series before the troops in France. Hell, he'd have offered to have benchwarmers knit hats for the troops if that would have helped. In short, the option provided a way for the government to give baseball what it wanted while at the same time giving the public something they could swallow.

Wheels were greased, arms were twisted, whiskey was drunk, and envelopes may even have been exchanged, but the headlines on July 26 all told the same story: "BASEBALL GIVEN REPRIEVE." Crowder didn't give baseball everything it wanted, but he gave them enough—or at least he gave Frazee enough. The "work or fight" order for ballplayers was stayed until September 1. The season could continue, truncated, but at least it gave the game another five weeks to try to make some money.

It was a big win for baseball but an even bigger win for Frazee and several other club owners, most notably Comiskey and Ruppert, who had supported him and found themselves in agreement with Frazee's estimation of Ban Johnson as not just biased against them, but inept. However, that still left the question of the World Series unanswered. Did that have to take place by September 1, or could they play it after the season ended?

Once again, Ban Johnson stepped in it. John Tener proposed to cancel the Series to play as many regular season games as possible, but Johnson favored a plan to end the season on August 20, which would allow the World Series to take place before the September 1 deadline.

Once again, Frazee led the insurrection. He entered into an alliance with several other American League owners and endorsed a National League plan to request permission to play the Series after the regular season. And he went public about the reasons why. "From now on the club owners are going to run the American league," he said. "[Johnson] is in great measure responsible for the cloud under which baseball has lain this year. From now on his 'rule-and-ruin' policy is shelved."

Continued pressure and pleas from Frazee and other owners, agreeing to limit the players' pay and make additional financial contributions to the war effort and other concessions, eventually worked. The War Department extended the deadline to September 15 for the two championship clubs so the World Series could be played.

That wasn't nearly as significant, in the long run, as the rejection of Johnson. It was as if they'd deposed the Kaiser. Frazee had shown not only that baseball didn't need Johnson but it was better off without him, and Frazee didn't mind letting everyone know it. After nearly two decades atop the game, first as president of the insurgent American League, forcing the National League to its knees and into a shotgun marriage, then as the most powerful man on the National Commission, no one had ever successfully crossed Johnson—at least not for long.

Now Johnson's position as the most powerful figure in the game was shaken. John Tener resigned from the commission, due in part to the controversy over the Series, and was replaced by John Heydler, who would one day prove less compliant to Johnson's wishes. For the first time, there was open insurrection and talk of a coup, and all of it emanating from one man: Harry Frazee. From that moment onward, the simmering enmity between

Frazee and Johnson went from simple dislike and disrespect to something approaching hate. Each was determined to oust the other from baseball, regardless of the consequences. In the end, their personal war would have nearly as big an impact on the game as the real war taking place in the trenches of Europe.

The impact on Babe Ruth would be part of the collateral damage.

4

○

Hijinks and Heroes

"Babe Ruth tried to win the bat from Whiteman before the latter started for Texas, but there was nothing doing, Whiteman and Ruth used this bat most of the season and it was considered the luckiest piece of wood in the bat pile.
—*Eddie Hurley*, Boston Record

All the while, as baseball and the War Department debated the future and how everyone could get what they wanted and still save face, for much of July the Red Sox had been getting by with a pitching rotation of Mays, Bush, and Jones, with only the occasional appearance by Ruth or someone else. Buoyed by their yeomanlike work, in one stretch the Sox went 15–3 and opened up a lead on the rest of the league.

Although the three-man rotation was temporarily effective, it was not sustainable. They continued to win, but toward the end of the month, the staff was showing signs of cracking up. The answer was in the outfield. The Red Sox needed Ruth to start pitching again. Regularly.

This, time, when they asked, he answered affirmatively. The mysterious sore arm and wrist suddenly and miraculously healed. He wasn't being magnanimous, but the combination of the bonus adjustment Frazee made to his contract and the possibility of earning some World Series swag suddenly made pitching a more reasonable proposition. Besides, now that it was settled that the season was going to continue, the shipyard leagues were collapsing as a major league alternative, and Ruth had no other options.

For the first time in months, his self-interest and that of the Red Sox were in alignment.

He'd also cooled at the plate. His last home run had come on June 30, and apart from a two-day explosion on July 11 and 12 against the White Sox, when he cracked four doubles and two triples, he was a mere mortal at the plate again. And even that explosion wasn't quite what it appeared— one double was a flare that fell in front of the outfielders and the other three opposite field hits to left against an outfield that was playing him to pull, while one of the triples landed on Duffy's Cliff and another rattled around the right field corner. None were the long drives Ruth had become famous for.

It might have been the deteriorating quality of wool and horsehide, but there is also some evidence that pitchers were starting to figure Ruth out, pitching around him when they could, and it was becoming clear that even though he claimed otherwise, left-handers still gave Ruth trouble. At any rate, as the season went on, Ruth's production dwindled. In August, he would hit .282, with only six extra base hits, all doubles, for a slugging percentage of .359, even worse against lefties. By comparison, in May he'd slugged .837. He went from being Babe Ruth to Heinie Wagner. In the final month of the season, Ruth hit no better than his fellow pitchers. All of a sudden, Ruth, with a bat in his hand, was just another guy.

The headline writers noticed. Ruth's name became less frequently used, and even the game stories, which earlier in the year had breathlessly recounted even his towering fly ball outs, now ignored him unless he really did something. Barrow noticed, too. By the end of the year, when Ruth wasn't pitching, George Whiteman often played left; that left Ruth's bat in the lineup, anyway—the two men shared the same stick. In the course of one short, strange season, Ruth had gone from a pitcher to a position player and then back to being a pitcher. It was as if some great unexplained spell, one that had made Ruth superhuman, a hitter the likes of which baseball had never before seen, had been broken. His 1918 performance is one of the most schizophrenic in the history of baseball, muddied at the start by the war, and made even muddier by the impact the war had on the season. By season's end, it was an open question as to whether Ruth's batting star would remain in the firmament orbit or whether he was some singular comet, never to return.

Fortunately, he still remembered how to throw. Down the stretch, he was once again one of the best pitchers in baseball and over his last 11 starts he went 9–2 with an ERA under 2.00. With Ruth in the rotation again, everyone else finally got a little rest and the Red Sox held on to their lead atop the American League as the Yankees collapsed and neither the Indians nor the Senators could overcome the slow decimation of their roster over the course of the season. Boston finished 75–51, in first place, two and a half games ahead of the Indians. Frazee's bold confidence coupled with Barrow's grasp of available talent—with a little help by their creative use of Ruth in the field—proved the difference.

After some further maneuvering, baseball finally received permission from the government to hold a World Series, but that didn't stop the drama. First, the owners figured out a way to screw the players out of the last month of their contracts, agreeing to release all but those playing in the Series, entering into a gentleman's agreement not to sign anyone released by another team. The players were powerless to complain, and baseball argued that a new way to divvy up the postseason money, imposed by the National Commission in the off-season that cut the second, third, and fourth place teams into the bounty, would make up for the loss. That argument was a lie, but the players were mostly kept in the dark and in the confusion of the season's final month, hardly had time to notice.

The Chicago Cubs won the National League and the right to play the Red Sox. Johnson threw down the first salvo of his war with Frazee by announcing that in order to save fuel during wartime, instead of having the teams travel twice between the two cities, as had been traditional, they would do so only once, and the Series would open in Chicago.

Frazee howled. While Boston would host four contests if the Series went to seven games, three home games to start gave the Cubs an advantage. It also set up the possibility that if they jumped ahead of the Red Sox either two games to one or three to nothing, that by the time the World Series came to Boston no one would give a damn. Then Boston wouldn't make any money. The *Globe* rightly called it "a Johnsonian slap at Frazee," and Frazee himself termed it "an insult to Boston fans," but one he was powerless to do anything about. Johnson, for his part, wrapped himself in the flag and took a shot at Frazee's patriotism, saying, "Someday Frazee will learn that the United States is engaged in a desperate war, the winning of which is the only thing that matters." He was speaking of the Great War, but he might as well have been talking about the escalating battle between himself and Frazee.

Had the Series taken place a month or so before, when Ruth's name was on the lips of every remaining baseball fan both in America or overseas, there might have been some excitement for what was to come. As it was, despite the fact that Ruth had finished with 11 home runs over the course of his 72 appearances on the field, by the time the Series began on September 5, interest was muted. All the posturing baseball had done over the course of the season, coupled with the perception that the players were money-grubbing, unpatriotic slackers eager to shirk their duty, dimmed interest. Compared to previous years, press coverage was relatively scant and not a single game was close to being a sellout. The Cubs' decision to play at Comiskey Park, with a larger seating capacity, instead of their own field, Cubs Park (better known as Wrigley Field today), was wasted. All they gained were more empty seats.

But the Cubs did worry about Ruth, and the larger dimensions of Comiskey Park, whose fences were 50 to 75 feet more distant than those at Cubs Park, might also have been at play in the decision. Yet despite the presence of Ruth, the Cubs were actually favored in the Series. Two of their top three pitchers, Lefty Tyler and James Hippo Vaughn, were left-handed. Together with right-hander Claude Hendrix, all three had won 19 games or more in the shortened season and the staff ERA was a stingy 2.18. Pre-Series speculation focused on whether the Cubs pitching could keep Ruth's bat quiet, as the press desperately tried to drum up interest in the games and sell a few papers. They hoped that when asked if the Cubs could quiet the battering Babe, everyone would forget that he had been *sotto voce* for more than a month.

Although the Cubs led the National League in runs scored, they were still a quintessential Dead Ball Era team, cracking only 21 home runs despite their home park's cozy dimensions; every man in the lineup was adept at playing the small ball style of play that still ruled baseball.

Unlike today, most managers kept their choice for starting pitcher a secret until game time, often gauging light, weather conditions, and even the size of the crowd before revealing their selection. Fastballers were favored when the weather was poor and the day was dark, presumably because the darkened ball was harder to pick up, or when it was warm and spectators might remove their coats, revealing a backdrop of white shirts.

Still, Ruth caused a stir and may have given Cubs manager Fred Mitchell some pause before the start of the Series. In batting practice, he strode to the plate, causing a ripple to run through the crowd, half either cheering him or razzing him, the rest falling silent and watching intently. Few Cub fans had bothered coming out to Comiskey earlier in the season to see Ruth play against the White Sox. Here was their chance finally to see the great Colossus.

Ruth thrived in such moments. He loved it when all eyes were upon him. As a boy, he had played for one reason—to get an admiring nod or a "nice job, George," from Brother Matthias or one of the others. Maybe that's why the moment never seemed too large for him. In every at bat of his life, he had always felt as if he had something to prove. He had always wanted to impress, to gain approval. In that regard, none was different from any other, whether it was batting practice or the World Series itself.

A strong cross breeze blew across the field from third toward first, billowing out the bunting hanging from the front of the stands and sending the odd bit of paper racing across the field. An over-the-fence home run was unlikely in Comiskey Park anyway, even if the wind was blowing straight out. It was 420 feet to center, 362 down the line in one of the few symmetrical parks in the big leagues.

One of Boston's position players or backup pitchers was on the mound. They knew the kind of pitches Ruth liked and he wasn't shy about telling them either. He rarely used batting practice for anything else other than an excuse to swing as hard and as often as he could. No bunts or smacking the ball the opposite way for him.

Massive bat in hand, Ruth took his stance, bat back and peeking over his right shoulder. Over the course of the 1918 and 1919 seasons, he would ever so slowly learn his swing and discover what worked and what didn't. Instead of standing square, his feet equidistant from the plate and spread wide apart, over time Ruth evolved a closed stance, his weight back, his bat rocking back. As the pitcher started his motion, and his weight shifted almost entirely on his back foot, like a rubber band being twisted, building up energy before being let go and simply uncoiling, stepping forward with his right foot and pushing off with his left, first his hips and then his torso and shoulders flying open, the bat lagging behind like the business end of a trebuchet, almost still at first, all his power and strength flowing through his shoulders to his forearms and wrists and hands, and then concentrating down the bat toward the end, the sweet spot sweeping through the strike zone at the point of contact faster and more powerfully than any other player in the game, a seamless dance, almost balletic in its precision.

It all happened in the blink of an eye, the resounding crack announcing success or failure even before the mind registered what had just happened, and that the ball was growing small. On this day, Ruth hit the first pitch he saw through the heart of the crosswind and into the stands in right field.

It was both breathtaking and frightening, but Ruth didn't much seem to care. He'd just watch for a second, maybe grin or yell something out to the pitcher and then beckon him to throw again, as if doing what no one else could do was nothing at all.

The Cubs were watching, too, thankful perhaps that they had made the decision to switch venues. If Ruth could do that in Comiskey, what might he do in Cubs Park, where the fences were 75 feet or so closer to the plate? They didn't want to think about that. But if Chicago manager Fred Mitchell was watching, the blast may have provided confirmation for a decision he had been mulling for days. As often as possible, he planned to pitch Vaughn or Tyler. At least a left-hander had a chance against Ruth. If he got hot, he could wreck a club all by himself, particularly against right-handed pitching.

Most observers expected Ruth to play every game in left field and perhaps not pitch at all. In the *Boston American*, H. W. Lanigan offered that Barrow "was to keep the Battering Babe Ruth on duty in the left pasture in all the games." Ruth expected to play, too, telling the *Herald*, "I hope I don't have to sit on the bench a single inning of the Series." He'd done that in 1915, appearing in only one game, as a pinch hitter, and hated it.

He had reason to hope he would remain occupied. Almost overlooked was the fact that during the last week of the season, Ruth experienced a personal tragedy: his father died.

The elder Ruth had run a tavern in Baltimore for years while his incorrigible son checked in and out of St. Mary's, but in recent years his fortunes had improved somewhat. After making it in the big leagues, Babe helped out the old man and bought a somewhat better joint on Eutaw Street.

The son even stood in behind the bar on occasion to help pull in customers. But the Ruth family's precarious social position was unchanged—they lived in a world where boozing and brawling came with breakfast, just as they had when Babe was growing up.

On the morning of August 25, one day after Babe last pitched and won, he received word that his father had passed away. The situation was both tawdry and sad. Ruth's mother was already dead and his father remarried and was living with his new wife, Martha, and her sister above the tavern. His wife's brother-in-law, who'd recently been charged with statutory rape, showed up uninvited at the bar. So did her brother, a fireman, and the two men soon got into it with one another. George Sr., relaxing upstairs in the family apartment, heard the row, came down to break it up, and eventually stepped outside to brawl with the fireman. He went down hard, and although few reports of the incident line up precisely, he hit his head, probably on the curb, fracturing his skull. He was taken to a hospital but soon died, leaving Ruth an orphan.

Ruth had missed a few days while attending to the funeral but returned to the team and never spoke of the tragedy publicly. Whether he was distraught, saddened, indifferent, or oblivious is not known. At any rate, it did not seem to affect his performance on the field. Baseball had long been his sanctuary and so it was again. If there was one wound Ruth carried forward in his life from his upbringing, it was his inability to place much trust in family relationships, particularly as a young man.

Before Game 1, with a crowd of just over 19,000 fans in attendance and thousands of seats unsold, Mitchell had both his left-handers, Tyler and Vaughn, go out and warm up, the kind of sleight-of-hand trickery still in vogue. Barrow countered with a man from each side, Ruth, and, oddly enough, Joe Bush, who had won only one of his last seven decisions. Either Mays or Sam Jones would have been more credible, but in those days, teams were loath to have a pitcher take time off before the World Series to set their rotation. Jones had pitched only two days before and on August 30, despite the fact the Red Sox had clinched the pennant, Mays, incredibly, had needlessly pitched both games of a doubleheader. Even then, a pitcher needed some rest.

When the lineups were announced by way of megaphone, there was little surprise that Ruth was on the mound and George Whiteman was in left field. What was surprising was that Ruth was hitting ninth, because even as he had slumped, Barrow usually hit him third. In fact, in two of his last three pitching appearances, Ruth had hit cleanup and Whiteman, playing left, had batted ninth. But this time, in the first game of the World Series, George Whiteman, he of the .266 batting average with one home run for the season, hit fourth.

Together, he and Ruth—well, mostly Whiteman—made Barrow seem like a savant. Ruth struggled on the mound, bending, but Whiteman, playing left field with abandon, kept him from breaking. He made a running catch with the bases loaded in the first, stopped another rally with another fine running catch with two on in the sixth, and smacked a key hit to move a runner along in the fourth, when Boston scored the only run of the game on a hit-and-run play. Shannon noted in the *Post* that "Three times this afternoon Boston's chances would have gone a glimmering" had it not been for Whiteman's play. He completely took the Cubs, and their fans, out of the game. The *Globe* reported that the crowd remained almost silent throughout and "the effect of the war was everywhere."

No kidding. Ruth was helpless against the lefty Vaughn, going hitless and striking out twice, but hung on to defeat the punchless Cubs 1–0. Game 1 set the tone for what would turn out to be perhaps the most desultory World Series in history, certainly the worst attended, and unquestionably the lowest scoring. Both teams played as if they were pinned down in the trenches and afraid to show their heads. Only Whiteman stood out.

That likely settled it for Barrow. He went with the hunch and the hot hand. The next day, when Tyler, a lefty, beat Joe Bush 3–1, Whiteman hit cleanup again and knocked in Boston's only run while Ruth, hardly able to remain still, stayed on the bench, even being passed over twice as a pinch hitter. And he stayed there for Game 3 when Mays beat Vaughn 2–1, as Whiteman again hit fourth, scoring one of Boston's two runs and robbing the Cubs' Dode Paskert of a home run. In the entire history of the World Series there has rarely been a stranger lineup decision, and never one that proved to be so effective.

The Cubs were feeling good, and even Chicago fans had started to warm to the Series, as more than 27,000 turned out for the home finale, leading players from both teams to think that they might make some money after all. Traditionally, the players' cut depended on ticket receipts. If the Boston crowd turned out—and the Series went to at least six games—there was a chance to make some dough.

Both teams boarded the same train at 8:00 p.m. for the long, twenty-seven-hour journey to Boston. Although clubs normally frowned upon frat-ernization, the long trip in such crowded quarters, with players of both teams mingling in the dining and smoking cars, made the admonition seem foolish. Besides, between the fallout from the collapse of the Federal League, causing ownership to cut salaries across the board, growing politi-cal awareness due to the war, and the histrionics of the regular season, some of the men realized they had much in common with one another. Perhaps it wasn't so much the Cubs versus the Red Sox, or the AL versus the NL, as it was the players versus the owners.

Yet there was no players union and, as yet, no organized push to form one. In the 1890s, the cooperative Players League had a brief trial run, but it was underfinanced and then undercut by the more established National League. Although there were periodic attempts by the players to create their own association and work for their mutual benefit, as of yet the play-ers were spread too far apart geographically, and communication too cumbersome for such a group to gain traction.

Most player careers lasted only a few short seasons and they took the attitude to make as much as they could as fast as they could and make as few waves as possible. The reserve clause bound them to the team that last signed them. The two major leagues had a virtual monopoly and there was little players could do about it. The average playing wage of just under $3,000 a year was more than double what most men earned at a time when 50 cents an hour seemed like a godsend, and a ballplayer's fame usually provided some additional opportunities to make money during the off-season. It just didn't make sense to cause labor trouble and put that at risk. There was a lot to be said for traveling in style and having your pick of girls in every town while the regular guys were either factory wage slaves or get-ting trench foot in Europe.

Before the Series, the players had all received a packet of documents from the National Commission. They had paid them little attention, but now as the train chugged through the night and they exchanged shots of rye and smoked cigars, a few players finally had the time to wade through the legalese. What they found lit a simmering fuse, and the flame got hotter on every subsequent page.

Prior to 1918, the players' share of Series money had been derived from 60 percent of the gate for the first four games, usually earning each player upward of $3,000 each—not bad for five or ten days' work. The National Commission and club owners took the rest. But before the 1918 season, the owners came up with a new angle. Winning teams had long tried to keep salaries down by arguing that players stood to reap a windfall if they won the Series, and now management tried to implement the onerous notion league-wide. Not only did they cut the players' share to only 55.5 percent of the receipts, but they further decided that only 60 percent of that money would go to the two clubs playing in the Series—the other first division clubs would divvy up the rest. That would allow every club owner in the league to argue that since most players would (or could) receive a postseason bonus, salaries need not rise. Why, in fact, they might even drop.

It was brilliant, particularly because the players had no idea the change had taken place and had no real way to do anything about it—or so the owners thought.

But there was even more. Before the Series started, Ban Johnson decided that each participating player in the Series would also donate 10 percent of his take to war charities.

The players got out their pencils and napkins and started ciphering. It worked like this: In the past, say, a winning share was $3,000. Given the cut in receipts, that now became only $2,763. But since the players now only received 60 percent of that amount, the remainder going to the other first division clubs, the share now became only $1,658. Take away the 10 percent "donation," and now the winning share dropped from $3,000 to only $1,493. In reality, it was even worse than that. Before 1913, the United States had no income tax. Due to the war, tax rates increased dramatically. For incomes above $4,000, a threshold most players in the Series would now breach, the tax rate jumped to 12 percent in 1918.

Altogether, that left a player who expected to earn $3,000 only a little more than $1,300. Factor in the small crowds, deduct their final months' salary, and by the time everybody passed around the napkins, they came to realize they would be lucky if they cleared even half of that. They could do the math, and the total players' share through the first four games came to just over $50,000, a sum that, due to the expansive rosters in place for much of the season, meant that between the two teams the money would be split among perhaps as many as fifty players instead of the usual thirty-five or so. They were playing the World Series virtually for free. Meanwhile, the National Commission and the owners were almost unaffected. They still got their dough.

The players weren't idiots. Contrary to most assumptions, many were well educated and aware—Harry Hooper, for instance, had an engineering degree. As the train chugged through the night and the liquor flowed, the mood went from one of dismay to insurrection. Over the course of the following day, even after the alcohol wore off, the players' dissatisfaction ossified. Harry Hooper and Dave Shean of the Red Sox met with the Cubs' Leslie Mann and Bill Killefer to discuss strategy. They were unhappy and planned to do something about it.

Well, most of them did. The one player who appeared both oblivious and unconcerned was Ruth. Nowhere over the next few days does his name appear anywhere near the word "disgruntled," and neither does he make any kind of comment whatsoever on the situation.

He probably didn't care and might not even have been aware. After all, compared to the others, he was well paid and Frazee had even given him a bonus after he jumped the team, and another one he qualified for by taking Boston to the pennant. It wasn't that Ruth was selfish, really—he tipped big and gave away money as if it was water—but he was so self-absorbed that he was almost unaware of any desires beyond his own. To his teammates, he was by turns exasperating and frustrating, but they generally did not hold it against him personally; they did, however, blame guys like Barrow and Frazee—mostly Barrow, for letting him get away with it. As for Ruth, it was hard to be upset with someone who was often unable even to recognize that he had done something wrong.

In fact, while many of his teammates and the Cubs were worried about each other, Ruth treated the long trip home like one big party. Even if he was starting to get something of a cold shoulder from other ballplayers, the rest of the passengers on the train thought Ruth was a riot. In addition to his usual carousing, Ruth and teammate Walt Kinney apparently found great sport in taking possession of the other passengers' straw boaters, the latest fashion in hat wear, punching a fist through the top, then placing the hat back on the owner's head. Ruth thought it was hysterical and so did the other passengers—well, most of them.

Concerning Ruth and the errors of his ways, one can never be quite sure if what made the papers was what actually happened, a heavily coded description that actually referred to something else, or an utter invention designed to enhance his reputation, draw crowds, and sell papers. So it was on the train trip back to Boston.

According to some reports, Ruth was simply too exuberant in punching through a straw hat and smacked his left hand into the side wall of the smoking car. Another claimed the train lurched and sent Ruth crashing against a window, breaking it. Another stuck with the lurch story and said that as Ruth grabbed for something to keep his balance, he bent back the third finger of his left hand. Another had him taking a "playful swing" at a fellow teammate—Carl Mays? Walt Kinney?—and missing, hitting some immovable object or perhaps even the side of someone's head or jaw. Or perhaps Ruth and a teammate got into an argument over the controversy about the World Series dough; potentially, no player was more influential than Ruth—he'd already proven he could make baseball management kowtow to his wishes. Had he wanted to, he may have been able to stop the Series on a dime.

No matter how he hurt his finger or precisely how it hurt—the words "bent," "broken," "cut," and "swollen" were all used—the end result was the same: Boston's best player, the man scheduled to pitch Game 4, had hurt a finger on his pitching hand by doing something he could have and should have avoided doing.

Barrow was livid. Had it been anyone else, or had the Red Sox trailed in the Series, there is no telling what he might have done. As it was, he could afford to gamble, and despite the fact that the middle knuckle was swollen and he had lost a chunk of skin, Ruth swore he could still pitch—Boston's trainer swathed the wound with iodine to prevent an infection. Besides, everyone else was so pissed off, Barrow may not have trusted another pitcher. The players were angry enough to consider striking—or if not that, maybe "arranging" a few games to make some money on the side. There had been rumors for years of exactly that taking place in the Series nearly every season.

At any rate, the players had already decided that if the commission didn't back down, they had no intention of playing Game 4. By the time their train arrived in Boston just before 11:00 p.m. the next night, the players had decided to approach Johnson and the other commissioners at their hotel, the posh Copley Plaza, the best in the city. So much for cutting back because of the war. The players designated Harry Hooper as their spokesman.

On Monday morning, he requested an audience with the commissioners. The three men agreed, and although they feigned surprise, they had likely heard about the grumbling from their friends in the press corps and had already decided on a strategy. Why fellas, they argued, the National Commission was just a lowly little group that worked for the owners, just like the players. The commission was powerless to change the rules now; that required all sixteen owners to meet, and they were spread out all over the country. They dismissed Hooper with a vague promise to meet again after Game 4.

The sleight of hand took Hooper aback. Before the game, he spread the news and told the players what the commissioners had said. There was still plenty of grumbling but by that time they were all already at the ballpark and fans were starting to show up. There simply wasn't time to take unified action.

No one was very happy about it, and as the players feared it was not the full house they hoped for at Fenway Park. Only 22,000 fans turned out and there were swaths of empty seats scattered around the ballpark. Even Boston's vaunted Royal Rooters, the group of fans and gamblers and politicians led by barkeep Nuf Ced McGreevey who had appeared at every championship since the 1890s, often singing their signature tune "Tessie," were nowhere to be found, an absence that was in no way accidental. They were fed up, too.

For his part, Barrow hedged his bet. During batting practice Ruth's finger seemed to cause him little trouble and he seemed to be swinging the bat well, but pitching was another matter. So in the event he did have to replace Ruth on the mound, he didn't want to burn a pinch hitter in the nine spot in the batting order, where he might be wasted. This time he hit Ruth sixth, although Whiteman remained in left and batting cleanup.

Ruth took the mound looking as if the world was on his shoulders, the yellowish stain of iodine making it impossible to ignore the swollen finger.

The Cubs teed off, getting a base hit and hard line drive in the first before Boston catcher Sam Agnew bailed Ruth out by picking a runner off base. In the second, Ruth gave up another two hits, and in the third, with a runner on second, Ruth picked him off. He was keeping the Cubs from scoring, but he was working hard, pitching from behind, not as sharp as he had been for most of the last month, clearly bothered by his injury.

Meanwhile the Red Sox weren't getting much off Tyler, either. Ruth grounded out in his first at bat, but in the fourth, first Shean and then— there's that name again—George Whiteman walked. Ruth came up with two outs. Mitchell got nervous and had Claude Hendrix start to warm up, but it was only a ruse. He had no plans to bring the righty in against Ruth.

In a similar situation today, Ruth would probably have been walked. The man hitting behind him, shortstop Everett Scott, was a singles hitter. But this wasn't the Ruth of the headlines and hyperbole. That guy had been gone for more than a month. Mitchell had Tyler pitch to him.

As Ruth held the bat, fans behind the screen could see him gingerly wrap his yellow finger around the handle. Had Ruth been a traditional batsman who pushed at the ball as much as he swung, the hand would have been a real bother. But Ruth didn't swing that way. In his style of hitting, the back hand, the top hand, did little more than help guide the bat and keep it on course; the front hand, the bottom hand, the only one that really needed to grip the bat tightly, provided the power.

Reports vary, but according to Shannon, Tyler pitched carefully and missed wide with his first two throws, then traded strikes and balls until the count was full.

The runners took off as Tyler wound and threw a fastball. This time Ruth connected, his right hand sweeping the bat through the ball. As Shannon wrote, "a report like a rifle shot rang through the park."

The ball rose on a line just to the right of center field, where outfielder Max Flack turned and started running. It was a long drive, but although the deepest part of center field, where the flagpole stood, was over 480 feet from the plate, in front of the bleachers the distance was much shorter and the stands were not located quite where they are at present.

Today, Ruth's hit, which likely traveled only about 370 or 380 feet in the air, would probably be gathered up by an outfielder and draw no comment.

But even though most outfielders played Ruth deeper than they played other players, they still often underestimated his strength; an extraordinary number of his long hits in his first year or two as a hitter didn't split the outfielders, as is often the case, but simply sailed over their heads, catchable had they only been playing deeper. Then again, Ruth was like a teenager batting against ten-year-olds.

So it was again. Flack was reportedly still 50 feet short of the stands when the ball cleared his head, took a bounce, and struck the fence to the right field side of the center field bleachers. Even so, the hit probably should have been scored only a double; a sloppy relay got past the Cub third baseman and as Shannon put it had to be "rescued" near the Cub dugout as Ruth chugged into third.

No matter, Boston fans were on their feet as McInnis and Whiteman scored. Ruth had a triple. The Red Sox led 2–0.

Over time, the drive would be celebrated out of proportion. It would be Ruth's last big hit in the postseason for the Red Sox, in a game in which he set a pitching record, in a World Series that would be Boston's last world championship for another eighty-six seasons. It also stood out because during the Dead Ball Era few World Series games had ever been decided by a long hit. More often, some error, catch, or act of daring had made the difference. But this was Ruth, and anytime his name was attached to anything, no matter how mundane, it became glorious. So it is with gods among men.

On the mound, his yellow finger standing out on the side of the baseball, Ruth soon started to fade. With each passing inning his control wavered, and only a fine fielding day by Everett Scott, who figured in three double plays and fielded 11 chances without an error, kept the Cubs at bay. In Ruth's next at bat, as he clung to the lead, with a man on, Barrow had him sacrifice, a measure of just how much confidence the manager had in Ruth and just how committed he remained to scientific baseball. Ruth continued to hold the Cubs scoreless, but wobbled and staggered as if he was lurching through the train chasing after straw hats.

It came apart fast. In the eighth, he gave up a walk and then Claude Hendrix, pinch-hitting for Tyler, singled. Ruth next threw a wild pitch, moving both men along.

They stayed there on a ground ball to first, as the infield played close, but the next batter hit a ground ball to second to score one, and then Ruth gave up a single to Leslie Mann to tie the score 2–2.

It didn't gain much attention at the time, but the runs were the first scored off Ruth in 29 innings of World Series pitching. After not pitching in the 1915 Series (in Ruth's three Series in Boston, he appeared in fewer than half the contests), in 1916 after giving up a first inning run he had thrown 14 shutout innings against Brooklyn in his only pitching appearance and in 1918 he had already thrown a shutout against the Cubs. The performance set a new record of 29 innings (since broken by Whitey Ford with 29 ⅔ innings), breaking Christy Mathewson's existing mark of 28. It was significant, but not as impressive as it would later seem over the years, when the lively ball made such a record even harder to achieve.

The game ended quickly. Shufflin' Phil Douglas came on in relief for the Cubs, gave up a single, and when Hooper bunted toward third, Douglas picked up the ball and threw it over the first baseman's head. It bounded off the stands down the line and Wally Schang raced home with the run that gave Boston a 3–2 lead.

Ruth tried to finish, but he was done. After giving up a single and a walk to start the inning, Barrow called on Joe Bush. With a man on second, he sent Ruth to left—Whiteman was a better fielder, but Ruth had the better arm and had a better chance of cutting down a runner at the plate. Bush only threw a handful of pitches—after a sacrifice, a ground ball to Scott started a game-ending double play, and Boston won, taking a 3–1 lead in the Series.

After Ruth's relative silence for the past month, his performance—in particular his hit—was praised all out of proportion. Virtually every headline sang his praises and heralded his triumph . . . with little mention made of the fact that his hijinks aboard the train had nearly cost his team a chance to win and had still likely adversely affected his performance. His mighty bat healed nearly all wounds. That was Ruth, and, increasingly, the way the press treated him; they needed him, baseball needed him, to sell papers and put rear ends in the seats.

Anointing anyone else a hero of the game would not have accomplished that. Shannon's breathless account began "big Babe Ruth's mighty bat wrote another page in the annals of World Series championships yesterday" and went on from there. He didn't mention another Boston player until eleven paragraphs into the story, another 600 words. With a single hit, Ruth got more ink than any other Boston player had the whole Series.

But all was not well. The players—at least the players not named Ruth—had not forgotten their issues with the National Commission. While most accepted an invitation to attend a play that night, likely secured by Frazee, Hooper and Everett Scott of the Red Sox and Mann and Killefer of the Cubs went to the Copley Plaza looking once again for the three commissioners. They should have gone to the theater. Reports vary, but after what might have been a brief meeting, Johnson, Heydler, and Hermann gave them the dodge, again falling back on the argument that they were just lowly employees of the owners and powerless to act without their direction. Afterward, they probably went to the play. They certainly went to the bar. The four players waited for them until after midnight and then gave up.

It was almost comical, a kind of vaudeville act played out in real life. The commission figured that if they just kept giving the players the runaround, in another day or two the Series would be over and the question would become moot. After all, what could the players do? Go on strike? To the National Commission, the notion was absurd. Players were employees who did what they were told. Period. Attempts to unionize or take any kind of collective action had usually died on the vine. Ruth's "me first" attitude was the rule, not the exception.

This time, however, the commission underestimated the players' resolve. The players' delegation returned to the hotel the following morning, but was put off once again. This time the commission told them they could meet after the game.

After the game? If Boston won, the Series would be over. Good luck finding the National Commission then. With that, Johnson and company retired to the Copley Plaza bar to celebrate breakfast and fuel up for the game. With a scheduled 2:00 p.m. start, that only left four or five hours for libations.

The players took a more sober view. By noon, most of them were at the ballpark and as the rest trickled in, each man soon learned what was going on and began to discuss the matter. A consensus soon emerged. If the commission would not even meet with them, much less meet their demands, well, the answer was simple; they would not play. It was not as if it was going to cost them very much.

As far as it can be determined, the players were united—or at worst, indifferent and willing to go along with the consensus of their teammates. No one openly sided with the commissioners.

The gates at Fenway opened a short time later and a good walk-up crowd turned out, hoping to catch the Red Sox win the world championship. They slowly began filling the stands, expecting to see the players sauntering out, taking batting practice and shagging flies. Instead, all they saw was an empty diamond, as if the off-season had already begun. Before long, word spread that something was happening and that the players were on strike. The long line outside soon scattered, while inside the park the mood turned ugly. If there was no ballgame to cheer, there was still plenty to make noise about.

Just before 1:00 p.m., word reached Johnson and the other commissioners in the hotel bar that the players weren't on the field and didn't plan to leave the locker room. The commission was so concerned it took them more than an hour to get to the park. They could have walked faster, but they could barely stand.

At 2:35 p.m., they stumbled and bumbled into the Boston dressing room, where Ruth and his teammates were still sitting around in street clothes as a clutch of sportswriters stood by eager to see the show. Johnson spoke first, blurting out to no one in particular that "if they concede anything to those—pups, I'm through with baseball," although the report in the *Boston American* made it clear he didn't really refer to the ballplayers as "pups."

The players' delegation, led by Hooper, and the commission, accompanied by a few sportswriters, retired to the umpires' room for a little privacy. Herrmann immediately launched into a soliloquy about how much he had done for the game and Johnson soon chimed in as well.

The players were incredulous. Both men were stone-cold drunk. "I made it possible Harry," Johnson blubbered over and over into Hooper's ear, nearly in tears. "I had the stamp of approval put on this series, Harry, I did it, I did it . . ."

Anytime the players tried to speak, the commissioners simply responded with more blather, ignoring them even when Hooper said the players would donate all their Series money to war charity, if only the old rules remained in place. It was a matter of principle, he tried to explain, not greed.

But the commission's ear was not just deaf to the players' pleas, they were so drunk they couldn't even hear them over their own blubbering. Herrmann blurted out "Let's arbitrary this matter" and then started talking again. Hooper and the others realized their threat was futile. If they didn't play, they'd be blamed. Hooper looked over at the group of reporters who watched, barely able to contain themselves, and said with disgust, "It is apparent we have no one to talk to." He and Mann reported to their clubs that the commissioners were too drunk to talk. The players said the hell with it and decided to play anyway. Mann and Hooper returned to the umpires' room, and after extracting a promise from Johnson that they'd face no punitive actions for the delay, they agreed to take the field.

While the players dressed, Boston mayor John "Honey Fitz" Fitzgerald took command of a megaphone in the stands and announced that the players "have agreed to play for the sake of the public and the wounded soldiers in the stands."

The crowd responded with a resounding chorus of boos. They'd been resentful of the players all year and now, begrudging the fact that the players were trying to wrap the flag around their decision to play, finally had a chance to vent. When the teams trotted out to the field, they were jeered as calls of "Bolsheveki" and "slackers" echoed over the diamond, as well as, J. C. O'Leary noted in the *Globe*, "a lot of other names that would not look nice in print."

Through it all, Ed Barrow stuck to his plan. Whiteman played left and batted fourth. As the left-handed Hippo Vaughn made his second start of the series for the Cubs, Ruth sat on the bench. The only time he left it was to coach first base when the Red Sox came to bat.

The Sox managed only five hits as Vaughn shut them out. Meanwhile, his Cub teammates touched Sam Jones for three runs, and would have had more had not George Whiteman continued to play out of his mind and make several more outstanding catches.

The paper the next morning told the story, and although most of the local reportage in regard to the strike was evenhanded, the national press sided with Johnson. The fans weren't in the mood for sympathy, and most backed the commission. In the *Boston Post*, Arthur Duffey summed up the dismay with the game almost everyone was feeling, writing "baseball is dead . . . killed by the greed of owners and players . . . the wrangling of the players and magnates yesterday over the spoils furnishes a disgusting spectacle . . . the game just reeks with scandal after scandal."

There was a lot of nodding in agreement over morning coffee and little wonder then that the next day only 15,000 fans turned out at Fenway Park for Game 6, most believing they were witnessing that last major league game that would be played in a long time. It was clear that as long as there was war, there would be no baseball, and no one was making plans for 1919.

By now, the players just wanted it to end, too. Who won? Who lost? *Who cared?* They were playing for free, for nothing. Any victory now would be purely Pyrrhic. Hell, the umpires, each guaranteed $1,000 for working the Series, would probably take home more than the players would.

The fans who did show up were surprisingly enthusiastic. No one was going to spend good money to jeer, so those who did turn out were the few fervent fans who remained—them, and the gamblers. The gamblers always showed up.

Still, after playing Game 5 in an hour and forty-two minutes, they played Game 6 as if in a contest to beat that mark. The Cubs played inattentive baseball—two of their three baserunners were picked off. The only player on the field who seemed to give a damn was the least likely hero of all, playing in place of an indifferent Ruth—George Whiteman.

In the third, with two on and two out, he came to bat against Lefty Tyler. For a moment, the Cubs paused and considered walking Whiteman to face McInnis, but in the end decided the career minor leaguer's luck was due to run out. It wasn't. He hit a sinking line drive to right.

Cubs right fielder Max Flack raced in and tried to catch the ball on his shoetops, but the dipping drive broke through his hands and hit the ground. Mays and Shean raced home, giving Boston a lead it would not relinquish.

Of course, it was Whiteman who provided the only remaining drama, launching himself in the air to snag Turner Barber's sharp drive to short right in the eighth. He caught the ball inches from the ground—a remarkable catch given the gloves of the era, and then tumbled head over heels. When he left the game one batter later, and Ruth, making his last World Series appearance in Boston, trotted out to take his place, a late-inning scrub, the crowd reacted with its most genuine outpouring of emotion and affection of the Series, cheering the only player who didn't seem to have a dollar sign on his back, Whiteman. Ruth and the others just watched.

It ended an inning later, with a ground ball to Shean, who made the short toss to McInnis. He held the ball in the air for a minute, and then, as Ed Martin wrote in the *Globe,* "Hooper, Ruth, Mays, Shean, Schang, Scott and others did a fade out. Down came the curtain and from out of the stillness that swept over the battleground came a lone voice piping up: Those Red Sox always were a lucky bunch."

Somehow, Boston had its fourth World Series in the past seven seasons, something no other team had done, and with three virtually different ball clubs—only Hooper remained from the 1912 club, and of the regulars, only Hooper, Ruth, Scott, and Mays from 1916. At the final out, a carrier pigeon was released to deliver news of Boston's 2–1 victory to the soldiers stationed at Camp Devens, some thirty-five miles northwest of Boston. For many there, it was the last good news they'd ever receive.

After a summer in some kind of remittance, the Spanish influenza was roaring back. There was a big outbreak in Chicago at the end of the summer, and circumstantial evidence suggests that those who made their way to Boston from Chicago for the World Series might have hastened the fall outbreak in Boston.

At Fort Devens, where thousands of soldiers lived in close proximity to one another, the pandemic that fall was particularly devastating, killing more than 700. Less than a month after the Series, baseball was the last thing anyone was thinking about. Death hung over Boston like a pall. In all likelihood, had the 1918 season been played to a full schedule, due to the pandemic a 1918 World Series would never have been played at all. By October, the city was in a panic and large gatherings of people rare. As it was, at least two members of the local sporting press fell victim to the disease anyway, the *Globe*'s Ed Martin and the *Record*'s Harry Casey. Their reports on the World Series would be among the last they would ever file.

Fortunately, the disease infected no Boston or Chicago players. They scattered as soon as the Series ended, the Sox earning $1,102.51 each and the losing Cubs $679.09, a touch more than they anticipated a few days earlier, but still only about a third of what players had earned in recent World Series. But that wasn't the worst of it. Despite promising they'd take no punitive action against the players for the threatened strike, the National

Commission refused to issue the players' Series medallions, the equivalent of today's ring. Despite petitions from a number of players, most notably Harry Hooper, for the next seventy-five years every baseball commissioner through Fay Vincent upheld the decision. Even a plea from Whiteman, who pled "I have never asked for anything in my life" and included a canceled check, proving he'd made his 10 percent donation to the war charities, was ignored. Not until 1993, when there was no official commissioner to say no, was the decision rescinded and the medallions belatedly awarded to the ancestors of the members of the 1918 Red Sox, including George Whiteman's ninety-four-year-old sister-in-law, and Babe Ruth's adopted daughter, Julia. By then, every player on either team was long dead.

Although history would later remember it as Boston's last world championship of the century, and for Ruth's record-setting pitching performance, in truth the only player anyone much talked about afterward was Whiteman. Compared to everyone else, the quiet, humble minor leaguer appeared almost saintly.

Ruth had a pretty good year personally, although in the end his overall value to the team in 1918, despite his histrionics at the plate, was offset by his diminished performance on the mound. According to most modern metrics, in terms of wins he was actually less valuable to the Red Sox in 1918 than he had been in 1917. When one factored in the disruptions he caused—jumping the team, balking at pitching—perhaps even less so. According to the numbers, the most valuable player in the league, for the fifth time in seven seasons—was pitcher Walter Johnson. Still, Ruth's stalwart pitching performance down the stretch had saved the season for the Sox— and, in some respects, his standing. Had Boston not won the pennant, Ruth may well have taken the blame and earned a reputation even he may have found difficult to shake.

But Ruth and everyone else learned one enduring lesson in 1918: home runs made news, made money, and made everyone overlook bad behavior. Remember, even after jumping the club, it was he, Ruth, who had gotten a new contract and a midseason raise, not anyone else. That didn't go unnoticed by the other Boston players.

After the Series, Ruth briefly returned to his gentleman's farm in Sudbury, and with the help of the press participated in photo ops that showed him chopping wood, feeding chickens, and standing next to his wife, the picture of domestic bliss. This fall, however, he postponed the usual post-season fare of barnstorming and partying. In addition to the pandemic, there was still that pesky "work or fight" order and players were no more eager to fight than they had been during the regular season.

Ruth could have easily found "essential" work around Boston, but instead he soon made a beeline to Charles Schwab's Bethlehem Steel plant in Lebanon, Pennsylvania, to secure a spot on the giant steel company's baseball team, joining White Sox outfielder Joe Jackson, Indians pitcher Stan Coveleski, and Cardinals infielder Rogers Hornsby. After all, there was still another month or two of decent weather and good money to be made down there, where the flu had abated. And if the war continued into the spring of 1919, the only place Ruth or many other major leaguers would be able to continue to play baseball would be in one of the larger industrial leagues. The big money for that wasn't in Boston, whose factories were smaller, but farther down the Atlantic seaboard, where the plants producing raw materials were closer together, employed tens of thousands, and whose owners liked to one-up each other.

Ruth didn't do much work for Bethlehem—he might never have even seen a single piece of steel. One Bethlehem employee later recalled that Ruth was given the makework job of "blueprint messenger," telling writer William Ecenbarger that "the whole gang of them [the ballplayers] was draft dodgers. They were supposed to be working for the war, but they didn't do any work. All they did was play baseball. Babe Ruth used to show up at the plant for an hour before practice. He'd be wearing fancy trousers, silk shirts and patent-leather shoes. He'd just walk around talking to people about baseball. There wasn't anything essential about what he was doing." In this, Ruth was not unique. As much as baseball and other professional sports like to wrap themselves in the flag today, the truth is, that with few exceptions professional athletes and leagues have little tangible to brag about when it comes to patriotism, unless it happens to intersect with profit.

Records are incomplete, but Ruth played, at most, only a handful of games in late September and early October before turning up back in Baltimore. He might have had another touch of flu or simply returned home to deal with his late father's affairs. At any rate, no one was trying to track him down and force him to "work or fight."

Then, the war ended. A German offensive in the spring had stalled and an Allied counterattack in August pushed the Germans back and eventually made it clear that they could not win the war. In September, various Axis smaller powers began to stand down and sign an armistice, leaving Germany isolated. In early November, they finally capitulated. The worst war in the history of humankind to that point, killing 16 million and injuring more than 20 million more, lurched to an end on November 11, 1918.

When the world awoke the next day, it was utterly changed.

5

Out of Left Field

"Ruth made a grave mistake when he gave up pitching. Working once a week he might have lasted a long time and become a great star."
—Tris Speaker

By the spring of 1919, America was a different place. Thousands of doughboys marched home both world-weary and now more worldly than before. Meanwhile, back home, the massive industrial effort that Americans put into the war changed almost everything. Women had entered the workforce and now their calls to vote gained traction. Airplanes flying overhead suddenly became commonplace. The world had gotten smaller overnight. The Victorian Era was dead. After years of nothing but death and destruction, Americans, particularly young Americans, wanted to forget, have fun, and cut loose.

Babe Ruth was the right guy at the right time, the symbolic leader of the party soon to get under way, the uncrowned King of what soon would become the Roaring Twenties.

Once the war was over, it didn't take baseball—and Ruth—long to start looking forward to 1919. Frazee and the other men who owned the game had taken a financial hit in 1918. Although the Red Sox had been the third biggest draw in the league, attendance, despite Ruth's prowess with a bat, had still tumbled by almost a quarter of a million fans from 1917. Now, no longer hamstrung by trying to make it appear that they supported the war effort while in reality acting in their own self-interest, all Frazee and the others wanted to do was make some money. So did the players. And so did Ruth.

Johnny Igoe, his financial counselor back in Boston, had his ear and while Ruth went through with the charade of being a steelworker, Igoe had been fielding offers. Not that he was particularly well qualified to do so, because he had little more than Ruth's trust and shared desire for cash to offer. Once he latched on to Ruth, he held on for as long as he could.

Nevertheless, Ruth was one of the few players who came out of the 1918 season in better shape than he went in—not at the waistline, but in earning potential. The press had touted him beyond proportion for his performance and by the end of the year Ruth, whether he deserved it or not, was the best-known player in the game. For those eager to forget the war and everything that went with it, he was also suddenly one of the most beloved. Ty Cobb? Joe Jackson? Walter Johnson? They were old news. Babe Ruth? In the parlance of the day, where new words were being coined every week, Ruth was "copacetic," the cat's meow.

Igoe and Ruth—or at least Igoe—sensed a change in the air and decided it was time to make a grab for more. If Frazee had been willing to up Ruth's salary in midseason after he'd jumped the club, they figured that now, after another World Series win and with life returning to normal, he might be good for another fat raise. All sorts of people were reaching out to Ruth with crazy offers of one kind or another—boxing, vaudeville, and anything else you could conceivably charge admission to—and at the same time shysters of all stripes were approaching Ruth determined to separate him from all that hard-earned cash. Not that he actually had much—he still usually spent it as soon as he got it, and sometimes even before. Ballplayers weren't paid in the off-season and Ruth was likely already feeling the pinch.

And the men who ran baseball weren't helping matters much. Once more, they cowered before the future. Instead of returning to business as usual after the war, they chose to act conservatively and tried to get rich by pinching pennies and saving dimes instead of chasing after dollars.

Well, most of them. After helping to save the season and then winning the Series, Frazee was feeling expansive. There was a rumor he was looking to sell the Red Sox. His asking price was a million dollars, and if he got it the New York Giants were reportedly available and Frazee wanted to put together a group to buy them, a notion that made Ban Johnson recoil in horror. To him, the only thing worse than having Frazee in baseball at all would be having him as an owner of a National League team in New York.

But behind the scenes—or, actually, not too far behind the scenes at all—Frazee, sensing weakness in Johnson, was sounding out other owners about dumping the National Commission altogether. He favored a single commissioner, someone more independent, who wouldn't be beholden to a single team or league. Johnson, if not already thoroughly corrupt, was at least compromised by personal relationships with so many club owners. Increasingly, he seemed to be basing decisions not on what was right, or what was wrong, or what was legal, or fair, or best for the game. Instead, his calculation usually started with himself: Was it good for Ban Johnson? And then he asked who else would benefit, a friend or a foe? Since the World Series, he'd already made one decision, to withhold the world championship medallions, clearly made for reasons other than moral courage. When Frazee found out, he thought the Red Sox were being singled out for persecution.

They were, and when Johnson found out that Frazee was trying to build a consensus among owners and was even sounding out ex-president William Howard Taft about becoming the first commissioner of baseball—and when that news ended up on the front page of the *New York Times*—the only war baseball was worried about now was between Frazee and Johnson. Only Archduke Ferdinand had been so bold, and although a number of owners agreed with Frazee's approach, few were willing to make their position public. *The Sporting News*, which acted as a mouthpiece for the National Commission, breathlessly headlined a story on Frazee's attempted coup: "Looks Like He's Playing Lone Hand." Just before the owners met for their annual meeting in early December, Frazee made it clear that he wasn't backing down, saying he'd rather "lose the World Champion Red Sox" than continue kowtowing to Johnson. Frazee may not have meant it, but that was precisely the result Johnson hoped to see happen.

At Johnson's behest, and in a play to increase profits in the upcoming season, major league baseball reduced rosters from 25 players per club in 1918 to only 21 in 1919, and then the teams conspired among each other to suppress salaries, effectively placing a limit on team payrolls, higher for those teams with already big payrolls in larger markets. As Jacob Ruppert of the Yankees noted, "The players can sign at the salaries noted or not at all." That was all fine and well, and even Frazee had no problem with that, although when Frazee proposed to pay players a small sum during spring training, the other owners shot down the notion as tantamount to socialism.

The next decision, however, was mind-boggling. After playing an abbreviated schedule of only 126 games in 1918 and taking a financial hit, Johnson doubled down and decided that instead of returning to normal as fast as possible like the rest of American society, baseball would behave as if the Hun was still lurking over the horizon. Instead of playing the usual 154-game season that had been in place since 1904, they would play only 140 games in 1919, and wait until April 20 to start playing. They then further complicated matters by deciding on an abbreviated spring training schedule that wouldn't begin until late March, losing out on a couple of extra weeks of free publicity that the newspapers pumped out each spring that got fans excited about the upcoming season.

By way of explanation, Johnson offered that the reason for doing so was to "eliminate the evil of playing double-headers" and to avoid early spring rainouts. It was like waiting to plant corn until the 4th of July to avoid frost.

To a guy like Frazee, it was insane. The Red Sox were defending champions, and with a host of talented players due to return from the service, they seemed well positioned to race to the top and rake in the cash. In theatrical terms, now baseball was closing the balcony and banning the matinee. For the second year in a row, it was as if baseball didn't want to make money . . . or at least it didn't want the Red Sox to make any.

Boston was not the only team that believed it was a target. In New York, the Yankees were finally out from under the odious impact of the blue laws and in 1919 would finally be able to play baseball on Sundays. Cutting back on the season likely cost them a couple of huge dates. The Yankees' co-owner, Cap Huston, called it a "foolish piece of legislation" and was joined in opposition by not only Frazee, but by Charles Comiskey of the White Sox, who also backed Frazee's plan for a single commissioner, and the Giants were known to be displeased with Johnson as well. There had always been a bit of friction between the two leagues, but now there was also a fissure beginning to show that ran horizontally, potentially splitting the American League in two camps and sending hairline fractures into the NL. Ever so slowly, the Red Sox, Yankees, and White Sox were lining up against Johnson and looking for support from other owners.

They hadn't forgotten that it was syndicated baseball and resulting favoritism that had infected the National League and eroded the public's trust in the 1890s, opening the door for Johnson's upstart American League. They had long suspected that was taking place again, that Johnson had invested personally in one or more ball clubs, that the onetime insurgent had adopted the same tactics he'd once railed against.

Frazee and Johnson didn't even speak during the meeting, but as soon as it broke up neither man could hold his tongue. Johnson fired the first shot, saying he had uncovered "Certified information . . . that gambling existed at Fenway Park" and claiming that gave him the right to terminate Frazee's tenure as owner.

Gambling at Fenway Park? Why there was green grass and infield clay and peanuts being sold in the stands, too, just as there was at every major league ballpark in the country. If not for gambling, the game wouldn't have survived the 1918 season: the only fans who had turned out in close to their previous numbers were the gamblers, who cared only about the action the game provided, and nothing else. It was a low blow, but Johnson had made his intentions and his strategy clear. In public, he would stake out the moral high ground and try to slur the Red Sox, while in private he'd get down on the floor and dig at the foundations.

Frazee saw it for what it was, "a war of extermination on the part of Mr. Johnson," with him and the Red Sox franchise Johnson's "particular target," a threatened species he hoped to hasten toward extinction. Johnson naively hoped Frazee would walk off in a huff and sell the Sox, but he underestimated both Frazee's resolve and his acumen. Frazee knew he was sitting on a valuable property and was in no mood to sell. Besides, he really couldn't. Although Frazee owned the Sox, and acted as such, his power was mostly on paper. He still owed notes to Joseph Lannin, and although few people outside the Red Sox knew it, once those notes were paid Frazee still wouldn't own the team completely free and clear. The Taylor family not only still owned the ballpark, but still retained some stock in the club, as did several of their cronies. Although it wouldn't become clear for some time, the tangled ownership situation would make it almost impossible for Frazee to sell the team for several more years. He wasn't going to be forced out; Johnson would have to take the team, and the legality of that, despite Johnson's threat over gambling, was untenable.

Over the next few months, the war between the two men would escalate. The result would leave Ruth as something of a refugee, another spoil of war.

For now Ruth was either oblivious, unconcerned, or both. Just as the player strike during the Series hadn't been his business, neither was the war between Johnson and Frazee. He installed Helen back at the farm in Sudbury and went on his merry way spending most of his time in Baltimore, Boston, and New York. He returned to the farm for ever briefer intervals as Mrs. Ruth became more and more accustomed to having the same kind of relationship with her husband as his Red Sox roommates; increasingly, she, too, was rooming with little more than his suitcase, all dirty laundry and cigar stubs. Ruth made most of his headlines in the off-season grousing about his contract and indicating that he was after a new one.

It wasn't long after the war that players who had been in the service or had left for war work began returning to the fold. At first, this apparently made a windfall for the Red Sox. They were already world champions, and compared to the competition the deepest team in baseball. Their returning veterans, such as outfielder Duffy Lewis, Jack Barry, and pitchers Ernie Shore and Dutch Leonard, promised to make them even better. Although Leonard had helped for a time in 1918 before taking a shipyard job, the Sox had gone the whole year without the help of Lewis and Shore. Lewis, a valuable outfielder and productive hitter, already had left a lasting legacy in Fenway Park, the earthen retaining wall before the left field wall, called "Duffy's Cliff" after his ability to scale the embankment to catch balls hit over his head. A potent hitter, along with Speaker and Hooper he'd been a part of what once was considered the best outfield in baseball, and a rare successful pull hitter at a time when that ability was not much appreciated. Shore, bought by Boston from Baltimore along with Ruth in 1914, had since proven to be a valuable pitcher, winning 58 games in four seasons. In 1917, he was credited with a perfect game after relieving Ruth when the starting pitcher was thrown from the game after walking the first hitter. Both Shore and Lewis had spent the 1918 season in the Navy, mostly playing baseball, Shore in Boston and Lewis in his native California.

Boston's windfall, however, didn't have a silver lining. With rosters reduced and the gentleman's agreement in regard to a salary cap (generally somewhere between $60,000 and $100,000, depending on the team), Frazee couldn't keep the men—if he did, he'd either blow past the cap and earn the wrath of his peers, including Comiskey and Ruppert, his two new best friends, or he wouldn't have enough money to pay anyone else, particularly Ruth. He couldn't afford to anyway—he needed to recoup his losses as much as the next guy did. It was almost as if the rules were put in place solely to prevent the Red Sox becoming a dynasty after the war.

Given the enmity between Johnson and Frazee, that might not have been far from the truth. Frazee had outmaneuvered every owner in baseball in 1918—now, thought Johnson, was the time to put the Red Sox back in their place.

And there was yet one more ugly little factor to consider. Among the men who owned baseball teams it was widely believed that Frazee, likely due to his ties to the New York theater, was Jewish. There were still occasional veiled references in the press to the "mystery of his religion," and that Frazee was "too New York." Frazee was not Jewish, but the lie was widely believed and Jewish owners were still not welcome in the game. It hurt Frazee and it stung. The single best-preserved document in his entire archive collection is a pristine copy of Henry Ford's anti-Semitic broadsheet, the *Dearborn Independent,* dated September 10, 1921. An article entitled "How the Jews Degraded Baseball" presents Frazee as a Jew, using much of Johnson's original argument against letting him in the league as evidence:

A few years ago the owners of the American League entered into a gentleman's agreement not to sell their holdings at any time without first consulting all the other owners. The name of a prospective purchaser was to be submitted and considered, and the deal was to wait upon the approval of all the owners in the league. In the face of that fact many people wonder how Harry Frazee became owner of the Boston American club. It is very simply

explained: the agreement was not observed in Boston's case, and thus another club was placed under the smothering influences of the "chosen race."
The story is worth telling.

Frazee, like so many of his kind, was in the "show business," a manager
of burlesque companies. Then he saw a chance in sport.

Regardless, the decision to make trades to rid the team of surplus
players—at least how to structure the deals—was never Frazee's alone.
Although Barrow would later try to parse his role during his tenure with the
Red Sox—decisions well received by history were his, while those that were
not were Frazee's—and try to claim credit all out of proportion for Ruth's
success, it wasn't Frazee who decided who to take on in trades; it was Barrow. So on December 18, Boston traded Lewis, Leonard, and Shore to
the New York Yankees for Ray Caldwell, Frank Gilhooley, Slim Love, Roxy
Walters, and what was variously reported as between $10,000 and $15,000.
Most observers thought the Yankees, whose manager, Miller Huggins,
pushed for the deal, got the upper hand. History, however, would not be so
harsh. Both Lewis and Shore would be out of the major leagues in two years,
and the deal would prove to be incidental to the success of either team.

Compared to Frazee, Ruppert was in a stronger financial position, both
personally and in terms of his ball club. His wealth dated back three gen-
erations, and even with two teams (three if one included Brooklyn), the
New York market was easily the largest in baseball. Sunday baseball promised a windfall and the Yankee payroll was bigger than Boston's, which
gave Ruppert more flexibility. But in December of 1917, a constitutional
amendment to ban the sale of alcohol passed Congress, and by the final
days of 1918 it was becoming clear that it would be ratified by the requi-
site three fourths of the states and soon become law. For Ruppert, whose
fortune flowed from his brewery and had a near stranglehold on beer sales
in New York, Prohibition was not good news. He had to transition, and transition quickly, making baseball, not beer brewing, his main business. The end
of the blue laws was a help, and the Yankees had challenged for the pennant in 1918 before fading. In order to compete with the Giants, make
some money, and get out of an onerous lease situation at the Polo Grounds,
he needed a winning team, a big draw, so he could make some money and
build his own ballpark.

Making a trade with Boston helped both teams, and had the added benefit of strengthening their alliance as they did battle with Johnson. Although the deal would later be characterized as the first example of some nefarious plot by Frazee to strengthen the Yankees on Boston's behalf (and some later observers would misinterpret the trade and mistakenly conclude that the Yankees paid $15,000 per player), that's not the case. Although the deal was further complicated when Leonard refused to report and was sent to Detroit, the Red Sox got some value back, both in cash and, potentially, in Caldwell, a talented frontline pitcher, albeit one with a drinking problem. Besides, Frazee had to lower his payroll. Interestingly enough, at this time the assumption was that Ruth would still be a pitcher in 1919. With a roster of only 21 men, his ability to do double duty might be even more valuable to the team—and necessary—than it had been in 1918.

Over the next few weeks, Boston's smoldering fire sale continued, as the Red Sox shed more returnees and worked a trade with Detroit to fill a hole at third base, picking up Ossie Vitt (and including Leonard in the deal). But as the new year reached into spring, Ruth began reaching out for more green. He let it be known he wanted a raise—and a big one. And by the way, he didn't want to pitch anymore.

In other words, he wanted more for less . . . yet the Red Sox had already made moves for the upcoming season under the assumption Ruth would be pitching—Barrow said publicly "he will probably pitch and pinch-hit. One thing I'm convinced of, Ruth will play only one position. He will not be switched from first to left field then back to the box. He will not be worked that way again." Had that not been the case, the club might have found a way to keep either Shore or Leonard. In late January, Frazee and Barrow were still talking about acquiring another outfielder—someone cheaper than Lewis, presumably, to play left field. A rare analytical feature in the *Globe* by Mel Webb made no mention of using Ruth solely as an outfielder, referring to him as a "remarkable asset . . . as pitcher, first baseman and outfielder, as well as a fence buster." Had Ruth not tailed off so badly the previous August, he might have been viewed as more of a hitter than pitcher, but that was not yet the case. In any event, in regard to Ruth, the Red Sox were keeping their options open.

Ruth, however, had other ideas, and he was never more unpredictable than when he thought for himself, or when someone had his ear. Ruth, although not unintelligent, was not particularly well educated or discriminating in his thinking. He often acted more on enthusiasm and emotion than on analysis.

First, there was the matter of money. After earning $7,500 in 1918, under the advice of Igoe, for 1919 Ruth wanted either a one-year deal for $15,000 in 1919—or a three-year deal for $10,000 a year. And that was just to play outfield. "I'll win more games playing in the outfield than I will pitching," he told the press. That wasn't true under any analysis, either the kind made then or now, but it made good copy, and once Ruth got an idea in his head, it was hard to turn him around.

Purely in terms of money, it was a strange request. If Ruth really thought he was worth $15,000 a year, why offer a longer-term discount? Because if he did think he was worth $15,000 for a single season, or could get it, he'd likely be asking for even more in subsequent seasons. Ruth wasn't the kind of guy who much worried about his financial security.

Frazee saw it for what it was, and what he saw in the theater all the time, a negotiating ploy—by asking for $15,000, Ruth revealed that he really wanted $10,000. He probably wasn't really interested in a three-year deal, either. That was designed to scare Frazee into offering Ruth $10,000 or so for a single year. Multiyear deals were rare at the time, and given recent events, who in their right mind would make such an arrangement? What if the flu came back?

There was no rush for the Red Sox. Ruth had few alternatives and wasn't known for his patience. Boston let him wait.

Over the next two months Ruth made occasional forays into Boston to talk contract and have some fun, then zoomed all over New England. All it took was a few days cooped up in Sudbury to get him fired up for a road trip. He spent a great deal of time in Meredith, New Hampshire, a resort town on Lake Winnipesaukee, where he cavorted with local schoolgirls and even broke up a fight between rowdies at a dance he attended with his wife. But Ruth may have found more to his favor in Meredith than the music. He'd return to the town for a number of years, and there are persistent rumors that the reason was that Ruth had fathered a child, a boy, with a local girl, and kept it secret the rest of his life.

In 1921, he and Helen would adopt an infant, Dorothy, and his second wife, Claire, had a child of her own, Julia, whom Ruth also adopted. Helen allegedly had several miscarriages, but Ruth never admitted to fathering a child. Given his extracurricular activities, that means Ruth was somehow incapable of being a father, incredibly lucky, or discreet.

The notion that Ruth had a son is not as far-fetched as it sounds. Respectable young women of the era were often spirited away to have out-of-wedlock children anonymously in special homes designed to protect their identity and virtue. Infants were then either taken at birth for adoption or their parentage laundered, appearing in the care of relatives or cooperative friends, a foundling left on a doorstop or presented as an orphan of some distant relative never talked about before or since. For the rich and powerful, it was even easier to accomplish. There is some evidence, for instance, that Red Sox owner Tom Yawkey's adopted daughter was, in fact, his own by another woman. Some believe the same was true of Ruth's first child, Dorothy, that she was the result of one of Ruth's affairs, then later "adopted" by him.

The prospect that Ruth might have had a son is tantalizing. The Ruth line ended with Babe and his sister, and the notion that Babe Ruth's DNA might be floating around leaves one wondering if there might be some ballplayer one day bearing Ruth's ancestral abilities. If so, it's probably best for the boy's parentage to stay a secret. Imagine the burden of being Babe Ruth's son?

In between trips, Igoe tried to float ideas that Ruth had other financial options—after all, as part of a cost-cutting measure, every player in the majors was given his release in 1918. Theoretically, Ruth could sign to do anything for anyone, although the baseball magnates all agreed not to poach players from one another. Ruth's only leverage came from offers outside baseball, but in this, he and Igoe were hardly sophisticated. They tried to trump up the notion that Ruth might give up the game for boxing, something made about as much sense as John L. Sullivan taking a turn on the pitcher's mound, and there was even a story that Ruth was thinking of putting his money and his talents into "roller polo," an early version of roller hockey, or play baseball in some industrial league.

None was realistic, and didn't worry the Red Sox in the least. In truth, Ruth had no other options, no ballplayer did, really, at least not any that were very realistic or would pay him anything close to what he could make playing in the major leagues. If Ruth wanted to play baseball, he would either play for the Red Sox or not play at all. The size of his contract would depend only on how much Boston could spend under the unofficial cap without drawing the ire of the other clubs, and how much either man would respond to public pressure to get a contract worked out.

Well into March, the local papers were still referring to Ruth as a pitcher, but as the off-season continued, the idea that he was only an outfielder began ossifying in Ruth's brain. Just months after leading the Red Sox to victory in the World Series and winning two ballgames and setting a World Series record for consecutive scoreless innings, based on 11 productive swings of the bat and the resulting roars of the crowd, Ruth decided to change the course of his career entirely. It wasn't inspired by a sore arm or a bad knee or anything else. Ruth just fell in love with the idea of hitting home runs, with the feeling that coursed through his body when he got ahold of one.

There is something to be said for that. Hitting a baseball square and then watching it go over a fence is almost transcendent. Once experienced, it is never forgotten. Pitching, for all the power and authority one can feel while blowing a fastball past a hitter, doesn't offer the same return. Its joys are primarily cumulative. Of all sports, the feeling that comes from hitting a home run is singular, and in baseball, particularly hitting, which includes so much inherent failure, so much that is dependent on the ball finding space between fielders, only the smacking of a long home run, which renders everyone else on the field irrelevant, seems to justify all the previous disappointments.

One can imagine how Ruth must have felt when he hit his first over-the-fence home run at St. Mary's, a place where he was confined and almost every moment of his day regulated and controlled. But when he hit a home run . . . well, it left the yard, and it never came back. That's the feeling he wanted, that's what he was chasing, and every subsequent home run was Ruth's pursuit for that sense of freedom, of that ephemeral possibility, once again. Even better, when you hit a home run, everybody loves you for it. What can possibly feel better to an unloved young boy than that?

Ruth's preference was all fine and well, but the Red Sox weren't about personal experience; they were about making money, and that meant winning ballgames. Ever since the end of the World Series, the Red Sox had assumed that Ruth was going to pitch in 1919. Barrow had penciled in a rotation of Ruth, Mays, Sam Jones, and then either Joe Bush, Ray Caldwell, or young phenom Herb Pennock—two bona fide stars and one front-liner, leaving him to choose his fourth starter from between a couple of veterans and one of the best pitching prospects in the game, Pennock—an eventual Hall of Famer. That's why they'd been able to shed Shore and Leonard and stay under the artificial payroll cap. But if Ruth didn't pitch, that changed the equation and felt a lot less secure.

Many of the Red Sox set sail from Boston on March 18 for Jacksonville, where they would then disembark and travel by train across the state to Tampa, where they planned to hold spring training. Local government there, eager for a tourist attraction, subsidized their travel to entice them to the area, and even planned to subsidize a visit by the New York Giants so the Red Sox and Giants could play some exhibitions. Tampa was already gaining a reputation as a winter home to snowbirds, those who could afford to flee the cold of the Northeast, and they were eager to pay to see some baseball. You couldn't spend every day at the beach.

While his teammates sailed south, Ruth lagged behind and met with Frazee in New York, where the owner held court with a number of Boston players still seeking contracts for 1919. He'd been offering Ruth $7,500— half of what he asked for. Ruth balked, but he wanted to go to Florida, too. That, coupled with his impatience, caused Ruth to accept when Frazee agreed to Ruth's request for a three-year deal at $10,000 a year. Although some reports indicated it was only $9,000 annually, that may have been just to make Frazee look good. With that business taken care of Ruth hopped on the train to Florida and joined teammates a few days later.

In agreeing to Ruth's proposal for a long-term deal, Frazee may already have been looking ahead. The big snafu in every trade of the era was always the ballplayer's contract. Most were single-year deals and teams hated making trades only to have their new player, making the logical assumption that his new team must think highly of his abilities, immediately ask for more money. With Ruth under contract for three years, if he were traded, the other team would know exactly what he would cost them.

Ruth may have been under contract, but he was not under control. He'd enjoyed the off-season and was heavy, twenty or thirty pounds over his usual weight, and neither his arm nor his legs were in shape to pitch. That may have been intentional on his part. By showing up coated in a nice layer of fat, that pretty much guaranteed that Barrow, by way of punishment more than plan, would use Ruth in the field in an effort to get him to lose a few pounds, at least early on. Sure enough, on March 24, when the team held its first workout at Plant Field, a ballfield laid out in the infield of a racetrack that also served as the home of the Florida State Fair, Ruth took part in Barrow's double sessions, working out both on the mound and in the outfield.

Although the Florida weather made it in many ways preferable to Hot Springs, Plant Field was an odd place to play, not even a real ballpark. The diamond was laid out in front of the track grandstand, facing the backstretch. Although the "fence" in center field was the track rail on the opposite side of the course, elsewhere there was a ramshackle barrier, leaving some room between the fence and the rest of the track rail. Ruth wowed spectators with several long drives that first day, but all fell well short of the ballpark fence, not to mention the more distant rail.

That should have been no surprise. In the spring of 1919, major league teams were likely still using baseballs manufactured the previous season featuring subpar wool and horsehide, the deadest of dead balls. Better quality baseball wouldn't be available until later in the season, and during spring training the Red Sox might have even been using worn balls left over from 1918. Hitting those would have been like trying to hit a lead-filled beanbag.

The fans of course, knew nothing about this and didn't care. Having heard and read about Ruth's exploits from the previous year, they were already speculating as to whether or Ruth or anyone else could hit a baseball over either the fence or the rail—and this was a racetrack, where wagering was customary. The infield at the standard half-mile racing track was only 400 feet across. Given that home plate was sited at the edge of the racetrack, a drive to dead center needed to travel just a bit less than 400 feet to clear the rail. It was much farther down the lines, but had the field been centered on the track infield, the rail would have been more than 500 feet away.

But that's not how the diamond was laid out. The grandstand overlooked the finish line near the end of the home stretch, which made the rail in right field much closer than that in left. Although it is impossible to determine precisely from period photographs, in right field the distance to the rail may have been as short as only 475 feet or so—still a long drive, but not quite as long as one might initially think. The configuration of the field and the fences would figure prominently into Ruth's story that spring.

Ruth got off to a quick start in intra-squad games that began almost immediately. Tellingly, when Ruth played the field it was for the squad referred to as "Babe's Busters," the scrubs, and not the regulars. He entertained crowds with his long hitting, but didn't hit anything close to the rail. But he also pitched against Boston's regular lineup, a sign that Barrow still viewed him as a pitcher first. Stuffy McInnis was still the first baseman. There was, however, a hole in left field. When everyone returned from the war, George Whiteman, the hero of the '18 Series, was deemed expendable. Although he went on to set a record for the most games ever played in the minor leagues and would remain active for another decade, he never appeared in the big leagues again. Veteran Del Gainer, back from the war, seemed to be Barrow's early choice to stand before Duffy's Cliff.

But in Boston's first exhibition game against the Giants on April 3, that all changed. For Ruth, it may well have been the most important home run of his career, at least to that point.

It rained a bit earlier in the day, but by afternoon the skies had cleared and the sun shone bright and hot. In racing terms, that left the field dry and fast. The evangelist Billy Sunday, a former ballplayer himself, was on hand to throw out the first pitch. More than 6,000 fans, a huge crowd for a city of 50,000, turned out for the game.

After a scoreless first, Ruth, batting fourth and playing left field after pitching the day before in a practice game, led off the second inning versus the Giants' Ivy Leaguer, pitcher "Columbia" George Smith. With the count 3-and-1, Ruth "leaned on it" as the *Boston Post* reported, and sent a drive to deep right center field. New York right fielder Ross Youngs started back but soon pulled up.

It was one of those hits that got small fast. The ball landed far over the temporary fence in right, then bounced and kept going. Ruth trotted around the bases as the huge crowd, who filled the grandstand and pushed up against the fence, gave him a rousing ovation. This is what they had all come out to see, and what the papers had been promising all week. While the

Boston and New York papers more or less put the drive in context, in Tampa it was another matter. The next morning the headline in the *Tampa Tribune* screamed "Ruth Drives Giants to Defeat and Makes 'Em Drink B' Gads!"

Perhaps no single Ruthian home run apart from his called shot against the Chicago Cubs has been written about more, yet at the time it was struck, the home run caused little special comment. Not that it wasn't hit a long way—it was. The *Globe*'s Mel Webb announced it would have cleared the fence in front of the bleachers at Fenway Park—that meant a drive of about 400 feet, at least, and worthy of attention, but he didn't go overboard. And in the *Post* Shannon noted that it was the mightiest home run swat that Tampa fans had ever witnessed, writing that it "fell far beyond the race track fence," whatever that was, leaving it unclear whether he meant the temporary fence or the track rail. But like Ruth's called shot, the lore around the home run would overshadow the hit itself. Most reports at the time stated the ball landed in front of the rail, but that was slowly inflated, the ball later described as landing on the track itself, and sometimes even clearing the opposite side.

Given the size of the crowd, it's unlikely that the press, sitting in the grandstand boxes near the base of the stands, actually got a good view of the hit. And although there were reportedly a dozen movie cameramen on hand because of the presence of Billy Sunday, none apparently trained their lens on Ruth and captured the blast. Had they done so, that would have been the end of it.

In regard to Ruth, the beginning of a story rarely matches the end, and over time, more and more details about the exhibition game home run emerged. Years later, in his own ghostwritten autobiography, Ed Barrow wrote, "After the game, Youngs marked as nearly as he could the spot the ball landed. Melvin Webb, baseball writer for the *Boston Globe*, got a surveyor's tape and measured it. It measured 579 feet."

Since then, the accepted, measured distance became 508 feet on the fly and 579 to the ball's final resting place. There's even a historical marker in place today, marking the spot on the campus of the University of Tampa. Yet some still insist the ball traveled closer to the second figure on the fly and rolled to a distance of more than 600 feet.

Interestingly enough, Webb himself never adopted the figure, at least not in his reports at the time, which calls the whole thing into question.

After first just describing the hit by saying it would have made Fenway's right field bleachers, a week later he referred to it in the *Globe* as a "550-foot homer." In subsequent references in 1919 he never put another number on it.

Over time, the home run—hit in an exhibition game on a substandard field—would often be referred to as the longest in baseball history—which is, frankly, absurd. Given the conditions of the day, even if a brand-new baseball were in play, such a drive was near to impossible. And given the configuration of the field, and the fact that observers were estimating both landing points, the veracity of the numbers is even more debatable. Let's not forget that Youngs didn't chase the ball and certainly didn't jump over the fence after it. Then again, there is no record of the atmospheric conditions that day—wind, temperature, and humidity can significantly boost the carry of a baseball. If a gale of 30 mph or so were blowing the right direction or a rogue gust arrived from the heavens, and it was both hot and humid, a perfectly struck baseball could conceivably travel 50 or 60 feet farther in the air than would otherwise be possible, turning a drive of 400-plus feet into one closer to 500. If that is the case, then perhaps—perhaps—the accepted distance is reasonably accurate. After all, the Giants' John McGraw reportedly later said "it was the longest ball I ever saw." And it so excited representatives of the nearby city of St. Petersburg that they changed their plans to try to entice the Giants to train across the bay in their city. Instead, they targeted the Red Sox.

Still, while it is theoretically possible for Ruth's drive to have traveled 500 feet or so in the air, it is important to understand that even with the lively ball, under optimal conditions, it is extremely rare for a home run to travel so far—the laws of physics just don't allow it. Using the standard ball from 1918, it would be even less likely. As an aside, it's interesting to note that virtually all of Ruth's really, really long home runs always occur in places where measurements are virtually impossible, over fences and roof-tops, and landing in lawns and on streets. Yet when he played in a place where his blast could be easily measured, say to dead center field in the Polo Grounds, he conveniently never hit one there.

But it's possible Ruth didn't hit a standard ball that day in Tampa. This was Boston's first exhibition game of the year, and the first time a major league team had trained in Tampa since 1914, and the city was eager to develop the area as a spring training mecca. Speculation over whether Ruth could hit the ball to the track had been appearing in newspapers almost daily, almost as if someone knew something in advance.

Could Ruth have been given some help to hit the home run, perhaps with a special, more lively baseball, in the hope of generating some publicity? It was, after all, only an exhibition. A long home run would help everyone, so why not slip a special ball into play when Ruth came to bat? And given the way Ruth would perform in the next few weeks, if it worked at that game at Tampa, then why not during the remainder of the exhibition season? A special, more resilient and livelier ball had been manufactured during the war for use by the troops overseas. Even though the Reach company made the official ball, there was no one to check or who even cared what ball they used in exhibition games. Every baseball manufacturer made baseballs any way they wanted, and some were undoubtedly livelier than the "official" ball.

Although the home run ball itself allegedly exists, signed by Barrow and Ruth and given to Billy Sunday, there is no way to ascertain whether that is actually the ball in question. While the possible use of a special livelier ball is purely circumstantial, and speculative, it is certainly possible. Yet one thing is certain: over the remainder of the exhibition schedule and, in particular, as the Red Sox barnstormed northward, Ruth put on a home run performance unmatched at any point in his career. Something was going on.

So much of what Ruth did and who he was is wrapped in so much mythology that it is often impossible to wade through to hard facts. Take, for example, his bats, which, according to the source and stage of his career, have been variously described as weighing between 40 and 54 ounces and were long assumed by many to be the reason he hit such long home runs, just as corked bats presumably make it easier. Yet physics tells us that it is not the weight of the bat that matters as much as does bat speed, and that it is simply not possible to swing a bat as heavy as those used by Ruth fast enough to hit such monstrous home runs as he is credited.

Accidental or not, no matter how far the ball was hit, it served its purpose for everyone, but for no one more than Ruth himself. For one, after hitting that first home run, it kept him on the field for the remaining exhibitions. The resulting press, not just in Boston but in New York where the

Giants' spring performance was of less interest than Ruth's, raised his profile even higher in the city where he performed like he did nowhere else and where—what a coincidence!—the Red Sox opened the 1919 season against the Yankees at the Polo Grounds. No fewer than eleven New York sportswriters traveled to Tampa with the Giants, and Ruth's hit gave them all something to write home about. Barrow even later credited the blast as the determining factor in his decision to turn Ruth into a hitter. As Boston played its way toward New England, something that first started to take place during the 1918 season continued. Until that time, the vast majority of fans reserved their allegiance to a team first, and a city or a region, not an individual player. Oh, they loved their stars, such as the Tigers' Cobb, the White Sox' Joe Jackson, but only a few players had been truly transcendent, their personal popularity spilling over the borders and crossing the competitive lines, an object of affection more important than a team. Christy Mathewson of the Giants had been one such figure, not only a fabulous pitcher but, with more than a little help from the press, a beloved symbol of all that was good in the game, the kind of player mothers and fathers held up as an example to their children. It was something of a lie—Mathewson was never quite the milquetoast he was made out to be—but even fans who rooted against the Giants had worshipped him. Pirate shortstop Honus Wagner earned a similar reputation, but lacked Mathewson's publicity machine.

Ruth was rapidly becoming another such transcendent figure. Fans cared more about him than the team he played on, and outside Boston and Baltimore, his peccadilloes were less well known and the myth of the big overgrown boy was easier to manufacture and sell. For the first time, the myth of Ruth was beginning to usurp the reality. And unlike Mathewson, Ruth played every day. On most mornings, baseball fans checked the scores of eight games, four in each league. Ruth's performance at bat—"Did he hit another homer?"—gave them one more thing to check each day.

The Red Sox looked good during the exhibitions, winning four of six games from the Giants as Ruth batted a robust .381, but Barrow continued to worry over his pitching staff. Mays and Joe Bush each nursed sore arms, and Ruth was still not in shape to pitch—Webb noted, "Babe doesn't feel right yet and is keeping away from the slab altogether." It didn't hurt him at the plate, however, as in almost every exhibition game he cracked a homer and references to the blast in Tampa kept growing a nose, long blasts ever more described in terms of how close they came to matching the legendary racetrack home run.

His spring performance peaked in Baltimore, where Harry Frazee joined the team and the Red Sox played Ruth's old Orioles club in two exhibition games. Once again, Ruth pushed the boundaries of believability.

They played at Baltimore's Terrapin Park, which had been the home of Baltimore's Federal League team. Although the dimensions are not known precisely, the outfield was long and narrow, deep in center field ending in a point. But it was a short poke down either foul line, and in exhibitions overflow crowds routinely lined the outfield in front of the stands, possibly making the dimensions even more cozy.

A good crowd turned out to see their hometown hero on April 18 and Ruth did not disappoint. He came to bat six times. He walked twice. And on the four other occasions, including his last three at bats, he hit a home run. One may have benefited from the close crowd, a rather routine fly that turned into a home run, but the other three were legitimate, at least in terms of clearing the existing fence. Shannon noted the next day, "The Red Sox are a great ball team, but there are two pairs of Red Sox, and only one Babe Ruth."

Once again, it was a performance that tested the borders of belief, made even more remarkable by the fact that it was a cool day. Over the last couple of exhibitions, Ruth was 7-for-8 with five home runs and two singles.

It got better the next day. In his first two times up here he homered again, giving him five consecutive home runs and making him 9-for-10 with seven home runs over his last four games, something hard enough to do in batting practice when he knew what was coming, not to mention in game conditions, even against minor leaguers. The Sox romped over the Orioles, winning 12–3 and 16–2—a not unexpected outcome given that the Orioles had barely practiced that spring due to poor weather. It's doubtful their pitchers were even throwing full speed by then.

Ruth's first home run in the second game is the drive that calls the veracity of the blasts into question. The best estimate of the distance to the fence in dead center is about 450 feet. Ruth's blast reportedly not only cleared the fence but the street behind it and then landed on the roof of a house. Webb called it the "next longest wallop to his 550-foot drive in

Tampa." That Ruth was the most powerful hitter in the game at the time is unquestioned. That he could hit home runs in six of eight at bats over the course of two games, including five in a row . . . raises some doubts. The evidence, once again, is circumstantial, but it is not unthinkable that Ruth might have benefited from a juiced-up ball with a nod and a wink from everyone involved, not only the Orioles, but also the press and even Harry Frazee. After all, the old theater adage "give the people what they want" still held true. His home runs made a lot of newsboys and sports editors happy. "Ruth Hits Home Run" sold almost as many papers as "Yanks Have Hun on the Run" once had.

What is also certain, however, is the impact the performance had in New York, where in less than a week the Red Sox would open the season. Baseball was worried how fans would react to players they had considered slackers only a few short months before, and anything that could distract them from that had value. The timing of Ruth's performance could not have been more fortuitous.

Still, despite what he would later say, Barrow considered Ruth primarily a pitcher. After another exhibition in Jersey City, where Ruth hit like a mere mortal, the press noted that he'd worked out on the mound before the game and was even in the running to get the ball on Opening Day if Barrow chose to start a left-hander and weather conditions favored his selection. When Ruth wasn't pitching, Barrow expected to keep him in the lineup somewhere, but he also indicated that might not be a permanent decision. He'd seen Ruth enough to know that his batting prowess ran hot and cold. Right now he was not only hot, but the number one topic of conversation throughout baseball. Although fans were over the moon about Ruth, many longtime observers were still skeptical. John McGraw, who had a chance to watch him up close, thought that if Ruth played regularly he would "hit into a hundred double plays."

6

①

Rebellion and Revolution

"As a batter, Ruth is an accident. He never plays inside baseball at the plate. He goes up trying to take a swing on every strike, a style that would cause any other player to be benched. He either knocks home runs or strikes out."
— Jack Doyle, baseball scout, Chicago Cubs

Thirty thousand fans packed the Polo Grounds on Opening Day, nearly four times the number that had turned out for the Yankees' opener a year before, and three times the number that greeted the Yankees and Red Sox on the first day of the 1917 season, when Ruth had pitched. This time he was in left field, and seeded fourth in the batting order.

Many in the baseball world favored the Red Sox to take another pennant. After all, despite the off-season deals, they still had a wealth of talent. Most figured their stiffest competition to come from Cleveland, or perhaps Washington, where Walter Johnson made even a bad club dangerous.

But the Yankees were making a move. The addition of Shore and Lewis from Boston was significant. Ruppert, not Huston, was taking over, the dominant party in the partnership, and he applied the same principles to running his ball club that had served his beer business so well. Ruppert's beer, led by the signature brew Knickerbocker, was more or less synonymous with New York, a branding strategy ahead of its time and one that, when combined with his political connections at Tammany Hall, of which the ex-congressman was a member in good standing, gave him an obvious edge over the competition.

He knew the value of an established name, and to that point, in baseball terms the Giants owned New York, with the Yankees and the Brooklyn team running a distant second. And if there was anything approaching "America's Team" at the time, a ball club nearly as popular on the road as they were at home, it was the Giants. They benefited from the contrasting personalities and public image of their two biggest stars—the recently retired Mathewson and their combative manager McGraw, who between them gave every fan someone to root for. But Mathewson was no longer active and McGraw was getting old. Although the Giants had won a pennant in 1917, they were in transition and not quite the juggernaut of years past. Ruppert sensed that he and the Yankees had a brief window to wrest New York out of their control—or at least make it a two-team town.

But they had to prove it on the field first, and as yet the Yankees didn't have what it took. The offense was fine—sportswriters later coined the term "Murderer's Row" to describe the 1919 lineup, which included Frank "Home Run" Baker, but the pitching was thin.

Harry Hooper opened the game for Boston with a single off veteran starter George Mogridge, but Jack Barry botched a bunt and Hooper was forced out at second. Barry then moved over on a wild pitch and was still standing on second when Ruth came up with two out.

The crowd buzzed; this was who they wanted to see, in just this situation—who cared if the Yankees fell behind? Ruth had always hit well in the Polo Grounds. He'd later note that it wasn't just the dimensions of the park that he favored but the hitting background. It didn't hurt that the prevailing winds, swirling down from Coogan's Bluff, often seemed to give the ball a push and keep it in the air.

Ruth took a cut at a pitch by Mogridge and lashed the ball to center field, where his old teammate Duffy Lewis was making his debut for New York. It went for a home run, a matter future biographers would make good use of when citing the hit, along with Ruth's blasts in Baltimore, as definitive proof for Barrow and everyone else that Ruth's future was holding a bat, and not a ball.

What many failed to note, however, is that Ruth's hit didn't even make it over Lewis's head. At contact, the outfielder started charging in after the hard hit, a sinking line drive. Then, as one paper reported, the ball "struck a hard spot on the turf [and] took a wicked hop over Duffy's shoulder." In other words, it hit the ground in front of him, little more than 200 feet from home plate, and then bounced over his head. Lewis's momentum carried him a few more steps in toward the infield as the ball bounded toward no-man's-land deep in center field. Jack Barry saw the miscue and trotted home easily, but Ruth, still carrying more weight than at any time in his career to this point, had a more difficult time. He was forced to run, and run hard. Sammy Vick, the right fielder, finally chased the ball down and threw it in, but by that time Ruth had crossed the plate standing up.

The official scorer could have given Lewis an error for overrunning the ball, but he hadn't touched it. Besides, now everyone got to put Ruth's name and home run together in a sentence or two, and in a headline. It worked for everybody and allowed the boyos in the press box an excuse to mention that a few days before Ruth had said that he planned to take aim on the home run record in 1919. Whether he had actually said so mattered very little, and in regard to Ruth, it's virtually impossible to verify anything he said, particularly early in his career. He cursed like a wharf rat and his language alone made every sportswriter a fabulist.

Regardless, the hit set the tone. The Red Sox romped to a 10–0 win and Ruth, who chipped in a single later in the game, was cheered madly every time he swung the bat. The Yankees looked forward to big crowds for the next two games of the opening series, as did Boston. As visitors, the Red Sox took about 20 percent of the gate. But by the following day the weather turned, causing the next two contests to be canceled, first due to the rain and then the cold that sent snow flurries skidding through the streets.

After Ruth spent several days trying to swallow Manhattan whole, the Sox headed south to Washington, and Ruth, who'd had the Mrs. in tow in New York, sent her home and set himself free. He hadn't had quite as much fun in Manhattan as he hoped, but in Washington he had plenty of cronies to run with from his days in Baltimore and at St. Mary's.

It was Sunday when they next played, and another big crowd turned out. Harry Frazee must have looked on mournfully. With no Sunday baseball in Boston, in terms of attendance he was already starting out behind.

The game unfolded much like the opener in New York—the Red Sox jumped out to a first inning lead—this time Ruth getting on by way of an infield error—and then rolled to an 8–0 win behind Sam Jones. Ruth found the headlines yet again, this time with a sixth inning triple after the Red Sox already had already built a big lead. And once again, he had some help. This time Washington center fielder Clyde Milan gave Ruth the assist, along with the official scorer, as he misplayed Ruth's routine fly ball. The Babe chipped in with two more extra base hits the next day off Walter Johnson as the Sox won their third straight 6–5, but Ruth's hits were of the garden variety, hard grounders and liners that skipped past outfielders. Walter Johnson, not Ruth, hit the longest drive of the game, a fly out to center field.

No one yet knew it, but Ruth was out of power, at least for a while. After the first three games of the season, with a home run, two triples, and a double to his credit, he appeared to be the greatest hitter in the game—and with an OPS (on base plus slugging percentage) of 1.467 and a slugging percentage of 1.000, by any measure he was (if one overlooked the bad bounce and the misplay). And the Red Sox looked like the class of the league.

But only for three games. Following that third game, with Helen shuttered up back in the big house in Sudbury, Ruth went out, just as he had the night before. And when Ruth went out—he went out and stayed out.

He was gone almost twelve hours, likely all the way back to Baltimore, although no one really knows. Barrow, who thought Ruth had the ragged look of a night owl earlier that day, supposedly sat in the lobby waiting to see when he would return. Getting madder by the minute, Barrow waited until 4:00 a.m. before storming off to bed.

When he saw Ruth at the park the next day, Barrow didn't say anything. As it would soon become clear, after fourteen years between stints as major league manager, both the game and the players had changed and Barrow was ill equipped to deal with either. His skill was in putting together a roster and knowing whom to call when he needed to fill a gap. Essentially, Harry Hooper managed the ball club on the field. Barrow had been adequate during the 1918 season—with so many marginal players on the roster, no one—except for Ruth and Leonard, really—had crossed him. But in his second season, the players started to tune him out. Hooper was the guy they listened to, went to for advice, and looked to provide strategy. Barrow was like the school principal who came in at the end of the day, glanced at the grade book, and then took credit for the student's performance. He didn't really know how to handle the players, particularly Ruth, who already had done as he pleased for a full year under Barrow, even received a raise for it, and saw no reason to change now. The fact that Barrow had him room with coach Dan Howley had no impact on him whatsoever. But such open insubordination made Barrow look bad, and now was costing him what little respect he had with veteran players.

Ruth looked ragged and went hitless the next day, a 4–2 Boston loss, their first of the season. Then he skipped out of the locker room and was off to look for more trouble.

Barrow figured he'd be late again—after all, the manager hadn't said anything the night before—but Barrow didn't want to wait—or face the consequences of a confrontation with Ruth, who was certain to come in drunk as he was to take a big swing at the plate. And when Ruth drank, while he was usually garrulous, in the wee hours he could get a little wild and a lot belligerent. You didn't want to be around Ruth when he was drunk and his temper was set off.

It's a measure of Ruth's enduring power that so few of his biographers have ever uttered the word alcoholic in the same sentence as the name Babe Ruth, because that's almost certainly what he was. Few of his hijinks weren't accompanied by either some highballs or pitchers of beer, and his pattern of bad behavior followed by quickly forgotten apologies, late-night car accidents, and rash decision making all point in that direction—in neon. But the character of the Babe that would soon be built would all but inoculate him from the charge and certainly inoculate him from the responsibility of his actions. Other guys who got drunk every night were lushes; Ruth got drunk every night and it was just a bad boy stealing a sip from a jar in the cupboard.

This time, Barrow paid the night porter to keep an eye out and told him to come tell him when Ruth came in. The knock on his door came at 6:00 a.m. and Barrow quickly dressed and went to Ruth's room. He found his star dressed and in bed, the covers pulled over his head, supposedly holding a lit pipe in his hand. Confronted about smoking in bed, fully clothed, according to Barrow's ghostwritten biography, Ruth allegedly sputtered some excuse about how smoking was "relaxing." Disgusted, the manager only shook his head and told Ruth he'd see him at the ballpark, leaving the impression of punishment hanging in the air.

The more Ruth thought about that, the madder he got, and by the time he got to the ballpark, he was ready to explode. He sat in the locker room venting to his teammates, who likely egged him on—watching Ruth get mad, as long as you weren't the one he was getting mad at, was great sport. It was easy to get him worked up. The more he talked the louder and more profane he got, and by the time Barrow walked into the locker room, Ruth had worked himself into a lather.

Now he had to act. If he didn't, he'd lose face with the boys. So Ruth rebelled. He called Barrow a "son of a bitch" and told him if he ever came checking on him again, he'd punch him on the nose—or a series of much more colorful words to that effect.

Barrow cleared the room and invited Ruth to stay and fight. A former boxer, Barrow could handle himself—or thought he could. Called out, for once Ruth backed down. At his size he could have broken his manager in half, and he left the clubhouse and joined his teammates on the field. When Ruth came in to the bench, Barrow told Ruth he was suspended. It was the first time the Red Sox were facing a left-hander that season, so Barrow was probably planning to sit Ruth anyway.

The Sox won, and after the game came one of the most famous moments of Ruth's career, the most famous in Barrow's biography, and a set piece for the great Ruth mythology, the one that converted every indiscretion into the innocent act of an impetuous child. As the train chugged out of Washington, a chagrined Ruth went to his manager as if he was going to confession at St. Mary's and apologized.

Barrow did everything but tousle his hair and get him a warm glass of milk before sending the little scamp to bed. The two soon reached an agreement. Barrow would end the suspension but thereafter Ruth agreed to leave a note for Barrow every night telling him exactly when he came in. It allowed both men to save face—at least Barrow got Ruth to agree to something. But Ruth was more or less given license to carouse—and in only a few weeks there would be press reports referencing Barrow's continued dismay over the frequency of Ruth's "extracurricular" activities. For all Barrow knew, he could have been sleeping in an opium den every night. Most importantly, however, it got Ruth back into the lineup. A player earning $10,000 wasn't worth a dime to anybody sitting on the bench.

Yet given the way Ruth played over the next month, things might not have been as copacetic as the boys' biographies would have one believe. Almost immediately after that meeting, Frazee, Ruth, and Barrow had another one, and they told Ruth he'd better be ready to pitch, because that's what he was going to be doing. Ruth more or less returned to the rotation, playing the outfield or occasionally first base between appearances.

Unfortunately, for the next month he also started hitting like a pitcher, who usually batted last in the lineup because there was no place lower. But Barrow stubbornly kept Ruth in the middle of the order. And in the meantime, the Red Sox slumped and slid, falling from second place, only one game out of first, to as low as sixth, and as many as 10 games out of first place. And although teams have come from 10 games back early in the season to win a pennant, few of them have successfully vaulted five other ball clubs. Remember, the season was already truncated to only 140 games, leaving Boston even fewer games than normal to recover. The end result? The Red Sox were out of it early, and although nobody dared utter it at the time, Ruth bore much of the responsibility for that.

After his hot start, from April 26 through May 26 he hit a paltry .180 with only four extra base hits—including one home run, as the Red Sox went 5–11. To be fair, although he struggled on the mound giving up 13 hits and walking eight in one 11-inning relief appearance, he did pitch and win three of those ballgames. But at the plate he was pathetic, nearly the worst hitter in the lineup as he played the worst baseball of his major league career. By the time Ruth hit his next home run on May 30 and really started hitting again, the Red Sox were essentially finished for the 1919 season. To win the pennant they would have had to play more than .700 baseball for the remainder of the year, a pace only seven teams have ever maintained over the course of the season, a list that includes the vaunted 1927 Yankees. The 1919 Sox, even with Ruth, weren't '27 Yankees.

Even worse—at least for Harry Frazee—was that Boston's poor performance early in the season killed fan interest in the team. With four world championships in seven seasons, Sox fans were spoiled. They didn't care to come out to the ballpark to see a loser. So while the attendance for other major league franchises rebounded in 1919—on average, more than doubling, meeting or even exceeding prewar levels—that was not the case for the Red Sox. After a good start at the gate—the club drew over 50,000 fans in their first home stand over six games—as the team slumped on the road and returned to Boston well below .500, so did attendance. The combination of a losing team and the lack of Sunday baseball suddenly left Boston at a huge disadvantage. While pennant contenders Detroit, New York, Chicago, and Cleveland all either set attendance records in 1919 or threatened to, the Red Sox lagged behind. Oh, they got some bounce from the end of the war, increasing attendance from 249,000 in 1918 to 417,000 in 1919, but that worked out to only another 2,000 fans a game, still an average of less than 6,000 a day. Meanwhile, teams like the White Sox, Yankees, Tigers, and Indians—all contenders in 1919—averaged nearly twice that. It was hard to compete.

So what happened? Why did Ruth stop hitting? Well, he was carrying some extra pounds, but throughout the month of May, there was no indication that he was injured—the only damage he'd suffered was to his feelings. And it wasn't the burden of both pitching and playing in the field that bothered him either—he usually hit better when pitching. And while it is possible that the physical rigors of pitching and playing every day wore on him, it is interesting that at virtually every other level of baseball, from Little League through college and in adult baseball and semipro baseball, it is not uncommon for some position players to also serve as pitchers and vice versa. Only in professional baseball, where pitching arms are treated like cut glass, do pitchers have a single mission, and the reason for that is as much due to economics and tradition as it is to physical health or fatigue. If a pitcher gets hurt running the bases, the manager, not the player, takes the hit.

The truth probably lay somewhere between his attitude . . . and the baseball. Ruth had made his preference clear—he didn't want to pitch anymore, he just wanted to play in the field and hit. Given his self-regard and self-centered, immature nature, it's not beyond the realm of belief that Ruth might have moped his way through the month giving less than his best effort. There were also occasional instances when the press intimated he might not have been giving his all in the outfield, and he made several poor throws, previously never a problem for the strong-armed Ruth. He was a brooding little boy, eating his spinach but making it clear he didn't like it and ruining the meal for everyone.

And then there was the baseball. Anecdotally, there's every indication that at the start of the 1919 season the old war-issue baseballs with the bad yarn and subpar horsehide were still in use. After teeing off on what might have been a different ball in the spring, the same swings Ruth took during the regular season simply weren't yielding the same results—and the pitching was better, too. There has to be some explanation—including his performance over the final two months of the 1918 season; in the last three months of regular season major league competition, Ruth had been just an average hitter. Over nearly 300 plate appearances, he had hit only two home runs, only one over a fence. That coincides nicely with when the subpar ball was first put into play and when, presumably the postwar ball, now wrapped tighter, made of better materials, and suddenly more lively—began to be used. Toward the end of May, it appeared that Ruth the "fearsome slugger" was running on reputation alone. The Babe had gone bust.

The fans noticed. In one mid-month contest, Chicago spitballer Eddie Cicotte toyed with him, making him look so bad as he struck him out twice in a 1–0 shutout that Chicago fans stood and jeered, laughing at his inept swings as he both missed badly and then awkwardly stumbled from the effort. A lot of wise guys around baseball looked at each other knowingly and nodded their heads: Ruth couldn't keep it up—they'd been right all along. As a hitter, Ruth was a flash in the pan, and now it appeared as if he'd fallen off as a pitcher as well. Ever since he'd entered the league, he'd been warned that his lifestyle would eventually catch up with him. Maybe that's what was happening now.

Then, just when it looked as if he might never awaken, be begun to stir. By then it was already too late for the Red Sox, the damage to their pennant dream and their financial well-being already done. Ruth crushed his second home run of the season in St. Louis on May 20, a long blast in Sportsman's Park that cleared the right field fence and landed on Grand Avenue, and over the last few days of May he started to heat up again. Although his power remained sporadic through the next month, giving him six home runs halfway through the season, at least he was finally getting a few base hits. Perhaps that new ball was becoming more commonly used.

Too little too late, at least in the standings. The Red Sox struggled to play .500 baseball. And when Ruth started hitting in June, everyone else stopped. When Boston fell to the Yankees at the Polo Grounds 7–4 on June 30, the Red Sox were in sixth place, 24–31, and already trailed first place New York by 12 games.

The only people making real money off Ruth were the Yankees—fans turned out in droves to see their club take three of five from Boston. Over the course of three days, including doubleheaders on Saturday and Monday, more than 70,000 swarmed over the Polo Grounds to see their first place club—and Ruth. He was making his first appearance in New York since Opening Day, and fans there remembered what he had done then. He didn't disappoint, driving what was called "the longest fly ever caught" at the ballpark in game one, backing Sammy Vick up again the fence in the deepest corner of left center, then about 450 feet from the plate, hitting a ball over the roof in right field in the second game—just foul—and then blasting a grand slam off Bob Shawkey in the first game of the final double-header. But it mattered not, as the Red Sox still lost the game. It was that kind of year.

The knives were coming out in Boston, where the same sportswriters that had been predicting that Ruth would set a home run record were now moaning that Ruth might never set the home run record for a season, making Ruth a victim of their own overly enthusiastic hyperbole. To this point in Ruth's career, he had hit only 27 home runs as a major leaguer, 17 since the beginning of the 1918 season. Fully one-third of those had been hit against the Yankees, eight at the Polo Grounds. So far only two—two—of his career home runs had been hit at Fenway Park. It was a small sample size, to be sure, but at this juncture, only in New York, at the Polo Grounds, did Ruth even remotely resemble the hitter he would soon become, or player we see him as today. In real time, Ruth's 1919 season had been a dismal failure; he hadn't come close to earning his salary, his reputation far outstripping his performance.

Now that it really didn't matter anymore, in a lost season, Ruth started getting really hot. With the season essentially over, Frazee and Barrow finally acquiesced to his wishes and his complaints about a bum knee he had wrenched in early June, and relieved him of mound duty. Over the final three months of the season, he would pitch only seven times.

It made no difference, because when he did pitch, he wasn't the pitcher who had once been one of the best in the game. He lacked control, was often hit hard, and rarely struck anyone out. He was still a battler, but he wasn't anything special, depending on his curveball to get batters out. Less than a year before, he had still been, arguably, a star, a World Series record setter. Now he wasn't even the best pitcher on the Red Sox staff. Herb Pennock, Sam Jones, and Carl Mays all had been more dependable and productive.

This time, instead of leaving for the shipyards, the Red Sox players were simply looking to jump ship. The mood on the team turned turpentine as they all took Ruth's lead and it became every man for himself. Ruth, clearly, didn't have to follow the rules, so no one else felt they did either. Now that Ruth wasn't pitching anymore, it was clear that Boston was throwing in the towel. What little camaraderie that remained on the team soon turned sour.

A brief four-game win streak over the A's gave some hope of a turnaround, but on July 5, despite two Ruth home runs, the Sox dropped a doubleheader and began another skid. So far, since Opening Day, Ruth had homered in only two Boston victories. The rest of his blasts had been wasted.

The Red Sox weren't just losing, they were playing poorly and it wore on everyone. Pitcher Carl Mays, frustrated by nonsupport, threw a ball into the stands at a fan who was heckling him. Ban Johnson jumped to fine him $100, and when he refused to pay, Mays was briefly suspended—the Red Sox eventually paid his fine. His loss, coupled with Ruth's removal from the rotation, left the Red Sox seriously undermanned. The Red Sox went into St. Louis and even dropped three in a row to the St. Louis Browns, Ruth costing Boston one game when he botched an easy fly ball. The Browns had long been also-rans in the American League, but it appeared the Red Sox were ready to give St. Louis some competition in that regard.

Everything came to a head in Chicago on July 13, setting off a series of events that, as much as anything else did, eventually led to Ruth's exit from Boston. And that's important to realize: it was not one reason alone or one single event that led to the selling of the Babe. It was a confluence of events, circumstances, coincidences, accidents, and fate. This portion of the story all started with a simple ground ball—Ruth wasn't even involved but standing in left field hundreds of feet away.

With Mays back on the mound for Boston after the suspension, and one out in the first inning, Chicago's star second baseman, Eddie Collins, singled. The next batter hit a double play grounder to Boston second baseman Red Shannon. Yet instead of throwing to second, or even to first, Shannon inexplicably held the ball and both runners were safe.

Perhaps he lost track of the number of outs and froze with indecision, or just couldn't get a grip on the baseball, but afterward, Carl Mays became unglued. Arguably the best pitcher in baseball history not to be a member of the Hall of Fame, since joining the Red Sox in 1915 he'd won more than 70 ballgames, his unique, underhanded "submarine" delivery proving almost unhittable when he was hitting his spots. But as a personality, he was just as much a cipher.

Reserved and remote from his teammates, Mays was a loner, dark and dour, a player the other Red Sox considered an odd duck, arrogant, suspicious, and standoffish, someone who exuded the attitude that he felt he was smarter and better than his peers. Socially awkward, yet supremely confident in his ability as a pitcher, Mays didn't think twice about openly criticizing his teammates when they made mistakes, then wondered why they didn't care for him. One noted that he had the disposition of a man living under the spell of a "permanent toothache." They appreciated him for his talent—Mays had proven himself in the World Series, but he didn't really have a friend on the team—or in the game. He may well have been the most disliked man in the major leagues—and this was before he became notorious for throwing the only pitch in major league history to kill a man when in 1920 he threw the pitch that sent Indians shortstop Ray Chapman to the grave.

After Shannon's miscue, Mays stomped around the mound, making his displeasure obvious. Shannon had erred, to be sure, but no player ever likes being shown up on the field. Angry, Mays began to throw harder. That was a mistake. When he was right, his submarine pitch dropped to the batter's ankles and resulted in ground ball after ground ball. But when he got angry and overthrew, the ball stayed up, and straight, and was easy to hit. The White Sox jumped on him and scored four runs Mays felt he didn't deserve to give up.

It got no better in the second inning. With two out, Eddie Collins hit another ground ball, this time to first. Stuffy McInnis bumbled the ball, and now Collins was safe.

Mays saw red once again. To him, it almost looked like McInnis had misplayed the ball on purpose, and in his mind he thought that maybe Shannon had, too. In fact, maybe his teammates had been sandbagging him for weeks, maybe it was all on purpose, and maybe they wanted him to fail . . . that's the way Mays's mind was working.

He threw another pitch and Collins took off for second. Boston catcher Wally Schang received the pitch, sprang to his feet, and threw toward second.

Mays, already turning to look at the play, took the ball behind his ear, hitting him solid then ricocheting away. It didn't look like an accident. At least Mays didn't think it was, and his teammates were fed up with him anyway. Maybe Schang did hit him on purpose.

Mays finished the inning, but when he got to the bench he just kept going, right into the clubhouse. Another player reported that he was sitting with his head in his hands, distraught and weeping. Barrow sent in another pitcher and by the end of the game, a 14–9 Boston loss, Mays was gone, already on a train back to Boston.

Over time it would come out that he was bothered by more than dissatisfaction with the indifferent play of his teammates—his wife was ill, they had been arguing, and their off-season home had recently burned down, something Mays thought had been done on purpose. There were also rumors that Chicago had been trying to trade for him. The combination of on-field frustration and off-field problems had sent Mays into a deep depression, something baseball was ill equipped to deal with at the time. Every year, several players would simply disappear from major league rosters due to "mania," "exhaustion," "tobacco poisoning," or other euphemisms for emotional and metal ailments, some never to return.

Over his last three starts Mays had pitched well but had lost by shutout three straight times, dropping his record to 5–11, which in an era that valued wins more than anything else was likely to cost him money at contract time. This further unsettled the already unsettled pitcher. Being struck by Schang's throw apparently pushed him over the edge.

Back in Boston the next day, Mays said he intended to go fishing and explained, "I'll never pitch another ball for the Red Sox. . . . I believe the team ought to be up there fighting for the lead right now but there is not a chance of that the way things are being handled." The local scribes let that linger, and none of Mays's teammates, including Ruth, either came to his defense or waved good-bye. Even the press, which usually sided with management, was strangely quiet and even tacitly supportive of his decision. A headline in the *Boston Post* put it this way: "Mays Refuses to Ride Longer on the Broken Donkey." The implication was clear: Who could blame him?

Jumping the team was a big deal but hardly unprecedented. After all, Ruth had jumped just a year before and after a few days had returned and even scored a raise. There was no reason for either Frazee or Barrow to think this would end any differently. And in the event Mays didn't return, well, he could always be traded. Even if he were nuts, as long as he could pitch he'd still be attractive to a contender. A team would put up with just about anything from a pitcher as long as he pitched winning ball—Ruth himself was proof of that.

But jumping the team was a big deal to Ban Johnson. The acrimony between him and Frazee hadn't gone away but was simply simmering under the surface. When the ball club paid Mays's fine a few weeks before, Johnson hadn't been pleased—he'd fined Mays, after all, not the team—but he had stayed silent. Now, however, he saw an opportunity to use his power and put Frazee in his place. Maybe he could piss him off enough to make him think about giving up on the game and selling out. Johnson knew the Red Sox were hurting at the gate compared to other clubs and this might be just enough to provide the final push. Then he might be rid of Frazee for good.

Mays was a valuable commodity, worth plenty to a contending team in a pennant race, and Frazee was in position to reap a windfall and not face much local criticism for getting rid of a problem. If he was able to sell Mays for a good price, it would go a long way toward keeping him going, and help turn a profit. Besides, although no one yet knew it, Johnson still owned a piece of the Indians, and if Mays was going anywhere, he wanted to steer him to Cleveland. The Indians were in third place and trailed the White Sox, who had surged into first ahead of New York, by only five games. Mays could be a difference maker.

Afraid Frazee might sell off Mays to either the Yankees or White Sox first, Johnson acted in his own self-interest. He ordered the Red Sox to suspend Mays indefinitely.

He might as well have asked Frazee to dress the Red Sox in drag and put them in one of his shows. The owner had long ago lost all respect for Johnson and saw through the ploy.

Then he did something that really angered Johnson. He ignored him. Instead of suspending Mays, he acted as if Johnson didn't exist, as if he had no power or authority at all, and began entertaining offers for his missing pitcher. Although Frazee spent a lot of time in Boston, he lived in New York and he and Jacob Ruppert had grown close. Along with Charles Comiskey, all three were serving a one-year term on the American League's board of directors. Frazee not only had Ruppert's office phone number in his address book but Ruppert's private line and home phone, as well. He knew the Yankees would be in the market for the pitcher, but wasn't going to give them any kind of sweetheart deal.

For now, he planned to hold his cards close to the vest, dangle Mays in front of all interested parties, and see the price go up. Ruth hadn't been suspended when he jumped the team in 1918—how was this any different?

In the meantime, the Babe played on as if blissfully unaware that anything at all was happening. He might not even have noticed that Mays was gone. The worse the Red Sox played, and the further they fell behind in the pennant race, the better he hit and the happier he was. There was no moping after a loss from Ruth.

He felt no compulsion anymore whatsoever to give a nod to scientific baseball and take a pitch, hit behind the runner, or drop the occasional sacrifice. Now he was free to swing from his heels, and that's exactly what he did. The weather had warmed and all of a sudden—was it the ball? The fact he didn't have to think but could just swing? Or that the Red Sox were out of the race and in games that didn't matter opposing pitchers were less cautious? All of a sudden, home runs began flying off his bat. Headlines like "Ruth Home Run Only Consolation" became commonplace as his blasts came ever more frequently and Boston fans began to focus solely on that, and not on the performance of the team. And with each subsequent home run, fans in other cities followed suit.

But Ruth wasn't let entirely off the hook—and neither was Ed Barrow. As Frazee and Johnson squared off and Carl Mays dug for worms and baited hooks on the banks of some stream, the sports editor of the *Boston Post*, Howard Reynolds, weighed in with a rare byline. On Sunday, July 21, the front page of *Post*'s Sporting Section screamed out "Barrow Responsible for Red Sox Downward Slide." In a scathing report, Reynolds analyzed Barrow's moves since the end of the 1918 season and found fault with every one, writing, "The real reason of the tumble from the top to a place near the bottom of the American League is Ed Barrow." Not only were his personnel decisions at fault—nearly every man the Red Sox either let go or traded seemed to play like a star when they faced Boston—but the Mays incident exposed his real weakness. Citing the earlier "Ruth dust-up," Reynolds cautioned not to blame Frazee, but that "Under him [Barrow] there is no discipline in the Red Sox ranks, the players have no respect for Barrow because they know he does not know baseball. . . . No one gives a rap for his manager as long as he does not tack on the fines, and the way things are breaking now he does not dare do too much of that. Off the field the players do as they please. There are no hours."

It was clear whom he was referring to. Ruth might have been writing Barrow a mash note every night telling him when he pulled down the covers, but it wasn't slowing him down, keeping him sober, or helping him stay in shape or win ballgames. Thus far, the occasional home run, while exciting for the fans, hadn't offset his indifferent play on the field and his abandonment of the pitcher's mound. The other Red Sox saw through the charade of the nightly note as special treatment for a player they didn't think had earned it or deserved it. They didn't really blame Ruth—hell, they'd have taken advantage of the situation, too—but they didn't like the way they had to follow rules and he didn't.

And Ruth wasn't just disruptive in Boston. On July 18 in Cleveland, the Indians erupted for four eighth-inning runs to break a tie and take a 7–3 lead into the ninth. To close out the game, Indians manager Lee Fohl inserted frontline pitcher Elmer Myers into the game to secure the win despite the fact that he'd just pitched a complete game two days before. The Indians needed mound help—that's why they were so interested in Mays.

However, Myers didn't have it, and gave up a walk, a double, a ground ball, and another walk, as Boston scored one and now had the bases loaded. With Ruth due up, Fohl got nervous. He called on another pitcher, Fritz Coumbe, a left-hander, to counteract Ruth, giving him the admonition to keep the ball low. A hit wouldn't lose the game, but a home run would. There was only one problem. Coumbe hadn't pitched in two months.

It showed. "Coumbe put everything he had on his first offering," wrote a Cleveland reporter, "and Ruth put every ounce of his strength into a terrific swing," but missed, spinning out of the batter's box with the effort. Then "Fritz apparently forgot that making fast ones out of slow ones is a Ruth specialty." Ruth turned on the change-up and launched it over the right field screen and onto a house on the opposite side of the street for a grand slam. Cleveland, fighting for a pennant, lost a game it should have won.

And Lee Fohl lost his job. The Cleveland papers excoriated him and by the time the team took the field the next day, he'd said the hell with it and quit. Tris Speaker took his place. Ruth made his old teammate look like a genius in his first game as manager, this time striking out with a chance to tie the game and end the contest.

Frazee and Johnson continued to spar over Mays. Almost every day the press reported that yet another team had made Frazee an offer for the pitcher or that a previous offer had been increased. The White Sox reportedly offered Frazee first $25,000, then $50,000.

The Boston owner liked this game; he just sat back and watched the price go up and up. Johnson, in turn, sent a telegram to every team in the league telling them not to make a deal because Mays was going to be punished.

Just as Johnson had earlier expressed faux outrage over the gambling in the Boston stands, he now claimed that George Hildebrand, the home plate umpire in Chicago when Mays jumped the team, said he had been told by other Boston players that Mays had been planning to desert the team for weeks and force a trade. If Johnson suspended Mays over that, he would have to suspend just about every player on the Boston roster. The atmosphere was so poor that everyone was hoping to leave.

The Yankees came to Boston on July 24 and Ruppert and Huston tagged along to talk trade with Frazee. In addition to the offer of $50,000 in cash from the White Sox, the Indians, Tigers, and Senators had all made bids, primarily offering Frazee players. He considered the deals, but wanted more in return than they were willing to offer. Besides, he didn't want to increase his payroll.

It was no accident that the decision came down to the Yankees and the White Sox, the other two teams aligned with Frazee against Johnson and the two clubs most willing to ignore his admonitions against acquiring Mays. Comiskey still wanted to make a straight cash deal, but Ruppert was so eager to win now that he put together a package of $40,000 plus promising and affordable young pitchers Allen Russell and Bob McGraw. Frazee and Barrow were already rebuilding and had just purchased eighteen-year-old Baltimore schoolboy Waite Hoyt. Paired with Herb Pennock, the new charges made it appear as if Boston had the makings of another top-notch

pitching staff in the waiting, and money was always useful—Frazee had
already said he hoped to invest much of it in another pitcher. He didn't,
but a month later he did outbid every other team in baseball for the player
considered the best prospect in the game, Joe Wilhoit, who after failing in
several earlier big league trials, had just set a record with a 69-game hitting streak for Wichita in the Western League and was suddenly a hot commodity. Unfortunately, he flamed out—and was much older than the Red
Sox or anyone else thought—but the move is an indication of Frazee's
financial health at the time. He wasn't sitting on his money.

There was also one more indication of that. A year before, Ruppert had
supposedly bid as much as $150,000 for Ruth. Later reports would claim
that now he wanted $200,000 for Ruth and Mays in a package deal.

The offer was breathtaking, three times more than any other transaction to date, yet Frazee had still said no. In fact, in addition to running the
Red Sox, although Frazee had once said he intended to stay out of the producing business for a while, he never really did. That was a spigot that was
almost impossible to turn off, even if he wanted to—there were shows in
production and contracts to be filled.

At the time he'd bought the Red Sox he was already managing a bona
fide big-ticket hit, *Nothing but the Truth*, which ran in New York for 332
performances, closing in the summer of 1917. By the end of 1918, with the
end of the war in sight, Frazee produced the musical *Ladies First*, which
captured crowds surging back into the theater after the end of the war and
it ran for 164 performances. Keep in mind that New York theaters seated
upward of 1,000 people. Frazee could get nearly as many people to see a
play in a season as to see the Red Sox in Fenway. Any show that ran for
100 performances was a hit, with every subsequent performance almost
pure profit. Failed shows shut down quickly before they could lose much
money.

Now he was in the process of getting another play together, this one
entitled *My Lady Friends*. In addition, even after buying the Sox, Frazee
had retained his interest and ownership in several theaters and other businesses. Although the economy had suffered during the war, in the end
Frazee's theater interests hadn't suffered very much; he'd protected his as-
sets and received rent for the theaters anyway, regardless of how well somebody else's shows did in them, and two of the three shows he produced at

the time were hits. In fact, there are indications in his archives that during this time he funneled money earned from the Cort Theatre in Chicago to help support the Red Sox.

With the war over and the influenza epidemic a horrible memory, people were starting to stream back to the theater. As yet there was no radio, and the only mass forms of entertainment were confined to live music, vaudeville, baseball, boxing, and the movies, and only in the theater could the entertainment of vaudeville and the drama of the silent movies be paired with the music of an orchestra. Broadway was about to enter a Golden Age, something Frazee already sensed, and people began attending shows with the frequency they do movies today.

Although Frazee was not exactly Max Bialystock, the character played by Zero Mostel in the Mel Brooks movie *The Producers* who fleeced investors for profit, he was a shrewd businessman.

Just as his tax records in his archive show that Frazee held on to the sentiment that taxes were for people who couldn't figure out a way to avoid them—and as his archives show, he could, Frazee was just as circumspect about the financial worth of his productions. In his tax records, wherever he had a big year, there are inevitably big losses written off, usually in the form of creditors who could no longer be located. It is much the same with his theatrical records. Few plays show a profit on paper, no matter how long they ran or how many people went to see them. It is almost comical. When the house increases and his plays draw big crowds, there are big expenses, just high enough to keep the show in the red. And when the house is down, miraculously, those expenses disappear, yet time and time again the plays just come short of showing a profit.

This is not to say they did not earn money, for the theater started the tradition of what is known today as "Hollywood bookkeeping," creative accounting designed to keep payouts to investors as low as possible, making vast profits look like something else, funneling receipts to shadow vendors and the like, something extraordinarily easy to do in businesses such as baseball or the theater where people paid cash for tickets every single day. Like many of his peers in both the theater and in baseball, Frazee knew how to cook the books to his liking. At any rate, Frazee was clearly in no desperate need for cash, and turned down the package deal for Ruth and Mays. Now New York focused only on Mays.

Very quietly, the Yankees and had been secretly been reaching out to the pitcher, checking on his health and making sure he'd report if they made a deal. He said he would, that his troubles were behind him. On July 30, Frazee, Ruppert, and Huston shook hands and it was done; for $40,000, Mays was a member of the Yankees. When he found out, Ban Johnson almost had a stroke.

Never before had his authority been so openly and brazenly not just challenged but blatantly ignored. Fighting him was bad enough, but this was insurrection, acting as if he didn't matter. Buying a team without permission was offense number one. Working behind his back in 1918 and calling for a single commissioner was unforgivable. But this, this thing, this was something else entirely.

Johnson sent a wire to Boston telling them to indefinitely suspend Mays. Frazee immediately sent one back to Johnson telling him where to get off and then started talking to reporters.

"This action of Johnson's is a joke," he said. "Evidently he is still trying to run the Boston club or make things unpleasant for its management. However, on this occasion big Ban has been a little late. I am no longer concerned in Mays' fate as a pitcher. He is the property of New York." Frazee went on to send a few more digs Johnson's way, chiding him for "Just waking up to what is going on." After all, his negotiations with Ruppert were hardly a secret: the newspapers reported them daily. As the *Tribune* noted a few days later, "war to the knife has been declared in the American League." Frazee was in the middle of it and it would take everything he had to keep from being mortally wounded, but neither would Johnson escape the blade. Knife fights are rarely tidy.

And Ruth was likely already a part of that battle, or at least Frazee had to think he might yet be. The Yankees has already shown some interest in him, and they'd just dropped $40,000 on a player everyone hated and might be mentally unbalanced and had just jumped his team. He had to wonder now how much they would pay for Ruth, his other problem child. Sure, he was starting to hit, when it didn't matter, but Ruth had already cost him plenty. There was no way he was going to earn it back, not in 1919, and perhaps not ever. Over the course of two seasons, Ruth had been a tease, with brief periods of explosive power followed by long droughts. Who was to say it wouldn't happen again? There might be an opportunity to sell high.

But for now, Ruppert and Huston went to court in New York. They had more influence there than Johnson had, and, pending a hearing, easily got an injunction that restrained Johnson from ordering a suspension, banning Mays from pitching, or anything else. Mays entered the New York rotation and Russell entered Boston's. Johnson fumed, his ire toward Frazee and Ruppert increasing by the day.

Oblivious to it all, Ruth only saw pitches coming over the fat part of the plate, long fly balls dropping over the fence, and pretty girls and parties waiting for him wherever he went. A home run surge at the end of July gave him seven for the month and all of a sudden, Socks Seybold's American League record of 16 home runs, set in 1902, seemed within reach.

Of course, it wasn't quite what it appeared. Seybold, a left-handed hitter for the A's, had benefited from playing at Philadelphia's home field, Columbia Park, where it was only 280 feet down the line and 323 in the right field power alley, far shallower than Fenway or any other American League park Ruth played in. Nevertheless, a record was a record, even a relatively obscure one at the time, and it gave sportswriters, bored with the Red Sox and with the court battle between the Yankees and Johnson, something else to write about.

It helped filled the stands, too. When the White Sox came into town on August 2 for a Saturday doubleheader, the combination of the league leader, fine weather, and Ruth's assault on the record brought out a surprisingly big crowd of more than 30,000. For the first time all year, Ruth was earning his keep.

That was fine with Frazee, because on August 1 he entered into negotiations to purchase Fenway Park from the Fenway Realty Group, a holding company created by the Taylor family. When they had sold the Red Sox to Joseph Lannin, they had retained ownership of the park, which they had just built, allowing them to see a nice return from the ball club well into the future. Frazee paid $30,000 a year in rent.

But the Taylors didn't own all the stock in the holding company. Lannin and a few of their business cronies owned some shares, too. Given the open war that erupted between Frazee and Johnson, Frazee had some fear that Fenway could fall into unfriendly hands and that the terms of his lease could be changed to make ownership of the Red Sox untenable. In addition, he was already in a spat with Lannin over payment on a note worth $262,000 due in November. Buying Fenway Park could solve several problems at once. Back in March, General Taylor and John Taylor had already told Frazee they were looking to get out of the ballpark business and terminate the trust. Frazee, who owned 150 shares, had balked at the time, but now, given the changing political situation, he was agreeable to move in that direction.

Conveniently enough for Frazee, Ruth picked the long home stand to go into another prolonged home run drought, one that kept the crowds coming out day after day, wondering if this was the day he would snap out of it and set the record. On August 9, 24,000 fans turned out at Fenway for another doubleheader, this time against St. Louis. They didn't go away completely disappointed, as Ruth tripled to the bleachers in dead center field, the place where it seemed all his long drives had been going the entire home stand. It almost seemed like he did didn't want to homer—when the Sox played out of town Sunday exhibitions, which they often did due to Boston's blue laws, Ruth suddenly seemed able to pull the ball and almost homer at will.

Not so at Fenway. Then again, pitchers had gotten smarter. As Ruth warmed up over the course of the summer, they pitched him more and more carefully, keeping the ball away, giving him nothing to pull, often satisfied by holding him to a base on balls. After walking only 31 times through June, over the last three months of the season he'd be put on base 70 more times. In fact, during the seventh inning of the final game of the home stand versus the Browns, with the game scoreless, the bases loaded, and Ruth at bat, St. Louis pitcher Allan Sothoron intentionally walked Ruth—forcing home a run that eventually proved to be the game winner in Boston's 1–0 victory.

For whatever reason, once Boston hit the road, Ruth's home run power miraculously returned. He didn't waste time, homering on August 14 in Chicago off Erskine Mayer, the ball clearing the right field wall and landing in an adjacent soccer field. The Red Sox' Babe, and not the A's Socks, was now the official American League home run record holder.

The next target was Gavvy Cravath's National League mark of 24, set in 1915 with the Phillies. Like Seybold, that record, too, had been set with a little help, for the Baker Bowl was one of the smallest parks in baseball, and Cravath hit 19 of his 24 home runs there. Still, it gave Ruth and the fans something else to look forward to, and in Boston that was all they had.

Now that someone was hitting home runs with regularity for the first time ever, everything about the hit was a potential record. Fans were enthralled. How far, how many times in a game, in a season, in a league, for a team, in a park, off a left-hander, off a right-hander, to center field, to left, to right, into the stands, into the bleachers, over the roof, almost anything you could think of in any combination potentially created a record . . . it was almost endless. All because of Ruth, fans and sportswriters alike began keeping track of ever more arcane marks. And as virtually the first practitioner of his craft, almost every Ruth home run was a potential record setter of one kind or another. It was almost as if he'd invented the hit.

From this point of his career onward, it seemed as if Ruth either set a record or broke a record hardly anyone had ever even known existed before. Consider this: before Ruth, baseball's all-time career home run leader was Roger Connor with 138, set during a career that lasted from 1880 to 1897, beginning when the ball was still thrown underhanded, but in general, his mark wasn't given much credence. In the so-called modern era, post-1901, the all-time record was held by Cravath with 118. Ruth broke Cravath's mark in 1921, and every single home run he hit thereafter, 596 of them, for a total of 714, set another all-time record. It was a similar situation with nearly every other possible home run record as well. There's nothing else like it in the history of professional sports. All of a sudden, relieved of the burden of pitching and trying to win, and able to focus on hitting for the first time, Ruth could not be stopped. For whatever reason, home runs rained down like raindrops, but the new, improved baseball and another road trip, where he took aim at fences more to his liking than those at Fenway Park, didn't hurt.

One day after Ruth set the modern American League record, the Red Sox went into St. Louis and Ruth cracked two more. Then it was on to Cleveland, where he failed to homer but still managed a long triple, as outfielders seemed to deny reality and reason and kept playing him in too close. A fair number of Ruth's other long hits, doubles and triples, were catchable but floated over the heads of fielders still unwilling to admit he could knock the ball over their heads.

It all took off. In a matter of a few weeks, Ruth had become bigger than the game. In fact, it seemed as if he was changing the game incrementally every day. Baseball was both powerless to stop it and didn't want to. In the finale in Cleveland on August 22, Ruth took exception to a strike called by his old nemesis, umpire Brick Owens, whom he'd famously punched back in the first inning of a game in 1917 when he didn't like the arbiter's calls and was ejected and then suspended. That was the famous game Ernie Shore came on in relief and pitched perfect baseball thereafter.

This time, Ruth wanted to take another crack at Owens. After the call, he stepped out of the batter's box and turned toward Owens, cursing him out and making sure everyone in the ballpark knew it. Owens listened, heard the magic word or two or three, and tossed Ruth from the game.

The Babe exploded, rushing the umpire and pulling his fist back to hit him again. Before he could unleash the punch, however, players from both teams got between the two men and true violence was averted.

Had it been anyone else, the player would have been fined and suspended. Ban Johnson had done that before, and Ruth had to know that another altercation with Owens might prove costly. But this wasn't just any old player, not anymore. This was Ruth, the Babe, and Johnson may not have wanted to risk another legal battle or the ensuing public relations fiasco a Ruth suspension would inspire. Besides, he'd just helped fill up the Cleveland ballpark and Johnson had a piece of the Indians. Ruth was making everyone money. It was a measure of Ruth's power that Johnson laid off, for suspending Ruth would have also struck at Frazee.

Yet Johnson did nothing. The message was clear: Babe Ruth was bigger than the game.

It was as if once Ruth realized that, he was even more inspired. The Red Sox went to Detroit and Ruth started hitting as he had while barnstorming back to Boston in the spring, cracking four home runs in three days. Ty Who? In the papers, Ruth and the word "another" seemed to appear in every other sentence. With 23 home runs, he was poised to knock Cravath and his modern N.L. and major league mark off the pedestal.

But once he did that, what then would fans have to look forward to the rest of the year? Unlike today, batting records, apart from batting average were almost unknown in 1919, and given the evolving nature of the games and it organization, there was little consensus as to what an actual record in a category truly was. Now sportswriters scurried through clip files and record books and soon unearthed two more marks to take aim at, Buck Freeman's 25 home runs hit with Washington in 1899, which was widely considered the NL record in its own right prior to 1901, and Ned Williamson's obscure mark of 27 struck with Chicago back in 1884. Both records had been given mighty assists from fences set at friendly distances, particularly Williamson's, but were home runs nevertheless. Ruth's pursuit gave all such records new currency and introduced them to a new generation. Every home run Ruth hit made baseball history come to life again.

As the *Globe* noted when the Red Sox returned home, "there will be some big crowds out and many will go simply on the chance of seeing 'Babe' Ruth add to his already long string of home runs." Ruth was suddenly such big news that when other players homered sportswriters scrambled to squeeze in a Ruth reference either in the story or the headline. After the White Sox' Eddie Collins hit a home run to beat St. Louis, one headline termed it a "Babe Ruth Act," as if Ruth had a trademark on home runs and others now had to give him credit when they encroached on his territory.

Ruth cooperated with the daily drama and failed to break Cravath's modern N.L. record on the road, building the anticipation in his adopted home city. As if afraid the recent Ruth fetish might end before they could do anything about it, the Red Sox labored to take full advantage of the frenzy. When the Red Sox returned home, although already assured of a good Labor Day crowd, they announced that Ruth would be on display during the doubleheader, not just to try to match and break Cravath's record, but that he would pitch as well. Given the way things were going, fans had to wonder if he would throw a no-hitter just for the hell of it.

The Sox didn't need Ruth to pitch; the pennant race had been over for months and it really didn't matter who took the mound for Boston anymore, but for the moment, the name Ruth attached to almost anything made money and if having Ruth pitch guaranteed a sellout, Ruth would pitch. If selling peanuts had done the trick, they'd have had him do that, too. As one newspaper noted clearly, the 30,000 fans in Boston that day were "lured by the reputation of Boston's home run king," and nothing else. Ruth, at last, was starting to pay for that big contract.

And maybe there was one more reason. It's not beyond the realm of possibility that the Red Sox had already have been thinking about trading Ruth, and wanted to showcase him and prove that, yes, he could still pitch, too. That would make him even more valuable. The prospect of a slugging starting pitcher turned outfielder on his off days was tantalizing, if not to Ruth, then to everyone else.

It was obvious: Ruth was now the reason for the season. In the National League, the Cincinnati Reds surprised everyone and, after hanging around for much of the year, surged away from the field in August and by September locked up the National League title, stripping the pennant race of real drama as only the Giants retained even a distant hope of catching up, one they would not fulfill. And in the American League, the White Sox caught the Yankees in early July and then held the lead like a plow horse plodding forward, increasing it in small increments. By September, they were already taking money on a Chicago-Cincinnati World Series.

Ruth immensely enjoyed the attention, which he found made him more popular than ever before. He responded to the spotlight, the almost orphaned and abandoned little boy finally getting his due, grinning widely, tipping his hat and waving at the crowd at every opportunity.

He started game one of the doubleheader, and after barely pitching for the past few months apart from a few emergency appearances after the Mays sale, energized by the crowd, Ruth threw what would become the last really good game of his career. The crowd screamed at every pitch, a throng so vast that not only did they fill the stands, but they also filled the spaces under it. For the 1912 World Series, the Red Sox had added several rows of box seats in front of the grandstand, which stopped several feet above the playing field. Beneath the original seating area had been a space about three feet high, open to the concourses underneath the stands, separated from the field by only a wire fence. In the 1912 season, during the famous pitching duel between Joe Wood and Walter Johnson, before the new box seats were built, the crowd had pushed their way into this cramped space to watch the game from virtually ground level. Late in the 1919 season, as the Red Sox played on the road, work crews tore the new seats out, which were now warped and rotten. That was becoming a problem almost everywhere at Fenway. Except for the center field bleachers, the right field pavilion down the first base line, and the main grandstand, the rest of the park, more than 10,000 seats hastily constructed of wood just before the 1912 World Series, was falling apart, increasingly dangerous to use.

The deconstruction once again revealed the space beneath the stands. Ruth proved such a draw, and the crowd so enormous, that now boys and young men looked at the empty space and saw a viewpoint much preferable to their own tickets in the upper reaches of the stands. The result was that when Ruth took the mound, he did not only see the stands stacked with people, he also saw a horde of fans under the stands, from the ground up, packed with a new generation of worshippers who considered him both their peer and hero, faces pressed against the fence and stacked atop one another like cordwood.

In most instances, such an overflow crowd would have caused the Red Sox to string ropes in the distant reaches of the outfield in right, and center, and in front of Duffy's Cliff, and allow fans to stand on the slope itself. Tiered like a stand of bleachers, it was possible for ten or twelve rows of fans to stand and see over each other's heads. But on this day, either caught unprepared by the first such crowd in years, or aware of the historical nature of the day, the Red Sox allowed no one on the field and instead crammed the overflow into the aisles, creating thousands of extra standing room seats and forcing fans in the stands to stay in their places for virtually the entire game. There would be no cheap home runs over the ropes on this day. If Ruth—or anyone else—hit a home run, it would be earned.

With the crowd hanging on every pitch, Ruth seemed to toy with the Senators, allowing his share of hits and bending, but not breaking, apparently able to summon the old magic at will to keep Washington from scoring. After all, a year before Ruth had been the choice to start the most important games of the season. So it was again, albeit with something else entirely at stake.

Whenever Ruth came to bat, the crowd roared on each pitch, surging back and forth in great undulating waves as a stumble on one side of the park flowed through to the other as shoulder pressed shoulder and each head jockeyed for a view. Like a master showman, Ruth seemed to tease the crowd, slamming a third-inning triple to center to drive in a run and send the crowd into a frenzy, a ball that had no chance of leaving the field but was hit so hard it seemed to promise better things to come, and then coming around to score the second run to stake himself to a 2–0 lead. A later single gave the crowd something else to admire, and after giving up a lone run in the seventh, Boston took the first game 2–1, Ruth scattering 11 hits for the win, and figuring in every Red Sox score. It was a glimpse of what had been for a brief time in 1918, a player dominant on both the mound and at bat, valuable beyond any measure of any player either before or since.

But Ruth had still not accomplished what the crowd craved, and in game two he took his place in left field as Russell, acquired in the Mays deal, pitched for the Red Sox. Although later held up as an example of the "rape" of the Red Sox by the nefarious Yankees, the deal had actually worked out well for the Sox, at least over the remainder of the 1919 season. After going to New York, Mays went 9–3 for the Yankees, who collapsed in the second half and fell out of the race. Russell, for Boston, went 10–4 for his new club, in many ways outperforming the player he was dealt for, easily pitching the best stretch of baseball in his career. As author Steve Steinberg's research later ascertained, that would prove to be a pattern in the deals between Boston and New York over the next few seasons: they were usually equitable at the time they were made, and Boston received value in return. But history is written by the victors, and since the Yankees went on to become a dynasty, the deals now appear to tilt dramatically in New York's favor, although by most measures the numbers tell a different story. Only a few deals would be truly one-sided, and even those mostly made sense at the time.

On this day no one cared about Russell; it was Ruth's stage and he was learning to command it like no one else, feeding off the attention that eluded him as he grew up on the streets of Baltimore.

The game was close as Russell and the Senators' Jim Shaw each kept the crowd on their feet. The score was tied at one apiece when Ruth came to bat in the seventh with teammate Braggo Roth on base. Shaw tried to slip one past Ruth on a 2–2 count. As the *Globe* noted, "the ball never got by."

Ruth turned on the pitch and hit it on a line, some 20 feet fair, down the right field line, not a towering shot that inspired awe, but a bullet that seemed both fearsome and dangerous. It burrowed into the crowd just a few feet over the fence and disappeared. Ruth had tied Cravath.

Now the crowd really went off, the ovation described as lasting nearly ten minutes, straw hats spinning down onto the field thrown by exuberant fans.

A young boy—it was always a young boy—vaulted over the barrier from the stands down the third base line and raced toward Ruth, reaching him after he crossed the plate. In Ruth's era, that was not a sign of danger but of devotion. Rarely has there been a player both so adored and so approachable. The big man bent over the youngster so he could hear what he was saying, and then the youth passed him something that Ruth accepted. What it was is lost to history. What it represented was the scepter of royalty. Ruth was now anointed the Home Run King, a crown he retains to this day. Although others have usurped many of his numbers, no one has ever approached his sovereign status. They kept cheering after the game resumed, reminiscent according to some of the way the crowd at Harvard and Yale tried to out-cheer each other at football games, as the fans in left and right battled to make more noise than each other. But this was not for one team over another, but one man over mortality.

The game did not matter. The blast gave Boston a lead they would not relinquish and the Red Sox won 4–1. Wrote Boston sportswriter James O'Leary, "It is not often that man has an opportunity to perform so well in the presence of so large a crowd and when he has the opportunity he rarely has the ability to deliver the goods." That was the player Ruth was becoming, someone who suddenly seemed able to dial up such performances on command.

Now it was on to the lesser records, those once obscure but now made famous by Ruth's approach. A few fans had been aware of Seybold's American League mark, and once that was bettered, Cravath's National League and modern major league mark gained currency. Now fans learned of Freeman, a name their fathers or grandfathers remembered from a generation before, and his mark of 25 home runs.

The Red Sox salivated at the prospect of the crowd that would turn out the next three days to see Boston play the Yankees—er, make that Ruth confront history. It was not unthinkable to expect another 20,000 or 30,000 fans for each game, a windfall that would put Frazee in what was then termed the clover, rolling in a field of rich green cash. In one week, he could sell as many tickets as he had in the last two months. And with a couple weeks left in the season . . .

It was a time unlike any other in baseball history, an apparently once-in-a-lifetime opportunity for record after record to tumble all at once like dominoes. That is something that in the entire history of the game would happen only a handful of times—DiMaggio's 56-game hitting streak in 1941, and 1998's now tainted battle between enhanced home run totals of Mark McGwire and Sammy Sosa. For fans, it was one of those "have to be there" moments, worthy of retelling for the rest of your life.

Ruth was game, and so were the fans. But the weather was not. Over the next three days, it rained and it rained and it rained. As it did, the fortunes that Frazee hoped to reap spun down the drain, waterlogged, sodden, and lost for all time, perhaps $100,000 worth of receipts. With them may well have gone any chance for Ruth to remain in Boston.

Boston went to Philadelphia, where A's fans, saddled with a losing team as Connie Mack chose to lose on purpose and save money, were not quite as enthusiastic, but Ruth still responded. As the Red Sox warmed up before the game, a fan got Ruth's attention and asked him if it was easy to hit home runs. Thus challenged, and feeling invincible, Ruth stepped to the plate, beckoned for a pitch, and hit the first one he saw over the fence and onto the front porch of a house on 20th Street.

At least that's what the paper said. Increasingly, it was becoming ever more difficult to separate reality from hyperbole. But then again, when he came to bat for the second time that day, he sent the first pitch he saw in a similar direction to match Freeman's mark, then nearly added another later in the game when he a hit a drive that caromed of the top of the wall and ricocheted back for a double. Then, as if exhausted from circling the bases, he added three singles. The first report in the *Globe* didn't even mention the score. The headline only read "Babe Ruth Equals Home Run Record." The final was 15–7, Boston, and for much of the rest of the season whether or not Ruth hit a home run meant more to the headline writers that anything else.

Freeman, who had played in Boston after Washington, was magnanimous and later admitted, "I could never hit like Ruth." He also noted that he believed hitters of his era "would be helpless against the spitter and some of the other deliveries pitchers now use."

The only other baseball news was coming from the courts in New York. Over there, the whole sordid little story of how baseball ran and operated behind the scenes was slowly being exposed. By entering into a legal war with the Yankees over the Mays deal, Johnson left himself open for legal discovery and what was being revealed stank. Forced to testify under oath, Johnson's long-rumored financial interest in the Cleveland Indians was exposed as fact, as was his desire to have purchased the Red Sox himself from Joseph Lannin after the 1916 season, one thwarted by Frazee. No wonder he had chosen his target. It was further revealed that when the Mays deal was made, Johnson, acting on behalf of the National Commission, communicated in secret with five American League club owners, freezing out what the press began referring to as the "Insurrectos"—the Red Sox, Yankees, and White Sox.

Johnson was in over his head. He thought he was connected, but in the New York courts he couldn't match Ruppert's and Frazee's political and personal power. The Yankees' attorney excoriated Johnson in front of New York Supreme Court judge Robert Wagner, a crony of Frazee (and later his divorce lawyer), and Wagner let him talk, then publicly called Johnson a czar and dictator.

They were hardly disinterested parties, but the Insurrectos charged that it was now clear that Johnson, for years, had "the entire league under his domination." Those he favored reaped the benefits in the form of favorable trades and other favors. Those he did not—the Yankees, Red Sox under Frazee, and now the White Sox as well—usually got the short end. Increasingly, everything the Red Sox, the Yankees, and, to a lesser degree, the White Sox did, had to take Johnson into account. He was cornered now, and although weakened and publicly humiliated, he was still dangerous. The man who "never forgets an enemy," now had three who felt the same way about him. Ruppert publicly called for Johnson to be "put out of baseball," and the Insurrectos worked behind the scenes to garner support from other owners.

For now, however, very little broke through the stranglehold Ruth held over the attention of the nation's baseball fans. *He* was revolutionizing the game. After playing Washington, Boston went into New York, and with the attention of the entire city focused upon him, Ruth rose to the occasion once again. In the eighth inning of the first game of a doubleheader, he hit a curveball to the deepest part of the right field stands and passed Freeman with home run number 26. It hit an empty seat back and rattled around the upper reaches as fans scrambled for the ball.

The guy that got it managed to get Ruth's attention between innings. The King made his way back onto the field and the fan threw the record-setting ball back to its rightful owner. As one writer noted, Ruth now owned two of baseball's most impressive records, the home run mark, for individual achievement, and the scoreless innings pitched mark in the World Series, perhaps the ultimate team mark. Even the fact that the doubleheader was played was a sign of Ruth's power. Johnson had not authorized the second game of the contest, a makeup of one of the Boston rainouts. The Yankees were so eager to insure a big crowd and cash in on Ruth they didn't even bother to ask permission.

That was all that mattered now—cashing in on Ruth. Frazee announced that on September 20, the first game of Boston's final home stand, the Red Sox would honor Ruth with his own day, yet another ploy to milk the Babe for everything he was worth. Now the press started to make ready mention of Ned Williamson's 1884 mark of 27 home runs, providing Ruth yet another target, one more reason for fans to continue coming out to the ballpark.

As if to sustain the drama, for the next eleven days Ruth hit only ground balls, line drives, and flies that fell short of the fence, increasing anticipation every day and suddenly making Williamson's record, which no baseball fan had even heard of a few months before, the most famous in the game. No one cared about the circumstances in which it was set.

What's nearly as interesting as what Ruth was doing was what the press wasn't reporting on, which is everything else in his life. It's not as if Ruth's home run binge coincided with a turnaround in his personal behavior, his sobriety, sexual abstinence, diet, or vocabulary. Oh no, he was still the same coarse, self-obsessed, unrestrained human animal as he had always been. But now Ruth was royalty, protected by his people—the press. They had as much at stake in him as anyone, including Frazee.

Now, apart from the rare, occasional, veiled allusion, the public was shielded from the whispered gossip of the streets. As long as Ruth retained his throne—which he would do for the rest of his life—this other Babe Ruth would rarely be seen. Like Christy Mathewson, whose All-American image was belied by his love of gambling and a few other pursuits never brought up publicly, Ruth would benefit from the same protection. Today, he'd be splashed over Deadspin or TMZ like a sour bucket of paint. In 1919, his life was already being rewritten for the pages of *Boy's Life*. In only a few short months, the transformation of Ruth as both a player and a public figure was remarkable. It needed only the finishing touches to elevate him from the mortal sphere to one inhabited only by the gods, but that was soon to come.

Frazee and the Red Sox pulled out all the stops for Ruth's big day. The Catholic fraternal charitable group the Knights of Columbus agreed to sponsor the festivities. Ruth likely hadn't seen the inside of a church for some time and by now had a list of sins to confess that that would embarrass a whole seminary of priests, but it didn't matter. There was a special song, "Look at Him Now," written by South Boston songmeister Jack O'Brien and sung by Dorchester tenor Billy Timmins, cash awards and cigars, flag raisings, and anything else they could think of. Hell, Ruth might even hit a home run.

No one went home disappointed. This time 31,000 fans packed already aging Fenway as the bleacher seats, reinforced before the game, sagged and groaned under the weight of the crowd, and the prose ran a gaudy purple. The *Globe's* James O'Leary, rapidly supplanting Webb and Shannon as Ruth's private press agent, wrote, "Rome may have been made to howl for some particular or sundry reasons in the long, long ago, but the efforts of the Roman populace were only murmurs compared to the vocal explosion . . . of 31,000 fans at Fenway Park. . . . Nothing like this demonstration was ever heard at Rome or Elsewhere." The day unfolded as if scripted.

Ruth started the first game on the mound with perhaps as many as 5,000 fans standing behind ropes in the outfield—special ground rules in effect to make sure no home run would be cheapened. Boston scored three, first inning runs—Ruth walked—but after the White Sox tied the score in the sixth Ruth was relieved and moved to left field. The score stayed tied until the ninth . . . and up came Ruth.

So far, Chicago's Cy Williams had mastered Ruth, the left-hander pitching Ruth carefully, knowing that his best chance came to get him out came from keeping the ball away from the pull hitter. If Ruth had made any change over the course of the 1919 season, it was that he had become more adept at pulling the ball. Yet at Fenway, that wasn't as effective; he'd only homered in Fenway eight times in 250-some plate appearances in 1919, as too many long drives, if not hard down the line, died in deep right, about where the bullpens sit today.

This time however, Ruth reached out toward a fast one going wide of the plate. He got the fat part on it, and lifted the ball not to right, but to left, toward the middle of the wall atop Duffy's Cliff. It first passed over the head of White Sox left fielder Joe Jackson—as a hitter a pure afterthought in Ruth's shadow—then the crowd crammed onto Duffy's Cliff, and then, as heads turned up to watch, over the top of the wall, just to the center field side of the clock perched atop the fence above the scoreboard. Then, according to the press (although none could really see it from the press box), the ball sailed over Lansdowne Street and into the window of a building across the street.

It won the game, it tied Williamson's record, it capped Ruth's career in Boston, and it provided an exclamation point to the season. The stands fairly exploded, not with the sounds of the crowd at the Roman Colosseum cheering the death of a slave thrown to the lions, but worshipping an emperor taking over before an adoring public, Ruth dutifully doffing his cap as he toured the bases. More recent Red Sox lore counts Ted Williams's home run in his final major league at bat as the most dramatic in Fenway Park history, or perhaps Fisk's home run in 1975, but neither had anything on the drama the 31,000 fans in Fenway on September 20, 1919, had just witnessed. If was as if Ruth could will himself to hit a home run on demand. No one had ever seen anything like it.

Then came the ceremonies. Ruth and his wife gathered at home plate and received tribute. Mrs. Ruth received a traveling bag—she'd soon need it—while Ruth accepted $600 worth of bonds from the Knights of Columbus. Then, as the two were surrounded by photographers and cameramen, ritual was made of the presentation to Ruth of the bat that tied the record. More ceremony followed, as Ruth magnanimously gave it back to a delegation from the Liberty Loan Newsboy Association, which planned to auction it off to support "Scotty's Newsboy Fund," a charity honoring a fifteen-year-old Boston newsboy who had enlisted and then given up his life in France.

Interestingly enough, who wasn't involved in the ceremony was almost as interesting as who was. Harry Frazee later claimed to have given Ruth a cut of the proceeds that day—$5,000—but he stayed out of the way and watched from his box. Generally, whenever a player had a "day" his teammates chipped in and made some kind of presentation, or at the very least were involved in the ceremonies. Not on this occasion. Tellingly, Ruth's teammates only watched. He received no gifts from them.

It was in all ways and every way Ruth's day, and his alone. He didn't limit his contribution to the home run; he also tumbled into the crowd and nearly made a remarkable catch, threw out a runner at the plate, and in game two hit what many fans thought was home run number 28 when he rocketed a ball into the crowd in right, only to have the umpire rule that since it didn't make the fence, it would only be a double. The crowd howled and a "Sergeant of the Military Guard" even went out and took statements from witnesses, which he later tried to present to umpire Billy Evans. The arbiter told him, none too politely, to "attend to your police duties and leave the umpiring to me."

A day marked by the spectacular ended quietly. When Allen Russell retired Buck Weaver to end game two, the Red Sox escaped with a doubleheader sweep. Ruth trotted off the field to applause, but no one, as yet, had an inkling it would be the last time he'd appear at Fenway Park wearing a Red Sox uniform.

Of course, the very next day, when the frenzy for Ruth was highest, the Red Sox played . . . in Bristol, Connecticut. It was a Sunday and once again the Sox lost a potential big crowd to the blue laws. Frazee had done what he could to compensate, scheduling exhibitions in the hinterlands as much as possible, taking the same approach he did with his Broadway shows, but it wasn't very lucrative and the players resented the travel. Taking into account the cost of sending the whole team back and forth several hundred miles to play before what was usually only 5,000 fans or so, it didn't compare to the 30,000 suddenly eager to jostle their way into Fenway to see Ruth.

It was almost as if everyone sensed that something special was taking place, something that was only a once-in-a-lifetime occurrence, and something bigger than Babe Ruth alone. At the precise time the country was changing, everything picking up the pace and becoming more modern, faster, quicker, bigger, and flashier, baseball was keeping up with the times and evolving from a game in which victory was wrung out like a snake coiled around a rat, a slow squeeze of defeat, to a sudden strike. It wasn't trench warfare anymore; it was a revolution. The air force had been called in and Ruth, the deadliest of aces, was leading the way by showing the awesome power contained in the home run, dropping bombs into the crowd.

And he wasn't the only one, either. The new ball was having its impact all around baseball as every hitter in the league was affected by a ball that traveled a little better, that rewarded a big swing with a big result. Home runs and offense were up almost everywhere. In 1917, the last full season of major league ball, clubs had combined for 335 home runs. In 1918, due to a combination of the war and the baseball, the total slipped to 235. In 1919, however, led by Ruth, clubs combined for 447 home runs in only a 140 game season, and the arc of their frequency more or less matched Ruth's, a relative handful in April and May and then a deluge later in the year as the new ball, and, to a new degree, a new approach took hold.

Perhaps the biggest impact had yet to be seen in the major leagues but was apparent everywhere on the sandlots and the other places where boys still played baseball from dawn until dusk. They didn't imagine themselves to be Cobb, or Jackson, slashing out singles and committing acts of daring on the bases. They were Ruth, grabbing the bat at the end and swinging for all it was worth, as enamored of Ruth and what he could do as Ruth himself had once been of Brother Matthias, dreaming of one day doing what had then seemed almost superhuman.

In a few short years, the first of those boys and young men who were now dreaming of being Babe Ruth would enter professional baseball and complete the revolution he had started from the bottom up. In only a handful of years the game would almost be unrecognizable, the impact of the home run as dramatic on the sport of baseball as the forward pass in football, or the jump shot in basketball. Transformative is simply not a strong enough word. Ruth didn't transform the sport; it remade itself in his image.

With only a week left in the season it was Ruth who dominated the headlines, not the upcoming World Series, the only drama remaining whether Ruth would actually hit one more home run and make the record entirely his own. By now, that seemed almost preordained.

And as if the baseball gods were listening, they sent Ruth and the Red Sox to New York, the capital of the world, to demonstrate that he conquered all he saw. In the second game of a doubleheader on September 24, with

Yankee fireballer Bob Shawkey helping to provide the fuel, Ruth added an explosive exclamation point to the season. Once again, it came in the ninth. The Red Sox trailed 1–0, and on Shawkey's second pitch, Ruth struck.

Bat hit ball and sent it up, up, and out, over the roof of the grandstand in right, leaving the park between the fourth and fifth flags that adorned the roof and then onto little Manhattan Field, a local park in the Polo Grounds' shadow. The consensus was that it was the longest home run ever hit at the ballpark. It tied the game, and although the Red Sox eventually lost in 13 innings, no one cared. The major league single season home run record, regardless of league or era, was Ruth's and Ruth's alone: 28 home runs. There were no others to break.

Now it was as if Ruth stood back, looked around, and asked if there was possibly any other kind of record he might set with his next home run. The Red Sox went from New York to Washington, where Ruth hadn't hit a home run all season long, the only place he hadn't done so. No major leaguer had ever hit a home run in the same season in every park in the league.

Ruth got it over early this time in ho-hum fashion, in the third inning driving the ball only four or five feet over the right field fence, this time not breaking up a ballgame or crashing through a porch or a window, just a plain old, garden-variety home run. Yet even that was special in its own way. Only a few short years before, every home run hit anywhere over the fence had been the cause of wonder, an anomaly that seemed both a bit magical and accidental at the same time. Now, Ruth had made it both spectacular and commonplace. The notion that there could be "just" an average home run had once been unthinkable, but not anymore.

Thirty was a nice round number, but on the last day of the season Ruth sat on his laurels—sort of. Actually, at the peak of his popularity, he jumped the club, walking out on his teammates, stiffing the fans, and giving everybody who cared about him a big fat raspberry. Right when every eye on the game was trained on him, Ruth told everyone where to get off and thought only of himself. He had been offered a pretty good payday to play an exhibition in Baltimore, so he left. Frazee later lumped it in with his midseason shipyard vacation in 1918 as another example if Ruth's me-first attitude.

Either way, the move was both ballsy and selfish. By playing for another team, Ruth was breaking his contract, and had the Red Sox chose to, they could have caused trouble for him, and so could have Ban Johnson. But for the time being, Ruth was more powerful than all of them put together. He pretty much did what he pleased, and on the last day of the season, on what would have been his final day in a Boston uniform, he ditched everybody, missing a chance to hit home run number 30 to play with a bunch of strangers for money.

That says a lot about just who Ruth was at the time. Nothing was ever enough for him, his appetite in all things never sated, and apart from women and food, nothing drove Ruth like money. For the chance to make a dollar, he'd risk his reputation. Maybe it was insecurity, maybe it was greed, maybe it was childhood poverty, maybe it was ignorance, or maybe it was genius, but there was little Ruth wouldn't do for a check.

For the record, Ruth finished the season with a 9–5 record on the mound, a record better than the way he pitched. At the plate, however, he recorded numbers not yet seen, finishing with a record 29 home runs, and also leading the league in runs with 103, and RBI, with 113, while batting .322, with an OPS of 1.114 and a cumulative WAR, as pitcher and hitter, of 10.2. History tells us that WAR mark was second in the AL only to Walter Johnson of the Senators, who was still proving that pitching was perhaps more valuable than hitting.

It has become something of a cliché to say that had there been an MVP award in 1919, Ruth would have won in a rout, but that's not true, not if one paid attention. The frenzy of record setting in the season's final few weeks masked a thousand ills. The Red Sox finished sixth, 20½ games behind pennant-winning Chicago, far out of the money, and after April, in which they went 4–1, only in September did the ball club have a winning record. Although the big crowds of the final month of the season helped the bottom line, a contending club for an entire season would have proven even more lucrative.

Ruth had an amazing season—of that there is no doubt and no question. But it was also aggravating. His was an individual accomplishment, with virtually all his production coming after the Red Sox were buried, and long after it could have made a difference in their season. Moreover, it was his failures, early on, that caused the Red Sox so much trouble and strife.

If one is going to credit Ruth with the remarkable, it cannot come at the expense of reality, and the truth of the 1919 season is that for all his achievements, Ruth also cost his team a chance at winning another pennant.

Now perhaps that was necessary, an unavoidable consequence of the transformative nature of his game, but when viewed through the lens of exactly where Ruth and the Red Sox were at the end of the 1919 season, before anyone knew what was about to come, it is a not insignificant piece of the puzzle that was still Babe Ruth. Over the past two years, across nine months of regular season play, Ruth had been a spectacular and extraordinary hitter for perhaps four months—six weeks in 1918 and then the last half of 1919. The rest of the time, he had been a troublesome and problematic player of almost average ability, someone who had shown he would leave in a moment's notice for a chance to make a penny more, team be damned.

Babe Ruth was being pulled in two directions, one way by his immense talent, and another way by his various appetites, the dimensions of each not yet known.

It was not yet possible to see which Babe Ruth was to come.

7

🪐

The Insurrectos

"A rabbit didn't have to think to know what to do to dodge a dog. . . .
The same kind of instinct told Babe Ruth what to do and where to be."
—Yankee outfielder Sammy Vick

The regular season may have been over, but for Ruth, the off-season
was nearly as important and just getting under way. His name was on every
tongue. He had been well-known before, a phenomenon in Boston and a
familiar name in baseball, but this was something else again. He was
crossing over, like only a handful of athletes before him—the boxer John
L. Sullivan, perhaps, into the realm of celebrity, famous far beyond his
field. People who didn't give a damn about baseball swooned when they
heard Ruth was in the room and craned their necks to get a good look.

It was time to cash in. Ruth and Johnny Igoe, still his de facto manager,
were overwhelmed but knew enough to try to cash the checks as quickly
as possible. The Spanish flu made it clear that nothing was for certain and
anything could happen, and as the Roaring Twenties came into focus, an
increasingly fickle public warmed to a celebrity and then forget about them
just as fast, moving on to the next big thing at a dizzying rate. He or she who
hesitated left cash on the table.

Ruth first embarked on a New England tour with the "Red Sox Inde-
pendents," a team featuring himself and other locals, such as Gloucester's

Stuffy McInnis and Dave Shean of Winchester. They were supplemented by some lesser talents, minor leaguers and good amateur players, but occasionally by major leaguers such as New York pitcher Bob Shawkey, willing to play a little more baseball for a few dollars to support Ruth in a starring role. The club toured New England—Sanford, Maine; Rutland, Vermont; Beverly, Massachusetts; and others. For most New England fans, the World Series taking place in Cincinnati and Chicago was just another set of games, and with no real way to follow it apart from the newspaper, a set of games in which they had no stake.

Ruth and his squad were the better draw, and the barnstorming series was almost as lucrative for the players as the real World Series. Such exhibition tours alerted the players to the amount of money that was really in the game—when they didn't have to share with management, they didn't have much problem earning big money. Ruth often cleared $500 a game while barnstorming. Most of the time, he satisfied the crowd with a long home run, likely often helped by a side arrangement with the opposing pitcher to make sure Ruth had a chance and received at least a few pitches to his liking. In fact, when he didn't hit a home run, such as in Troy, New York, it produced a headline. No local barnstorming tour to date had ever been more successful. One Boston writer made note of the "barrels of shekels" the ballplayers were earning and further mentioned that Ruth was such a draw that "if the warm weather continues, he can book many more engagements."

The success of the tour likely played a role in Ruth's next move. He was increasingly dissatisfied with his pay. The three-year deal he had signed before the 1919 season, even though it had been his suggestion, now seemed like a con. He wanted a new deal, and told the press he thought he was worth $5,000 more a year, $15,000.

For the time being, Frazee rolled his eyes. He was used to this by now: Ruth could wait. He had more pressing matters.

The knives were out between him and Johnson. After the league president's humiliation in court in New York, his had been withdrawn, but Johnson could only sharpen the edge. He had Frazee in his sights and fully intended to back him up against the wall and watch him squirm as he slowly stuck the blade into his chest—at least that's what he dreamed. But Frazee would prove to be an elusive and worthy adversary. A lot was happening behind the scenes as each man tried to outmaneuver the other, extract revenge, and survive. There were wheels within wheels and the advantage would change week to week and even day by day as each built alliances and jockeyed for position.

In a sense, the Red Sox were the target of a very unfriendly takeover attempt. Everything Johnson did in regard to Frazee was designed to remove him from the game. And everything Frazee did was designed to keep control of his team and remove Johnson from office. Ruth was just a piece of the property, a pawn in a series of decisions made partially for baseball reasons, partially for political reasons, and partially for financial reasons. One thing can be said for certain—no single reason, no single fact, and no single condition led to the sale of Ruth. To argue otherwise is to deny the reality of the time in favor of the rose-colored glasses of hindsight.

The complexity of the causes has long defied analysis and led many observers to try to reduce the Ruth deal to the simplest possible terms, ending their most elementary and misleading calculation within the conclusion: that Frazee was broke and simply "needed the money," that he "raped" the franchise due to greed, ineptitude, and dishonesty. The truth is more complicated, but tells a far better and richer story, but one that also happens to be built from facts.

In the simplest possible terms, in the fall of 1919, Frazee's situation was this: He owned the Red Sox but had yet to pay off all his notes to previous owner Joseph Lannin. The team had been purchased on something like the installment plan, and Frazee owed Lannin $262,000 in November of 1919. He did not own Fenway Park—yet. The Taylor family, who owned the *Boston Globe*, had once owned the Sox and built Fenway Park before selling the club to Lannin. They retained ownership of the park, charging Frazee $30,000 a year for a facility that was rapidly deteriorating—the Taylors' own paper reported at the end of the season that the bleachers needed to be torn down and "many of the present seats are in bad shape." Lannin, too, owned shares of the Fenway stock, as did some of the Taylors' business cronies, and no one was eager to spend their own money to fix up the park. In an ideal world, Frazee wanted to own both Fenway Park and the Red Sox outright. If he did, he would be protected from the reach of Ban Johnson. But he did not, and until he did, he was at risk. He was afraid that Lannin might sell his shares of Fenway, that they would fall into

Johnson's hands, and that might force him to sell at an inopportune time, costing him hundreds of thousands of dollars.

Johnson's state of affairs at the time was one almost purely about retaining his own power. Frazee, Ruppert, and Comiskey had all aligned against him, believing that Johnson, acting in his own self-interest, had damaged the value of their franchises and cost them all money. Johnson's goal was to force either Frazee or Ruppert to sell his team, which would enable Johnson to retain control, protect his own investments in the game, and, most importantly, retain his power.

Ruppert, on the other hand, had some cash, for the Yankees turned a profit in 1919, but with Prohibition on the horizon, he was was worried about the future. He, too, was in an onerous ballpark situation, paying exorbitant rent to the Giants for the use of the Polo Grounds. His lease ran only through the 1920 season and he, too, was worried about losing a place to play.

And then there was Joseph Lannin. He was in financial trouble, which is the only reason he had agreed to structure the deal with Frazee the way it had been in the first place, having invested heavily in real estate whose value suffered during the war. He was depending on the payment from Frazee because he was already mortgaged to the hilt to other debtors and had entered into several financial agreements for which he now lacked capital—he needed Frazee's money to buy his way out of debt.

The overall situation was this: Frazee needed to keep his team and oust Johnson, Johnson needed to force Frazee to sell to keep his power, Ruppert needed Frazee's support to find a way to keep his team, and Joe Lannin needed his $262,000.

And the Babe? All he wanted was more dough and he was more than willing to break his contract in order to do it. Over the next three months, each of these figures would spend enormous amounts of energy and no small sum of money trying to get what they wanted, complicated by the fact that while they were all rich in their own way, none had the ready cash to fully realize their plans. Yet, rather incredibly, in the end, most of them would get what they wanted. Only Ban Johnson and a generation of Red Sox fans who were later sold a bill of goods about the history of their team to excuse the failures of the next generation of management, rather than the truth, would be left holding the bag. Boston would go eighty-six seasons between championships as a result.

As soon as the season ended, there were rumors that the Red Sox had suitors looking to buy the team—there were every year, as the battle with Johnson was common knowledge. Most were either hoping to pick up the club on the cheap or just looking for a little publicity—the race driver Barney Oldfield was supposedly part of one bid with former player Frank Chance. They reportedly offered $500,000, less than the purchase price of the club, a bid that might have been made at the behest of Johnson. To no one's surprise, Frazee turned them down. He had made it clear in the past that although in theory he wasn't averse to selling the Red Sox, he would only do so if he got a price that would recoup his investment, plus a good deal more.

In fact, however, it is unlikely that Frazee could have sold the team at this time even if he wanted to, or even if he had to. There were too many fingers in the pie, and too many strings attached.

In early November, several events taking place almost simultaneously threatened to cause a crisis. For one, Joseph Lannin's note became due on November 1, and he wanted his money from Frazee. At the same time, Frazee, Ruppert, and Comiskey, all serving their one-year term as the American League board of directors, called a special meeting with the other owners. Detroit, likely acting on Johnson's behalf, protested that since Mays should have been suspended, the games he pitched should not count in the standings and that the Tigers, who finished fourth behind New York, should have finished third and therefore deserved the third place share of Series money won by the Yankees. And by the way, the second game of that doubleheader against the Yankees near the end of the year? That shouldn't count either.

By opening a probe, it allowed Comiskey, Ruppert, and Frazee to do a little more investigating and relitigate everything. And although they couldn't act on their own, as a board they could pursue investigations and inquiries and then set the agenda with the other league owners, and Detroit's complaint gave them an excuse to do just that. They hoped to accumulate enough evidence of Johnson's poor leadership to entice one of the other club owners to jump ship and join them, creating a quorum that could lead to Johnson's ouster. But that was a tough challenge.

There was a lot more money at stake than there had been in 1918. In the 1919 Series, in something of a surprise, the Cincinnati Reds, significant underdogs, had knocked off the Chicago White Sox. A best-of-nine affair designed to milk as much money from the public as possible, the Series went eight games, the Reds winning five games to three, with the winning club taking home $5,207 per man, and the losing White Sox $3,254, about five times more than the Red Sox and Cubs had received a year before. The three runners-up who finished second, third, and fourth, also earned a nice chunk.

It had not been a particularly memorable Series—at least not yet—and although there were rumors of a possible fix, well, there were similar rumors after every postseason series and had been since the first World Series in 1903. But this time, the fix was in, at least for a few games, the plot actually hatched in the shadow of Fenway Park by notorious Boston gambler Joseph "Sport" Sullivan when he set everything in motion in a meeting with the White Sox' Chick Gandil at the Hotel Buckminster. Sullivan, well known in Boston gambling circles, had been hanging around baseball in Boston for almost two decades, a man everybody in Boston knew. Although he'd been arrested numerous times, he was often still sought out by Boston newspapers to give odds on the World Series. Sullivan was familiar to every Red Sox player of the era—he liked to have an edge, and if a conversation with a player revealed an injury or something else of significance unknown to the public, all the better. He had to know Ruth, even if Ruth did not know him by name. Sullivan reportedly cleared $50,000 on the World Series he helped fix. And while it would later become a baseball cliché to say that Babe Ruth saved baseball after the scandal, that's not true. By the time the scandal came to light, Ruth, the lively ball, and the home run had already saved it.

By the end of the month, however, no one was talking about the World Series anymore in any capacity. New York Supreme Court justice Robert Wagner ruled on Johnson's attempt to block the Yankees from using Mays. He issued a permanent injunction barring him from doing so and further found that Johnson "did not evince a desire to do equity to all parties concerned."

The ruling cut Johnson off at the knees, something that esteemed baseball historian David Voigt accurately called "a blow from which he would never recover." For the first time since forcing his way into major league baseball, Johnson had lost an important battle and seen his authority legally diminished. He would take a while to fall, and was still far from defenseless and still capable of throwing a few damaging haymakers, but the ruling marked the beginning of the end.

And he blamed Frazee for it all. The battle lines were drawn more sharply than ever, with revenge his only remaining option. With more than a month until the annual league meeting, there was plenty of time to make plans for that.

And what of the Babe, now that the season was over? As usual, he was out in pursuit of two things, money and personal pleasure.

His first order of business was money. Any added fun along the way was simply a side benefit. After the barnstorming season ended, he stayed in Boston to attend a dinner sponsored by the Knights of Columbus. The group showered him with gifts, including a diamond ring worth $500, in the hope Ruth might one day return the favor to the group or the Church in the form of some fat checks. Then he and Johnny Igoe traveled to California. Until recently, it had been sort of standard fare for baseball's flavor of the month, a recent World Series hero or batting champion, to tour the hinterlands of vaudeville usually embarrassing himself by singing a few songs and then taking questions or reciting a stilted script while miming his recent achievements on the diamond before a painted backdrop. It wasn't high art, but it was a way to earn some extra money and give fans outside the major league cities a chance to see their heroes in the flesh.

But this was a new age. Ruth was the hottest commodity in the game and in the wake of the war, the film industry was really starting to take off. Over the last decade, the industry had abandoned the nickelodeons that showed relatively simple shorts to an industry that now produced full-blown extravaganzas shown in some of the largest theaters. Production had started to move from New York to Hollywood. There was big money to be made and Ruth had some offers. Who needed vaudeville?

He wasn't asked to appear in any extravaganza, however. Shorts and lighter fare still made up a substantial part of the film industry, and just as newspapers learned that the name Ruth in a headline or on the lips of a newsboy could sell papers, Hollywood understood that Ruth's name on a marquee would draw a crowd. That he wasn't leading man material was clear, as film seems to emphasize the worst features of his face, but that didn't matter—Hollywood wanted his name, not an actor. While Ruth dreamed of the silver screen, he and Igoe also overestimated his value, asking $10,000 per picture. A lot of meetings turned into "don't call us, we'll call you" affairs. Meanwhile, Ruth went back to playing ball in exhibitions with other major leaguers. Although Pacific Coast League baseball was popular, Californians still turned out to see major leaguers when they had a chance, and it was a lucrative market for barnstorming.

Ruth joined major leaguers Buck Weaver of the White Sox, the Phillies' Irish Meusel (older brother of Bob), and some members of the PCL Vernon Tigers and toured the coast. Ruth alone received a guarantee of $500 a game—coupled with the barnstorming trip in New England, Ruth had already earned nearly his regular 1919 salary. He had to ask himself why he wasn't worth that much in the majors.

Ruth, reported *The Sporting News*, "was played up like a movie actor," on the tour. He even arrived in San Francisco ahead of the rest of the team and held court at the ballpark, demonstrating his prowess by taking batting practice and knocking six balls over the fence in a matter of minutes. One correspondent noted, "During the entire season of 1919 Coast League players did not put six balls over the same fence."

Although fans warmed to Ruth, the press wasn't quite as smitten. "Ruth is a big, good natured boy," wrote one reporter, "and he is unquestionably a marvelous ballplayer. But he could endear himself a little more to those he comes in contact with by the cultivating of a trifling of modesty. . . . . We may appreciate just how big a person Babe is, but we'd appreciate it more if somebody other than the Babe told us about it." Ruth, asked about Ty Cobb, had responded dismissively. "Cobb, he gets 'em [hits] beating out bunts and the scorers help him out. He gets 50 to 75 hits every year he isn't entitled to. . . . I have to hit 'em and hit 'em a mile to get my hits."

Once Ruth and Igoe saw that Ruth was just as big in California as he was east of St. Louis, their eyes grew big. "I feel I made a bad move last year when I signed a three-year contract to play for $30,000," said Ruth. In all likelihood, Ruth was already out of money and probably borrowing against the future of the contract and spending his barnstorming money as fast as it came in. After earlier saying that he wanted a raise to $15,000 a year, now Ruth upped the ante to $20,000.

On November 3, he went public. "Frazee knows what I want and unless he meets my demands I will not play with the Boston club next year," he said to a reporter, Igoe likely moving his mouth from behind the curtain. "I'm signed up for two more seasons but I deserve more money and I will not play unless I get it." He and Igoe even brought up the possibility of boxing again, floating a report that said Ruth was in training for a potential bout with Jack Dempsey, which was about as likely as Jack Dempsey taking over for Ruth in the outfield. Still, it underscored Ruth's desire for a bigger contract—and, perhaps, to leave Boston altogether. He certainly wasn't begging to stay, but spoke only of his desire for more money, and he seemed willing to go almost anywhere—and any length—to get it.

Although Ruth had no legal leverage—he was under contract to Boston for two more years—Frazee had to be concerned. Ruth had held out for more money in 1918, gotten it, jumped the team and been given a raise, then been given a new contract and still moped his way through the first half of the season, and according to some reports had been given a bonus of $5,000 by Frazee on Babe Ruth Day. Now he wanted more. First $15,000, then $20,000. When would it end? Actors signed contracts and when they left a show, you got a new actor. Was any amount enough to keep Ruth happy?

Frazee and Barrow may well have started to wonder just how much Ruth was worth to them, as opposed to what he was worth to others. Five cities in baseball supported two teams—New York, Philadelphia, Chicago, St. Louis, and Boston; and of those markets, Boston was the smallest. The Red Sox already had a tough time making money with the Braves only a few trolley stops away. The Red Sox payroll hovered around $80,000 a year—and wouldn't substantially increase, compared to the other clubs, for another fifteen years. If they gave Ruth $20,000, that would leave only about $60,000 to spread among everyone else—about $3,000 each, guaranteeing a thoroughly disgruntled club. The Sox were further hamstrung by the blue laws; Boston and Philadelphia were the only two cities in the league where playing on Sunday was still banned, and other cities were adding more Sunday dates every year. It was already hard to compete and getting harder all the time.

As Frazee sat pondering the upcoming season, he had to keep coming back to the same thought: How could he afford to keep paying Ruth? Would he ever be able to draw enough fans to support a player who was already demanding nearly a quarter of his payroll? And if he played hardball and held him to his contract, given Ruth's petulant nature, he might just start swinging with his eyes closed. Frazee had to wonder whether it was even worth keeping an unhappy Babe Ruth.

It mattered not to Ruth. His loyalty was to himself, not the Red Sox. A hometown discount was as foreign to him as turning in before midnight or leaving half a steak on a plate.

The owners' meeting to discuss the Mays case settled nothing except to bring up a series of festering complaints against Johnson by his adversaries, and for Johnson to demand loyalty for those who remained aligned with him, and ossify the position of everyone involved. Try as they might, Frazee, Comiskey, and Ruppert, the three Insurrectos, could not gain a fourth in their alliance and the league remained divided, the Insurrectos on one side, and the "Loyal Five" on the other. Ruppert correctly assumed that Detroit was acting on Johnson's behalf and made a countercharge that the Tigers didn't have any problem with Mays until they fell behind the Yankees in the standings. After all, they even made a bid for him and then accepted the protection of the court injunction. The Insurrectos voted to formally award third place money to New York and asked that the Yankees receive their share from the National Commission. When the commission ignored them, as *The Sporting News* noted with a sigh, "Then presumably there will be another lawsuit."

For now, apart from public posturing, everything was tabled until the official league meeting in December. The Insurrectos weren't backing down, but behind the scenes they were concerned. They looked at one another and decided they had the nucleus of a pretty good league, and started making noise about breaking off and forming their own circuit. Press reports claimed they had the backing of big money from investors Edsel Ford in Detroit, Harry Sinclair of Sinclair Oil in Pittsburgh, and others in Cleveland, Baltimore, and Montreal, and they hoped to poach a few other existing teams from the National League as well. *The Sporting News* dismissively termed the notion "the Pipe Dream League."

Each was worried about his own survival, for this battle with Johnson was a game of chicken that was certain to cost someone everything. The Yankees, despite Ruppert's wealth, were still as vulnerable as the Red Sox, perhaps even more so due to their ballpark situation, beholden to the Giants, continuing to pay approximately $60,000 a year in rent. They tried to negotiate a long-term lease, but the Giants, blanching at having to share those new lucrative Sunday dates, were ready to let the lease run out after the 1920 season and let the Yankees worry about the Yankees.

Johnson saw opportunity. Behind the scenes, he tried to gain control of the lease, which he could then use to force new ownership on the Yankees; they'd either have to sell or have no place to play. As a measure of his desperation, Johnson was even ready to do business with the Giants. To gain their cooperation, he was offering to make owner Horace Stoneham president of the National League. It was all veiled threats and conspiracies, strong-arming and posturing, lawyers and lawsuits . . . mostly over money.

The pressures on everyone, both politically and financially, increased by the day. Lannin wanted his money, unintentionally—or perhaps with a little nudge from Johnson—helping his cause by putting the squeeze on. Frazee however, likely had the money—or most of it, or could have raised it in any number of ways. His real estate holdings alone were easily worth well over a million dollars, he had a standing offer to sell film rights to an earlier production, *A Good Bad Woman*, for nearly $10,000, and he had enough money to launch a new play—*My Lady Friends* was scheduled to open in early December. Less than a month later he would receive lucrative offers to take the play overseas. He was also preparing to buy the Harris Theatre in New York and had already turned down Ruppert's $200,000 offer for Ruth and Mays. These were hardly the actions of a man on the verge of financial collapse.

The main reason he wasn't paying—or at least the reason he offered publicly—was due to a dispute over who was responsible for payments resulting from a lawsuit filed against baseball by the Federal League. When Frazee bought the Red Sox, Lannin was supposed to be responsible for all existing debt. Although the league collapsed, it had won in the courts and been paid off, only to appeal and have the judgment increased. Frazee had paid, but now wanted to deduct those costs—more than $50,000—from what he owed Lannin. The question was whether this was an existing debt. Lannin didn't think so, and was threatening to put a lien on Frazee and force him to come up with the cash at auction. The two eventually filed suit against one another, to the absolute delight of a gaggle of attorneys on each side, none of which were eager to make anything happen too quickly.

Over the next month, everyone involved was paying lawyers and plotting their next move. For the time being, Frazee had Lannin held at bay. As lawyers for both men negotiated, Frazee and Lannin had agreed to an extension of the November 1 deadline to pay off the notes, first to December 4, then to January 15. Lannin was not really in a position to hold a gun too close to Frazee's head to pay. He'd made an offer on some property based on the assumption he'd be paid, and was also committed to making an investment in the Mercedes automobile company. In the meantime, Frazee was having Fenway Park appraised in anticipation of making an offer to buy everyone out.

By the end of November, the notion that Ruth might be traded or sold was one of the worst-kept secrets in baseball. Sportswriters weren't stupid and kept asking Frazee if Ruth was on the market. He kept denying that he was, but at the same time, Frazee had made it clear that there were always offers too good to ignore, telling the press that the only player he wouldn't consider trading was Harry Hooper. With the official American League meeting scheduled for New York on December 10, everybody in baseball knew that would inspire a time of intense horse-trading, just as the Winter Meetings inspire a similar frenzy today. Then, as now, speculation often centered around the biggest and most controversial figures in the game. Ruth fulfilled both definitions.

In early December, just before what promised to be the most tempestuous meeting in the history of the game, Christy Mathewson penned a syndicated story "Big Baseball Trades Due" on what deals fans might expect to take place during the off-season. Mathewson, the rare player who actually wrote many of the articles that carried his byline—or at the very least, wrote an early version of them—dropped a widely broadcasted hint. He wrote, "This week will see some of the biggest trades pulled off in baseball for years, I know of one of very large dimensions almost certain to go through; it should startle the followers of baseball."

Hmm, that's an odd way to put it. What could he possibly mean by "very large dimensions"? *The Sporting News* was even less circumspect. It offered that Ruth "had been analyzing the celebrated Mays case and has arrived at the conclusion that a contract is not binding." The article went on to say that there was some indication that "Babe has picked his club, ala [sic] Mays, that he too would join the Yankees." Remember, he'd already been barnstorming with Bob Shawkey and Bob Meusel's brother. He knew what was happening in New York.

It wasn't only Mays doing the picking, either. Owners in other cities, particularly Clark Griffith in Washington, learned that talk about trading for Ruth generally received a welcome reception in the press, and more or less pushed everything else away for a few days and guaranteed positive coverage. Such was the power of the Home Run King—he could make the other team look good even when he didn't play for them.

The magnates gathered in New York on December 10. By then, Frazee, Ruppert, and Comiskey had to know their plot to oust Johnson would collapse; they'd failed to get any of the Loyal Five to join them, and were now almost powerless to do anything. At the start of the meeting, the three were ousted from the board of directors, which meant they could no longer set the agenda for the remainder of the meeting. Had they been able to, they planned to present a case arguing that Johnson was not fit to remain in his position, that his long-term contract as American League president was illegal and in violation of league bylaws, that his personal financial interest in ball clubs in the league was the equivalent of syndicate baseball, and that he had, for years, acted unfairly. It was all true, but it was also now meaningless without the votes. In the end, they hoped to convince the other owners to oust Johnson and move toward naming a single commissioner of baseball, one elected by all the clubs, and prohibit the commissioner's office from having a financial interest in any clubs, serving only for the betterment of all. It was a bold, forward-thinking proposal, one that baseball eventually would adopt, but one for which the Insurrectos themselves would rarely be credited.

Detroit owner Frank Navin was named league vice president, leaving the Insurrectos thoroughly out in the cold. Unable to entice any team from either league to join them, their quixotic quest for a third major league simply faded away. Now that Johnson had exerted his control, he suspended the rest of the meeting until February. To fill the time, everybody filed another round of lawsuits.

In their one substantive act, the owners voted to ban the spitball, later expanding the ban to all sorts of other trick pitches, like the shine ball and emery ball. For the first time since the spitball had first been developed nearly twenty years earlier, beginning in 1920 batters would only have to worry about breaking balls, fastballs, change-ups, and the rare knuckler. Although spitballers were grandfathered in, everybody else had to learn to get by with their real stuff. That meant almost every pitcher in the league would have to adjust. For Ruth, it was an early present. A lot of pitchers who had given him trouble before now had to take the mound missing a few bullets. Ruth's value only went up.

All the Insurrectos could do now was talk, mostly to one another, about what to do next. They'd been at this long enough to have some contingencies already in the works, plans C and D in case plans A and B didn't work. And there is every indication this is the time the Red Sox finally decided Ruth was available for acquisition as part of that contingency. But this would be no Carl Mays scenario, in which they'd hold some kind of public auction. By this time, Frazee knew who the serious players were, who had the money, and, more importantly, who he could trust. That was a very short list that included only the White Sox and Yankees.

But really, why trade Ruth at all? The answer to that lies not so much in the financial aspect of the deal as it does the political and the personal.

8

⚾

For Sale

*"The owner who trades or sells a star player must expect criticism.
It is the law of the game."*
                              —Harry Frazee

**So why was Ruth traded? If Frazee didn't need the money after
all,** like everyone has long assumed, then why not keep him? What had
changed? These questions vexed and distracted historians for decades.
But in a sense, these were the wrong questions to ask, or at least it was
wrong to think that the answer to the second question fully answered the
first. The logic behind the selling of the Babe is not bound up in a single
reason any more than the secrets of Ruth's success as a batter. The answer
lies in the complicated confluence of events.

Did Frazee really need the money? Well, who didn't? But to men and
women of means, wealth doesn't mean the same thing it does to you or me,
who feel anxious when the credit card bill is more than the figure in the
checking account. To the one percent, a pile of cash in the bank is not nearly
as important as the ability to get access to cash when needed. Frazee had
both cash and access to cash, just not enough to do everything he wanted
at the time, which was pay off Lannin, buy Fenway Park outright, and
purchase the Harris Theatre. That building, which had cost a half million

dollars when it opened in 1902, had done nothing but make money for its owners ever since.

Was the sale made out of financial desperation? Hardly. *My Lady Friends* had just opened to great reviews and was making $3,000 a week. Any financial problems he was having were of a temporary nature, a cash flow problem only because he had plans bigger than his bank account. Adding in his various legal battles, or potential legal battles, with Johnson, and cash was always a good thing to have. But, significantly, right up to the time of the sale, Frazee still did business as usual, and that did not materially change once the Ruth deal was made. He neither went on a spree nor acted particularly frugally. What has been missed is that the financial aspect of the deal was not entirely a question of Frazee's personal finances, but that of the Boston franchise, and its future value.

Still, had there not been the political situation to consider, or real and serious questions about Ruth, both as a ballplayer and a person, it is extremely doubtful any deal would have been made, or if it had been, that it would have been structured as it eventually was. Had there not been political considerations, Ruth may have commanded an even higher cash price. And had there not been questions about Ruth's talent and his character, perhaps he may not have been sold at all. Ultimately, the sale of Ruth to the Yankees was an elaborate package wrapped in a complicated bow that, once consummated in a secure knot, took care of any number of loose ends, particularly for the owners of the Red Sox and Yankees.

Tellingly, Frazee first rejected an entreaty from Comiskey, who reportedly offered him left-handed hitting outfielder Joe Jackson and $60,000 for Ruth. At first blush, the offer might have appeared tempting. Sixty thousand dollars was a lot of money, and Jackson's career batting average was nearly .360. Together with Ty Cobb, George Sisler, Tris Speaker—and Ruth—he was considered one of the greatest hitters in the game. Earlier in his career, with Cleveland, Jackson hit as high as .408. If Frazee wanted both cash and value back in exchange for Ruth, Jackson seemed to fit the bill.

Or did he? Joe Jackson was thirty years old. In both 1915 and 1917 he had hit barely .300, and had never played particularly well in Fenway Park, where the left-handed hitter, like Ruth, showed less power than elsewhere and owned a batting average nearly 50 points lower than his career mark.

There may not have been a statistician on the payroll, but Boston pitchers had to be aware of that. Furthermore, Jackson's slashing, Dead Ball Era approach to hitting wasn't likely to result in many home runs or extra base hits. And Jackson would be costly to keep. Comiskey, a notorious skinflint, had kept Jackson as more or less an indentured servant and he'd been earning only $6,000 a season, but he was certain to ask for more from Frazee.

There was also the Black Sox scandal, the one that eventually would lead to Jackson's lifetime banishment from baseball. Although Jackson's level of involvement is still debated today, he eventually paid the price and was suspended for life. Precisely how many whispers were taking place in the late fall of 1919 is uncertain, but it's likely Frazee would have heard something by then. Remember, Frazee had strong business ties in Chicago, and Sport Sullivan was well known in Boston. If guys like the sportswriter Ring Lardner, who'd been dropping hints about a fix into his stories during the Series, thought something funny was going on, Frazee had to have heard the rumors as well. And with Johnson already breathing down his neck about gambling at Fenway Park, the last thing he needed was to acquire a player who might be wrapped up in that.

He turned Comiskey down. Taking the player and the money just didn't make much sense. Eventually, much of the money would have to be paid to Jackson in salary, and Joe Jackson wasn't going to make the Red Sox a pennant contender anyway—as a hitter, even Ruth hadn't done that. And if he didn't play well, the Red Sox would be stuck with an underperforming and perhaps tainted star, one who would prove to be a constant reminder, if Ruth succeeded elsewhere, of what might have been.

Still, Comiskey's offer, which some have questioned in regard to its veracity, is likely true. In order to cut a deal with the Yankees, the Red Sox needed another suitor, or else they'd have had little leverage. Fortunately for Frazee, the Giants were in pursuit of St. Louis Cardinals infielder Rogers Hornsby and reportedly offered the Cardinals $70,000 and four players for the future star, who had yet to fulfill his immense potential. If Hornsby was worth more than $70,000 based on potential alone, what about Ruth? Moreover, the fact that the Giants were in the market so aggressively had to be a concern to Ruppert. He was still trying to catch up to his rivals and could not afford to fall further behind.

The question of whether Ruth would have succeeded elsewhere is another question that has rarely been asked about the sale, but had to be the foremost question in the mind of not only Frazee, but also Ruppert. The way each man may have factored that calculation may well have been the deciding factor behind the eventual sale.

This demonstrates the degree to which "the Babe," the player that Ruth had yet to become, has overwhelmed and overshadowed the player he was at the time. When one looks at Ruth's baseball biography today, the notion that one could doubt his future at the time seems insane. But coming off the 1919 season, even after setting a record, that was not the case. One, as previously noted, Ruth's offense had blown hot and cold over the last two seasons, hitting streaks sandwiched between slumps. He'd hit better when it didn't matter than when it did, he showed absolutely no loyalty to his team, and had proved to be a disruptive presence in the clubhouse. There was no guarantee his prowess at the plate would continue—and given his lifestyle, he showed every sign of being a fast-burning candle. There were already signs his body was starting to betray him; he'd had arm trouble, the wrenched knee he'd suffered in June was a cause of some concern, and he had already put on a great deal of weight. Ruth had already gone from lean and rangy to solid to stout. How far behind were just plain pudgy and then fat?

His performance in 1919 had also been so far outside the norm over the last months of the year, how reasonable was it to think that it would continue? Could it? Had he already reached some imaginary ceiling for hitting home runs that couldn't possibly be reached again or sustained? Jack Chesbro won 41 games in 1904 and no one had come close to that mark since. That sort of thing is common in baseball. Remember, 1918 World Series hero George Whiteman was already back in the minor leagues, and it was only normal to wonder whether Ruth's unexpected, unprecedented explosion could be repeated.

Through 1919, Ruth had hit 49 career home runs, but only 11 in Fenway Park. There, he hadn't often been BABE RUTH—at least not yet, and not for a sustained period. There is every indication, in fact, that had Ruth stayed in Boston and played the bulk of his career in Fenway Park, while he still would have been a record-setting home run hitter for his time, it might have impacted his career home run totals by as much as 25 percent. There's a big difference between 714 home runs and 530 or so. The ballpark, with its distant right field fence, simply did not suit him.

And what if the Red Sox kept Ruth and he deteriorated, got hurt, or became just another guy—after all, even Gavvy Cravath never came close to hitting 24 home runs again. Ruppert had already indicated he'd pay as much as $150,000.00 for Ruth. A wrenched knee, a broken wrist, a car wreck, a case of syphilis, or some scandal could move the decimal point on that number several places to the left and make Ruth worth far less. From Boston's perspective, Ruth might never be worth more. To suggest that ANYONE knew he would become the legendary Babe is utter fantasy. In fact, while there are those who believed he could become the greatest player in the game, or already was, no one dared put any kind of number on that.

Or if Boston was wrong and Ruth sustained his high level of production or even got better, Frazee might also have wondered how he could ever afford to keep paying him. Remember, he was hamstrung by the Boston market, competition from the Braves, a ballpark that he did not own, and the increasingly onerous handicap of not being able to play baseball on Sunday, costing the team perhaps one third of its potential gate. Under any calculation, it was hard to see the Red Sox of the era drawing much more than 600,000 or so fans a year. Had Ruth stayed in Boston and still become BABE RUTH, would the team have been able to pay him what he was worth? What would the team do if he hit 40 or 50 home runs and asked for half of the proceeds? Surround him with refugees from Boston's semi-pro Park League who all hit .200 and finish last every year? That would be like keeping a hit play in Boston's 500-seat Beacon Theatre instead of taking it to one of New York's 1,200-seat venues; it just made no sense. In fact, it would not be until after World War II, when the Red Sox, with Ted Williams, annually challenged the Yankees for the pennant, that the club would finally draw in excess of one million fans, something the Yankees became the first team to do in 1920.

Boston was a great baseball town, and a rabid one, but a small one, and relatively frugal. Roughly speaking, teams of the era could afford a payroll of perhaps 20 percent of the receipts from their attendance. Just as small market teams today are forced to sell off high-priced talent to wealthier clubs, that's likely what would have happened in Boston. In a sense, it's no accident Ruth ended up in New York; it was just economics.

And there was still one more factor. The recent battle with Johnson had been sparked over Frazee's refusal to suspend a player who jumped the club. The Red Sox and the Insurrectos had prevailed on that, but only because they had all been on the league's three-man board of directors, which allowed them to set the agenda and stretch out the battle until the season had ended, making the question of whether Mays could play moot until the court ruling.

Meanwhile, jumping the team was becoming something of an annual occurrence for Ruth, only now the Insurrectos no longer controlled the board; Johnson and the Loyal Five did. If Ruth jumped the team, what would happen now? He was already claiming that his contract was meaningless, the ultimate challenge to professional baseball. Would Johnson force a suspension, and this time, would one be upheld? How much would that cost? Sending Ruth elsewhere was a way to avoid an almost certain migraine.

Ruppert and the Yankees may have shared some of Frazee's baseball concerns, but they were viewing Ruth more through the lens of his performance at the Polo Grounds, where he was already BABE RUTH and mostly had been for the last two years. They may have been concerned about other issues, but Ruppert, from the time he had made his first offer for Ruth more than a year earlier, had already set those concerns aside. He had little choice. To make it in New York, to topple the Giants, to get his own ballpark, and make enough money to offset the losses the brewery would suffer from Prohibition, he either had to take a chance or sell the club, admit defeat, and do something else with the rest of his money. He could afford to take a chance and acquiring Ruth was the best option he had to build another fortune. Besides, he wasn't going to fail; he was a Ruppert.

Yankees manager Miller Huggins had already given the deal his blessing. When asked by Ruppert what he needed to win a pennant in 1919, Huggins had answered bluntly "Get me Ruth." He'd seen what Ruth had done in the Polo Grounds, and since taking over as New York manager

Huggins had witnessed the birth of the power game. His Yankees were already one of the most potent teams in baseball, and Ruth would only help.

He also knew that if he had Ruth, that meant no one else did. Even if Ruth didn't turn out to be as dynamic as hoped, if nothing else Huggins wouldn't have to worry about playing against him 22 times a year. That's a part of every trade; it's not only what it does for your club but what it does to another. Decades later, when the Yankees acquired Mike Torrez and Luis Tiant as free agents, taking them from the Red Sox was as much a part of their thinking as adding them to the Yankee roster.

Once the Red Sox and Yankees agreed in principle to a deal, they now had to decide how to make that happen, how to structure it to serve the needs of both teams and their owners. Frazee wanted to take advantage of Ruppert's eagerness and willingness to take a risk and get a good return, one that would also help extract him from his current difficulty with Lannin yet still leave his ball club intact, firmly in his control and well positioned to ward off any attacks by Johnson. Ruppert, too, wanted Ruth at almost any cost, and he, too, wanted help against Johnson. Although the Insurrectos had lost out, they knew they'd wounded Johnson and neither man thought for a minute that Johnson would forget that or was through with them. And since both Frazee and Ruppert planned on remaining in the American League, neither man was done trying to get rid of Johnson. They'd lost a major skirmish at the league meeting, but both were ready to go forward and fight again another day.

It's useful to consider what might have happened had the two men *not* made the deal, a question rarely asked, at least in its full dimension. The assumption is often that Ruth would have gone on to hit another 665 home runs for them, and creating a dynasty in the Hub while leaving the Yankees as a second-rate franchise. While that is certainly a possibility, given the events of the 1918 and 1919, and Ruth's recent behavior, there were other, more likely scenarios. Ruth may well have held out well into the spring, then been traded away in anger or jumped the club and causing some kind of protracted legal battle, one that might have cost Frazee his ball club, or sent Ruth to Detroit, or Cleveland. In any case, the entire history of the game may well have been changed. But a scenario that simply supplants a Boston dynasty for one in New York might be the most far-fetched and unrealistic of all, a false equivalency. There were simply too many moving parts, and history is rarely so tidy.

When the two men started talking seriously about the deal, it quickly became primarily a financial discussion. Much has been made of Ed Barrow's later, ghostwritten assertion that when Frazee asked him if there were any Yankees players he wanted in exchange for Ruth, and he responded that "losing Ruth is bad enough, but don't make it tougher on me by making me show off a lot of ten-cent ballplayers that we got in exchange for him. There's nobody on that ball club I want." If that's true, Barrow was either deluded or already secretly on the Yankee payroll. The 1919 Yankees were better at nearly every position than the 1919 Red Sox and had a number of valuable players who remained productive for several years to come. Pitcher Bob Shawkey was already a star and would put up a WAR of 7.8 and win 20 games in 1920, while first baseman Wally Pipp and second baseman Del Pratt were probably the best two players at their positions in the league, and rookie outfielder Bob Meusel, just purchased from the Pacific Coast League where he hit .337 for Vernon, was one of the best prospects in the game. Any team in baseball would have taken any of them in any kind of deal, and would have been a fool not to. It is also interesting that Barrow frames the deal only in terms of himself, saying "don't make it tougher *on me*" while evincing no concern about either the Boston fans or the performance of the team. If anyone was acting in his own self-interest, it was Barrow.

So who was the bigger fool? Frazee for asking for Barrow's advice, or Barrow, his baseball man? Despite later writing his own revisionist history of events, let's not forget that Barrow initially wanted to keep Ruth on the mound, that his management of the team had been widely and publicly criticized, that he'd taken a world champion into sixth place, and that his failure to rein Ruth in had played a huge part in the demise of the 1919 Sox. Barrow didn't become a genius until he followed Ruth to New York a few years later. There, armed with the money Ruppert made off Ruth, Barrow suddenly got a whole lot smarter. Barrow, acting as the team's general manager, was usually able to outbid every other team for young talent and spend his way out from behind mistakes. That's long been the Yankee way, and it started with Ed Barrow.

Although Ruppert had offered $150,000 or perhaps even more for Ruth in the past, that number wasn't on the table any longer. Prohibition was scheduled to go into effect on January 17, 1920, and he may not have been as eager to part with as much cash as he had been a year or so before. In fact, the way the deal was eventually structured, as a cash payment of $25,000 and a series of $25,000 notes, totaling $100,000, indicates that Ruppert had a bit of a cash flow problem himself. If he lost his lease on the Polo Grounds, he had to be able to move fast.

Regardless of whether they cut a deal or not, Frazee was moving forward anyway in the event the deal fell through. On December 15, he made a formal offer to the Taylors to buy out their shares of Fenway Park for $150,000—$25,000 in cash and three notes payable at one-year intervals. If the Taylors had accepted, that would have given Frazee control of Fenway Park and therefore leverage against Lannin—he would not have needed the mortgage, and may have considered keeping Ruth. But the Taylors turned him down.

The more Ruppert and Frazee talked, the more likely that each realized that one of their problems boiled down to the ballpark issue— neither man owned their own park, and both faced a situation in which they could potentially end up with a team that had no place to play, something that would have forced a franchise sale or the mother of all legal battles. If Frazee didn't pay off Lannin soon, Lannin was threatening to auction off his shares of Fenway. Since the Taylors wouldn't sell, that likely would have put Fenway out of Frazee's reach forever, leaving him to pay rent in a park that was already falling down, making it even more difficult to make money, and hurting the value of the franchise in any subsequent sale.

A Ruth deal offered both men a path out. As they batted ideas back and forth, a plan began to take shape that could solve all problems—those of the ballpark, the war against Johnson, and each man's cash flow issues. A series of "what ifs?" slowly started turning into "why nots?"

What if the Yankees bought Ruth outright, not for $150,000, but for somewhat less—say $100,000? Ruppert would have his player, his draw in New York, Frazee would be rid of a problem and have some cash. It was a risk, but one that helped each man—Ruth might either thrive or fail, and the Red Sox already knew it was as possible to lose with Ruth as it was to win. And then, to make up the difference, what if New York offered Boston a side deal some months later, like . . . provide a mortgage a little while later, if needed, on Fenway Park? According to information in Frazee's archives, they had already been discussing the mortgage as early as October as an entirely separate item, but now the changing situation with Johnson upped the ante.

Why not just fold it all together into one package? That way Frazee could pay off Lannin and acquire Fenway, further inoculating him from Johnson's wrath. Then—and this was the genius of the deal, really—even if the Giants canceled the Yankees' Polo Grounds lease after the 1920 season or Johnson somehow got his hands on it and tried to use the ballpark issue to force Ruppert into a sale . . . Well, the Yankees had a ballpark, *Fenway Park*. That, in turn, would at least give them some leverage with the Giants. Boston could even waive their territorial rights and allow the Yankees to play in Boston: Welcome back, Babe. While that would undoubtedly result in a legal battle that would make the current knife fight look like a series of paper cuts, it was a potential possibility.

It was ambitious, bold, audacious, and ingenious, a triple-bank shot off the rail, perhaps the most inspired baseball transaction ever. If it worked, and Ruth played at least reasonably well in New York, everyone won—but Johnson. And if it didn't work, and Ruth bombed, well Ruppert was "only" out $100,000, plus whatever he paid Ruth. That was far better than losing his team. Frazee only lost if Ruth became superhuman.

For years, few observers ever really factored in the benefit that holding the mortgage provided the Yankees, but it's beyond the realm of belief to think they just so happened to take out a mortgage on Fenway Park at the precise time their own lease on a place to play was being threatened. That was no accident, and there is evidence to that effect in Frazee's archives. After the deal was made, one of Frazee's attorneys, Thomas J. Barry, took him to task in a letter, writing that he had been a fool to take the Yankees' terms on the mortgage, that he could have easily gotten far better terms from a bank. "I had in mind that if you did not take Rupert's [*sic*] money you could get $25,000 more from him on the Ruth deal, and also Wise would not be so technical as the present attorney's, and that we could get our money quicker from him." But getting better terms from a bank wouldn't have served all Ruppert's needs and the deal wouldn't have worked. Besides, by eventually taking a mortgage from the Yankees at a higher rate of interest than was commercially available, Frazee would, in effect, be paying the Yankees more than $100,000 for Ruth when one included the mortgage payments . . . but those interest payments were tax deductible.

Their timing was impeccable—at least for Frazee. He locked in his rate with the Yankees, and beginning that same month the United States economy entered a brief but extreme two-year recession that some economists now refer to as a depression. Within months, credit dried up and commercial credit rates nearly doubled. In the long run, the rate Frazee got from the Yankees actually turned out to be a bargain. Had he waited and then tried to get a loan from a bank, he may not have received one at all. By the time the mortgage was finally executed in May, Frazee's rate was actually lower than what he would have gotten commercially. On almost every financial level, the deal worked. All that was left was for the attorneys to look over everything—and to get Ruth on board.

That was the one potential holdup. Ruppert didn't want to make a deal and then have Ruth balk at agreeing to come to New York or hold out for a new contract and then leave him holding an empty uniform. Five months earlier, the Yankees had made sure that Mays was on board before pulling the trigger on that deal, and they planned to do the same on Ruth. He was as volatile and unpredictable off the field as they hoped he would prove predictable on it, and they didn't want the deal to come as a surprise and have Ruth throw a tantrum. That was a real concern, because while the details were still being worked out, a story in the *Boston Post* threatened to mess things up. Somebody was talking to Paul Shannon.

He didn't know everything, but he knew enough to know that something was up. The headline on December 20 screamed "BABE RUTH IN MARKET FOR TRADE."

After saying that neither Frazee nor Barrow wanted to discuss it, Shannon warned Boston fans not to be "astonished if the burly batter is allowed to pass through." He noted that the contract differences between the Red Sox and Ruth were real, and while admitting that Ruth was a talent, he also pointed out that Ruth wasn't always easy to get along with, writing that "he had hurt morale considerably" and offering the opinion that Ruth's attitude had "put a big dent in his popularity in Boston" and estranged

Boston management, "who are beginning to loop in the burly batter as a second Frankenstein."

The story inspired widespread debate on not only Ruth's value, but, given the Giants' recent bid for Hornsby, that of any ballplayer. The top baseball salary at the time was likely Ty Cobb's annual $20,000, a figure it had taken him nearly two decades to reach. Ruth had only played five full seasons, and wanted more than that. In the *Globe*, Arthur Duffey crowed that no ballplayer was worth that kind of money, not even Ruth. Then, as now, the notion of someone becoming fabulously wealthy just for playing ball offended a certain portion of observers.

All the while, Ruth enjoyed the sunshine and the fine weather in California, soaking up the rays and playing golf. However, he was not completely oblivious to what was taking place. Every day brought more indications that something was up, and baseball's rumor mill has never been particularly discreet. If Ruth didn't hear the whispers, Igoe certainly did. By late December, there were even more veiled references in the press that something was happening. Ruth's future in Boston was the subject of almost daily debate in the local papers.

Ruppert and Frazee talked and talked, and then finally sent everything off to the attorneys. Although Ruth had yet to be informed or signed on, worried that the news might leak prematurely, they went ahead and closed on the sale. Each had looked at the tax situation, and there were advantages having the deal dated in 1919. If Ruth backed out, they could always just tear it up.

The five-page contract transferring Ruth to the Yankees was dated December 26, 1919, between the Boston American League Baseball Club and the American League Base Ball Club of New York. The price was $100,000—$25,000 cash, plus three promissory notes for $25,000 at 6 percent interest for each, the first payable November 1, 1920, the next two on the same date in 1921 and 1922. Frazee already planned to sell the notes at discount and receive the cash up front, a sign not so much of desperation, but of the way each club was responding to the needs and desires of the other. Putting up only $25,000 in cash kept Ruppert fluid, and Ruppert even made the arrangements with one of his banks so Frazee would not have to wait too long to sell the notes.

It's important to realize that the mortgage on Fenway Park is not specifically mentioned in the document. Apart from the cash and notes, the remainder of the sale price is described as only "other goods and valuable considerations." That's because the mortgage could not be put in place until Frazee actually acquired title to Fenway Park. And it's possible each party still held out some dim hope that, perhaps, that part might not even be necessary, in which case "other goods and valuable considerations," could mean almost anything, including more cash or players. Besides, why mention a mortgage in a deal and watch Ban Johnson, who as member of the National Commission approved all contracts, think of some reason to block it, or otherwise tip him off about their ballpark plans?

The agreement to secure a first mortgage on Fenway Park was actually handled in a separate letter of agreement between Ruppert and Frazee. Although some subsequent biographers have tried to assign a total value of more than $400,000 to the sale, that's not quite the case. Remember, when Frazee sold the Red Sox he eventually paid off the mortgage, and money was sent back to the Yankees with interest. In the end, the deal cost the Yankees "only" $100,000 and a temporary loan by way of the mortgage, and Frazee actually ended up receiving even more back in value. His final acquisition of Fenway Park would eventually allow the Red Sox to be sold for somewhat more than if he had not owned the park outright. Land values in Boston skyrocketed in the early 1920s and as purely a real estate deal, Frazee made a pretty good one. Selling Ruth for $100,000 eventually helped him sell the Red Sox for more than $1 million, nearly twice what he initially paid.

And once and for all, let's put to rest the tired, spurious, hoary old chestnut that proceeds from the sale of Ruth financed Frazee's production of the seminal hit musical *No, No, Nanette*, the production that more or less created the modern musical comedy, helped usher in the Golden Age of the Broadway musical, and earned Frazee millions. There is simply no thread that connects the Ruth sale and *Nanette*. Between the sale of Ruth and the creation of *Nanette*, Frazee produced a number of other successful Broadways shows that ran hundreds of performances and grossed hundreds of thousands of dollars. It's not like Frazee set aside the money from the Ruth sale in some special account, then pulled it out four years later.

While it is true that *Nanette* was based on an earlier show, *My Lady Friends*, that play was already in production—and a verified hit—at the time of the Ruth sale, years before Frazee ever had the notion of using it as the inspiration for *Nanette*.

The sale of Ruth eventually helped Frazee purchase Fenway Park free and clear of any mortgage. *Nanette* was actually financed, at least in part (for theatrical producers generally use other people's money—investors—to bankroll their shows), by the sale of the Boston Red Sox in the summer of 1923 to a syndicate led by Bob Quinn for nearly $1.2 million. That transaction not only took place just prior to the first stages of the production of *Nanette*, but put nearly ten times the amount of money into Frazee's pocket than the Ruth sale ever did. Selling the Red Sox eventually freed Frazee of what had become a burden, and within a few months allowed him to turn his full attention to the idea of turning *My Lady Friends* into a musical, an idea that had been percolating for some time. To argue that the Ruth sale financed *Nanette* is a leap that lacks both facts and logic. It's a fantasy that simply allowed Boston fans to excuse generations of losing baseball, bad management by Frazee's successors, and simplistic, poorly researched, agenda-driven history.

Now all somebody had to do was tell Ruth about the deal and convince him that going to New York was a good idea. The job fell to his new manager, New York's Miller Huggins. The former major league infielder retired as a player with the Cardinals after 1916 but managed the club from 1913 through 1917 and was credited with helping make Rogers Hornsby a major leaguer. He took over the Yankees in 1918, not only being in charge on the field, but making most of the personnel decisions as well. A smart baseball man and a good judge of talent, Huggins would eventually receive credit, like Barrow, for keeping Ruth in line in New York.

Huggins had the owner's full trust, and, conveniently enough, was already in California, sent there earlier to sign several Yankees, including new acquisition Bob Meusel. He may well have known the Ruth deal was in the works when he left New York. Now they wired Huggins to deliver the news to his new star. While he was on his way, Frazee made his first move post-Ruth, trading for hard-luck left-handed Washington pitcher Harry Harper, a move roundly praised in the Boston press.

Babe Ruth and Boston teammates Ernie Shore, Rube Foster, and Del Gainer, circa 1915. By 1920, Ruth's days as a pitcher for the Red Sox would almost be forgotten. *Library of Congress Prints and Photographs Division*

Theatrical producer and Red Sox owner Harry Frazee (center), the man who sold Babe Ruth . . . and had good reason to. Stuffy McInnis is to his right; Jack Barry is to his left. *Leslie Jones Collection. Courtesy of the Trustees of the Boston Public Library*

American League founder and President Ban Johnson, rightly referred to as the "Czar" of baseball, and a man who "never forgets an enemy." *Michael T. "Nuf Ced" McGreevey Collection. Courtesy of the Trustees of the Boston Public Library*

Philadelphia Athletic owner and manager Connie Mack. Before the 1918 season, Mack dealt several stars to the Red Sox, delivering a pennant to Boston. *Michael T. "Nuf Ced" McGreevey Collection. Courtesy of the Trustees of the Boston Public Library*

Chicago White Sox owner Charles Comiskey joined Frazee and Ruppert in opposition to Ban Johnson. *Michael T. "Nuf Ced" McGreevey Collection. Courtesy of the Trustees of the Boston Public Library*

Yankee co-owner Jacob Ruppert, (left), standing next to New York Giants manager John McGraw (center), saw how Ruth performed at the plate in the Polo Grounds and set his sights on the emerging star. With Prohibition on the horizon, the beer baron needed his ballclub to win … and draw fans. *Courtesy of the Trustees of the Boston Public Library*

Catholic religious ceremony at Fenway Park, circa 1919. This photo is perhaps the best view of Fenway Park as Ruth transitioned to the outfield. Built in 1912, by 1919 Fenway already looked worn and tired. It was no Polo Grounds, which featured an inviting right field porch. *Boston Sports Temples Collection. Courtesy of the Trustees of the Boston Public Library*

Fenway's left field wall circa 1919. Fenway Park didn't suit Ruth, and not until 1919 did he even begin to use the left field wall to his advantage. *Boston Sports Temples Collection. Courtesy of the Trustees of the Boston Public Library*

Harry Hooper. Ruth's teammate, Red Sox right fielder, and onfield leader. Hooper, not manager Ed Barrow, had the respect of the players. *George Grantham Bain Collection, Library of Congress Prints and Photographs Division*

Babe Ruth with the Red Sox at Fenway Park, 1919. *George Grantham Bain Collection, Library of Congress Prints and Photographs Division*

Babe Ruth, 1921. In New York, Ruth became baseball's most-beloved figure. *George Grantham Bain Collection, Library of Congress Prints and Photographs Division*

What was the difference between Boston and New York for Ruth? In New York, he became "the Babe," the man everyone, even President Warren G. Harding, wanted to meet. *Leslie Jones Collection. Courtesy of the Trustees of the Boston Public Library*

It took Huggins several days to make it to Los Angeles and track down Ruth. He reportedly found him playing golf at Griffith Park, and met him in the clubhouse.

The subsequent meeting has been described in almost absurdly apocryphal terms: Huggins introducing himself, Ruth wondering if he'd been traded, then Huggins sagely giving Ruth some fatherly advice about how he would have to behave in New York, with Ruth promising to play his best, before getting around to the real topic of interest: How much was he going to be paid? All they left out was Huggins promising Ruth a new pony.

Such is the power of mythmaking, and the instant Ruth became property of the New York Yankees the mythmaking machine of the city that never sleeps went to work 24/7 to make a man equal to whatever myth it could manufacture. But there are other accounts. According to wire reports, Ruth actually learned of the deal on January 4, likely from an inquisitive reporter, whom Ruth told he had yet to meet with Huggins or even hear from the Yankees at all.

About the trade, Ruth responded, "I am not surprised. When I made my demand on the Red Sox for $20,000 a year I had an idea they would choose to sell me rather than pay the increase and I knew the Yankees were the most probable purchasers." It seems that maybe the deal may have been something Ruth and Igoe wanted all along, that by asking the exorbitant salary increase they may have hoped to force Frazee's hand, already knowing that New York was the likely destination, the only team that could afford him.

When Huggins and Ruth did meet and Ruth asked for more money, Huggins told Ruth he couldn't talk specifics but that the Ruppert and Huston were agreeable to working out new contract terms to give Ruth his $20,000. That was all it took. Had Ruth wanted to stop the deal, with his power and influence, he probably could have forced Ruppert and Frazee to tear up that little five-page document. Ban Johnson might have even given him some help, just to stiff Frazee. But he didn't because he didn't want to.

Ruth agreed to the deal. There is nary a mention that he found it necessary to talk things over with Mrs. Ruth or anyone else, another sign that he likely knew what was coming all along.

Ruth's time in Boston was over. He would never wear a Red Sox uniform again. George Herman Ruth was no more.

He was Babe Ruth now, and he belonged to the Yankees and, soon, to New York.

Now would come the other part of the selling of the Babe. But first, everybody had to sell the sale.

9

○

Welcome to New York

*"I told you Boston was some town, but this [New York] is the real one.
I never seen nothing like it and I been going some since we got here."*
—*Ring Lardner,* You Know Me Al

There was, perhaps no better time to be a young man of means
coming to New York City. The Roaring Twenties were just getting under
way and New York was the epicenter. Over the next decade, no other place
would roar as loud and as often. Prohibition was right around the corner,
sparking the era of the speakeasy, dresses were creeping up, morals were
loosening, and young people were taking over. The city was electrified
and suddenly never slept, Broadway was on the precipice of a golden age,
the Jazz Age was tuning up, and prosperity was right around the corner.
Horses disappeared from the streets, a million cars would be added to the
city, and the last great public works building boom was about to get under
way, as in the next decade the West Side Highway, the Holland Tunnel,
the Triboro and George Washington bridges would all be built or start
construction. Buildings with central heat, running water, and indoor toi-
lets were replacing tenements. The nose-to-the-grindstone philosophy of
life was being replaced by one that valued leisure and excitement. The middle class was starting to grow. Manhattan supported eleven daily newspapers

and Brooklyn had four of its own. Every street corner featured a newsboy screaming out the headlines.

Over the next decade, no name would be on their lips more often than that of the Babe, that one name the epitome of the age, larger than life, limitless and over the top all at once. In a city that worshipped personality, celebrity, and oversized everything, the Babe was all of that and more. His roar may well have been the loudest and most sustained of them all. Journalist Westbrook Pegler dubbed it "the Era of Wonderful Nonsense," a time when flagpole sitting and dance marathons and long-distance swimming would soon capture the public's fancy. If there was ever an athlete made for a particular place at a particular time, it was Babe Ruth and New York City in the 1920s. Any account of either the city or the man must include a portrait of the other. The city made Ruth and Ruth helped make the city. They were inseparable, and together, they remade the game.

In January of 1920, Boston and New York could not have been more different, and the reaction to the sale in each place speaks to those differences. Boston, a city that still clung to its self-image as the Hub of American democracy and everything else despite the fact that it had been usurped in almost every category by not only New York but other more vibrant cities such as Philadelphia and Chicago, feigned shock.

After not having turned out for Ruth like they had in New York, and after Ruth himself had intimated that he would like to be sold or traded, when the deal broke Boston acted as if something had been stolen, the sale a kind of moral affront. It was a blow to the city's self-image, not just as the home of championship baseball—for if one included the Braves, Boston teams had won the crown in five of the last eight seasons—but of everything else. New York had already taken over as the center of American commerce and culture; now this.

The headlines screamed, and no one took it more to heart than Boston's sportswriters, who suddenly realized that over the past year or two Ruth had made their lives a whole lot easier and a whole lot more entertaining. Now that he was gone, well, they had to get to work again, and that wasn't going to be much fun.

It was front page news, bumping Governor Calvin Coolidge's announcement that he would not seek the presidency because "the presidency must seek the man" to the side rail. So it was with Ruth. If Boston would not seize him, then New York would.

Reaction in the Hub was best epitomized by two cartoons, one emblematic of the knee-jerk, emotional reaction to the sale, and the other by those few who bothered at all to try to understand what had taken place, not just over the past few weeks, but the past few years, and not just in Boston, but all baseball. The first, in the *Boston Herald*, showed Ruth as the latest Boston monument being toppled by an ax-wielding caricature of Frazee, with "For Sale" signs posted in front of revered Boston symbols such as the Boston Public Library, Boston Common, and a statue of Paul Revere. A sign in front of Fenway Park read "House Lots for Sale" and was captioned, "Why not finish the job?"

The second, which appeared in the *Boston Post*, offered the alternate view. Titled "The Bull in Frazee's China Shop," it showed Ruth, a bull amid shattered glass labeled "team discipline," "team morale," and "disgruntled players." As Frazee desperately held tight to the bull's tail, Jake Ruppert magnanimously held open the door, a bag of cash in hand, saying, "This way out, Harry." But only one day later a third, more evenhanded appraisal appeared in the *Herald*. This one showed Ruth being dragged away by two cops, Frazee and Barrow, one saying, "We can't manage him." In the background a fan muttered, "Well, get somebody who can."

For most of the Boston press, over the next few days they did the most reporting they had done in months, finally starting to put together the basic framework of Frazee's situation in context, and taking a longer view of Ruth. Some almost seemed astonished finally to realize that the Red Sox had finished sixth with Ruth in 1919. Despite the 1918 world championship, their record over the past two seasons with Ruth more a hitter than a pitcher was 147–133, barely above .500.

In a rarity for the time, some writers actually went out and asked fans and notable baseball figures of the city what they thought about the deal. Baseball insiders like former players Fred Tenney and Hugh Duffy, and ex-manager Bill Carrigan, all supported the deal. Most fans, such as Royal Rooters supreme Mike Nuf Ced McGreevey and Charley Lavis offered the opposite view. "I figure the Red Sox is now practically ruined," said Lavis. But the breakdown is telling. Almost to a man, the ex-ballplayers viewed the deal in terms of the team, while the fans, whose love of Ruth had come to replace their love of the Red Sox, usually spoke only of how much they would miss watching the Babe. They hadn't cared that the team had finished sixth. They may not have realized it yet, but they loved the home run more than winning baseball, and for much of the next century that would be their only solace.

Although history would try to tell a different story, and present the entire city in an uproar, prepared to chase Frazee through the streets and string him up, in reality reaction was split. The *Boston Post* seemed unable to decide which side to take and stayed more or less neutral, while the *Boston Globe* (whose owners, the Taylors, stood to benefit financially from the deal) and the *Boston Transcript* supported the sale. Of the others, the *Herald* and the *American* were most critical.

An editorial in the *Boston Post* managed to capture the scope of the sale better than just about anything else. Admitting that there were reasons that both supported the transaction and argued against it, the editorial also noted, "this is not the first time Boston has been shocked by the sale of a wonderful player—Cy Young and Tris Speaker went their ways, much to the disgust of the faithful, but the club did not suffer materially. But Ruth is different. He is the class of ballplayer that flashes across the firmament once in a great while and alone brings crowds to the ballpark whether the team is winning or losing." Really, for the first time, now that he was gone, it was finally possible to acknowledge Ruth's unique appeal. He was beyond the game, but that had only become apparent toward the end of his Boston reign, and was not yet completely certain.

Interestingly enough, no current Boston player made a public comment at the time, nor would one for some months, until long after Ruth had reached success in New York. Like Barrow, players like Harry Hooper would wait until the verdict of history was in before claiming, after the fact, to have been on the right side all along. But their silence at the time is telling. Shannon noted in the *Post* that "it is believed that practically every man on the Boston team is pleased at Ruth's sale to New York. Popular as Ruth was, on account of his big-heartedness, the men nevertheless realize that his faults overshadow his good qualities." That was Ruth, as teammate, the past two seasons.

Frazee didn't remain silent. He knew that if he didn't provide some explanation, others would put words in his mouth. That eventually happened anyway, but it didn't stop him from trying. Besides, Boston was owed an explanation. He released a statement on January 6 to the *Boston Post* that, without revealing much at all about the financial and political aspects of the deal, which were both not yet complete and litigious, gave his logic for the trade:

> Ruth had become simply impossible, and the Boston club could no longer put up with his eccentricities. While Ruth without question is the greatest hitter that the game has ever seen, he is likewise one of the most selfish and inconsiderate men that ever wore a baseball uniform., and the baseball public, according to press reports from all over the country, are beginning to wake up to the fact. . . .
>
> Some people may say that the Boston club sold Babe Ruth simply because of the tremendous sum of money handed over by the New York club, but let them listen to a few facts and perhaps they will change their mind. Ruth is a wonderful box-office attraction and he drew many thousands of people to see the Sox play all over the circuit. Had he been possessed of the right disposition, had he been willing to take orders and work for the good of the club like the other men on the team I would never have dared let him go, for he has youth and strength, baseball intelligence, and was a popular idol. But lately this idol has been shattered in the public estimation because of the way in which he has refused to respect his contract and his given word. But I shall enlighten the public some more.
>
> Twice within the past two seasons Babe has jumped the club and revolted. He refused to obey the orders of the manager and he finally became so arrogant that discipline in his case was ruined.
>
> He left us in the lurch many times and just because of his abnormal swatting powers and the fact that he had been given such tremendous advertising by the newspapers he obeyed none but his own sweet will. At the end you could not talk to him. . . . Fans, attracted by the fame of his hitting, went out to Fenway Park unmindful of the steady work of [Stuffy] McInnis, [Harry] Hooper, [Wally] Schang, [Everett] Scott and others who were playing the same steady and brilliant ball, oftentimes handicapped by injuries that should rightfully have kept them out of the lineup. There was no longer any

interest in the pennant race. And these same faithful, loyal players really
felt it. . . .

How many games can you point out that he [Ruth] won single-handed and
unaided last season? He won some, I will admit, but many a time it has been
some other player on the team that contributed the deciding smash. Only
Babe's long hit always got the credit. We finished in sixth place in spite of
Babe and his 29 home runs. This will bring out, I think, very clearly the fact
that one star on a team doesn't make a winning ball club. Cleveland had the
great [Nap] Lajoie for years and couldn't win, Detroit has its Ty Cobb and
Boston had its Ruth. A team of players working harmoniously together is
always to be preferred to that possessing one star who hugs the limelight
to himself. . . .

Harmony had departed when Ruth began to swell and I doubt if we
could have kept out of the second division this year with Ruth in the lineup.
After all, the baseball fans pay to see games won and championships
achieved. They soon tire of circus attractions. And this is just what Ruth has
become.

I might say in conclusion that the New York club was the only outfit in
baseball that could have bought Ruth. Had they been willing to trade players, I would have preferred the exchange, but to make a trade for Ruth, Huggins would have had to wreck his ball club. They could not afford to give me
the men I wanted.

Although Frazee would later release a longer, even more nuanced statement to *Baseball Magazine*, and news about his protracted battle with
Johnson provided additional context to his remarks, this would mostly be
ignored in Boston, where over time the sale would be viewed through an
ever more distorted lens, ever more out of the context of its time. Once
Ruth succeeded, once he became THE BABE in New York, none of that
really mattered.

In New York, reaction was far different.

There it was all huzzahs and champagne corks and streamers, celebrations and brass bands. The press had been waiting for SOMETHING to
happen with Yankee baseball for years, and it never had. They had all spent
the last twenty years writing the legend of Giants manager John McGraw

over and over again: they were pretty much sick of it, and sick of him. And while Ban Johnson had been promising to "help" the Yankees become a competitive team for almost twenty years, apart from 1904, when they lost the pennant to Boston on a wild pitch thrown by Jack Chesbro, that had never happened.

In fact, they even had a name for it, the old "hoodoo," the Yankee jinx, because every time it looked as if the Yankees were about to become a great team, or even a good one, something always happened. Discards from New York became stars in other places, while in New York, stars became discards. Chesbro, the best pitcher in the game in 1904, was out of baseball a few years later, his arm dead. Stars like Frank Chance and Wee Willie Keeler and Kid Elberfeld came to the Yankees only to flame out and fail. And when they did develop a star, like Birdie Cree, who for a time was everything Tris Speaker was and more, something always happened—Cree had his wrist broken by a Walter Johnson fastball and was never the same. Owners Frank Farrell and William Devery were crooks who fleeced their own ball club. For years, the Yankees had been what the St. Louis Browns would later become, an afterthought in their own town, virtually colorless, the beat no sportswriter wanted.

Now perhaps it would be different. Now maybe, at last, the Giants had some competition.

The sale was front page news in New York, too, albeit in smaller font, where the reaction ranged from the sober in stodgy papers like the *Times* and *Tribune* to the entirely over the top. In the *American*, Bugs Baer went overboard and noted, none too delicately "But how that gorilla glanded baby can whamm that Spalding [sic] pebble! . . . Ruth has stung many a homer at the Polo Grounds, but more in sorrow than in anger. Now everything he slams . . . will be all velvet." Guys like Baer and Westbrook Pegler and Damon Runyon, who later wrote the show *Guys and Dolls*, bridged the gap between the baseball world and Broadway.

In Boston, that had been a cause of concern about Frazee, but in New York it was accepted, the line between sports and entertainment already blurred, burgeoning celebrity culture an umbrella already covering each pursuit. In Boston, they wrote about baseball in terms of Fenway Park, and what went on in the white lines. In New York, the only borders that mattered were the circulation area, and with guys like Baer already syndicated all over the country, that meant almost everywhere. Ruth hadn't played a second—hell, he hadn't even come to town yet—and just because he was going to play in New York he was already bigger than he ever had been in Boston, or would have been. They had cartoons in the New York papers, too. One in the *New York Evening Journal* showed him as a Colossus, looking benevolently down on his new city.

In New York, anyway, Yankee players sounded nearly as happy as the press. "We'll sure make life miserable for those pitchers," said Ping Bodie to the *Tribune*. Neither Ruppert nor Huston had to defend the deal. It was the Yankees, after all. They'd never won a pennant, they'd finished third in 1919 but had thoroughly collapsed the second half. In a sense, they were beyond criticism. Anything they did was fine with the press and their fans, as long as they did something.

And the truth was that Ruth was joining a better team than the Red Sox. The 1919 Yankees were ahead of their time and had led the league in home runs with 45. Even according to the standards of the Dead Ball Era, the 1919 Sox had been rather pathetic. Boston hit only four home runs all year clubbed by someone not named Ruth. No one knew it yet, but that was no way to win anymore.

The only criticism that did come Ruppert's way was concerning the price he paid. Oddly enough, in most reports in each city the price was announced as $125,000, a figure neither party bothered to correct but lingers to this day. Even at that level, criticism was tempered. Big money was everywhere in New York. Millionaires lined Fifth Avenue. In Boston, where the Brahmins on Beacon Hill pinched pennies, a dime left on the street was a sign of ultimate extravagance. In New York, they dropped dollars and never bent to the ground.

Ruppert needed the good news, too. The same day the Ruth sale hit the papers, a last-ditch effort to produce near beer, a low-alcohol brew of only 2.75 percent, was shot down by the courts. Prohibition was two weeks away. It was now baseball or nothing.

The only caution expressed anywhere, really, came from Grantland Rice, America's best-known sportswriter, whose syndicated column,

"The Sportlight," appeared in hundreds of newspapers all across the country. Rice alone bothered to take the time to make even the most rudimentary analysis of Ruth's home runs, and he alone noticed something. Rice noted Ruth's three notable home run lapses in 1919, the first lasting 37 days early in the year when he slumped badly, the second of 16, and another in September, of 12 days. "Just what homerless germ became installed in his batting eye is not known," he wrote. "The ways of genius are beyond any cold, scientific analysis." The Yankees hoped that observation was true.

For the time being Ruth remained in California and Huggins took his time returning as well. Meanwhile, lacking access to the player or the manager, the New York press focused on where Ruth would play, something that Ruppert and Huston left hanging. Tellingly, they had not abandoned the idea that he might do some pitching—the rotation was a weak spot. In the *Tribune,* W. J. Macbeth wrote that "Babe is willing to 'double in the brass,' i.e. take his regular turn in the box when he is not cavorting elsewhere." But unless there was a trade or some other transaction, just where that elsewhere would be was of some concern.

Even though Barrow gushed to the New York papers that first base was Ruth's natural position, that was out. Wally Pipp was considered one of the better first baseman in the league, both at the bag and at the plate. Left field was a possibility, but not only was that Duffy Lewis's spot, but as Macbeth noted, at the Polo Grounds, "Left field is a terrific sun field . . . and orbs as precious as those sported by Mr. Ruth should scarcely be expected to be placed under unnecessary strain." Right field was out, he argued "because unless the fences are moved back . . . he is likely soon to exercise the ambulances," as Ruth was known to forget about fences when playing the outfield. Still, it was crowded out there, with Lewis, center fielder Ping Bodie, Sammy Vick, the rookie Meusel, and now Ruth. But make no mistake: there would be a spot for Ruth somewhere. A giant contract ensured that.

Before Ruth returned east, however, he—or more likely, Igoe or a Boston sportswriter working on their behalf—decided to throw a few bombs Frazee's way. After all, Ruth still hadn't officially signed with the Yankees, despite Huggins indicating that they had come to an agreement. The criticism from Frazee stung, and Igoe was also likely feeling the heat from his Boston friends for helping steer Ruth down to New York Harbor. Thus far, Ruth had stayed rather quiet. He didn't like the way that story in *The Sporting News* had taken him to task for having such a high opinion of himself.

Ruth struck back in the papers in both cities, claiming that he had always hustled but "Frazee is not good enough to own any ball club." Ruth apparently forgot about the raises he had gotten after jumping the club, and now complained that he had to buy his wife's ticket on Babe Ruth Day and claimed that all he had received from Frazee was a cigar. He couldn't keep his mouth closed and ended the screed by telling everyone he intended to change his batting style, choke up and go for base hits in 1920 instead of home runs.

It was a telling exchange . . . and the kind Ruth would soon stop engaging in, more or less. Anytime he got into a public spat in the newspapers, particularly over money, it made Ruth seem small, sometimes even petty, and cut across the image of the boyish, benevolent, freewheeling slugger without a care in the world. In Boston, such back-and-forth exchanges had been part of the reason, anyway, that some had sided with Frazee. When Ruth spoke out, he seemed to see everything through a lens that included only himself, and platitudes about his team and teammates sometimes rang hollow. In New York, he would soon start receiving better advice . . . and much better press.

Today, he'd have shuffled off to New York almost immediately, gladhanding everybody and making sure he got off to a good start with local journalists, but he stayed in California with Igoe for the better part of a month, golfing in the sun. When he came back, he went first to Boston, mostly for the money, making an appearance at a testimonial dinner in his honor and picking up some spare change making small promotional appearances while sniping at Frazee. He and Igoe wanted part of his purchase price from the Yankees—they figured about 10 or 20 percent was about right, another $10,000 or $20,000. But Frazee had no obligation, legal or moral, to give Ruth part of the sale price. He was property. All ballplayers were.

While Ruth took his time packing, Huggins finally made it back from California, and entertained everyone with tales of Ruth, whom he said he planned to play in right field and that all the talk that Ruth would change his batting style was "bosh." And sadly, one lineup problem soon solved itself. Yankee third baseman Frank "Home Run" Baker, who before Ruth had passed for a power hitter in the AL, leading the league in home runs three years in a row while with the A's from 1912 through 1914, never striking more than 12 in a season, announced he would retire from the game. His decision had nothing to do with Ruth, however. His wife contracted scarlet fever and died, and his two infant daughters were ill. Although he eventually reconsidered and returned in 1921, for 1920 that opened up a spot at third base, and Huggins indicated he intended to give Meusel a shot there.

Moreover, there remained just one final battle with Johnson. The Yankees filed a suit against him for $500,000, charging that he was trying to drive them from baseball by convincing the Giants to cancel their lease, leading the Insurrectos to reinvigorate the notion of their Pipe Dream League. When the American League meetings resumed on February 10, it was all Sturm und Drang and tumult and shouting. By now, even the Loyal Five were getting weary of Johnson, who seemed unable to keep the league free of litigation. Everyone was exhausted, sick and tired of the whole mess, but the lawsuit was not frivolous and the Yankees had some evidence, enough to force a settlement. Even Johnson's supporters were tired of going to court.

Over the course of one very long day and into the night, the various factions pounded out an agreement. Mays was officially reinstated. The Yankees were awarded third place. The league created a two-man "board of review" that included Ruppert to dispense fines and penalties, stripping Johnson of significant power. If they couldn't reach a consensus, a judge would decide. In exchange, the Insurrectos agreed to drop all their lawsuits and legal actions against Johnson and the league. The Yankees estimated their battles had cost them $60,000. Frazee was probably on the hook for a similar amount, but the war was all but over. Johnson had been defeated. Before the year was out, he would be rendered almost completely powerless, deposed almost completely.

Ruth spent the next month settling his affairs in Boston and preparing to come to New York, arriving just a day before the whole club was scheduled to head south for spring training.

To this point, Ruth had come to Manhattan only as a visitor. Now, he was coming as the Home Run King, ready to claim a new capital.

Neither New York, Babe Ruth, nor the game of baseball would ever be the same again.

10

○

The "Infant Swatigy"

"Everybody interested or connected with baseball in New York has been building castles in the air for the Yankees with Babe Ruth the Foundation. It would be a terrible state of affairs, therefore, if Ruth should fail to come through with the usual home run wallops, would it? But stranger things have happened."
—The Sporting News

On February 28, 1920, Babe Ruth arrived in New York for the first time as a member of the New York Yankees.

He breezed into the Yankee offices on 42nd Street all bluster and bravado, handing out cigars, talking a mile a minute, greeting everybody and forgetting who they were a half a second later. Huston and Ruppert, were waiting to meet him, as was Huggins. Ruth would play under the terms of his old contract with the Red Sox, for $10,000 a year, but a side deal consisting of bonuses over the next two years totaling another $20,000 would bring his annual salary up to that amount. After a round of pleasantries, they all took off for Pennsylvania Station, where their train to Jacksonville, Florida, was scheduled to leave at 6:20 p.m.

Ruth entered Penn Station the same way he entered the Yankee offices, full of swagger, coat trailing behind him, a porter straining under the weight of his bags, which included his ever-present set of golf clubs, the press and a growing entourage of New Yorkers pressing close and trying to keep up with what was already the most exciting thing in the most exciting city that day. Ruth noticed one thing straight off: this was not Boston. Although he had been to New York, it was different now.

He soon realized that some of the freedoms he'd enjoyed as a member of the Red Sox were no longer available. In Boston, although he'd been somewhat confined by the town, he'd had it easy with the press. They had grown up together, more or less, and Ruth's relationship was pretty free and easy. They asked a few questions, he answered, and that was that.

Now, almost every New York paper had someone on the train and everyone wanted to talk and ask questions and then ask the same questions again. He would eventually get used to it, and the New York press would eventually become his greatest protector, but at first it was a little much, like flies buzzing around his head all day. A later account, undoubtedly ghostwritten by one of those same writers, likely Westbrook Pegler, who by the end of the year would write Ruth's 80,000-word autobiography without hardly using a single word Ruth uttered, nevertheless captured some of Ruth's concern. "After we got away for the spring training, I found myself up against something that puzzled me a lot more than Walter Johnson's speed or Eddie Cicotte's snake ball. This was the sport writer. They asked me all kinds of things about my bat and how I held it and how I swung it; they wanted to look at my eyes and one fellow got me to strip off my shirt to give my back muscles the once over. At first I thought they were kidding me, but it didn't do me any good to find out they weren't."

He had to get used to it. In New York, everything was bigger, brighter, and more intense. Of course, there were benefits to that, as well. New York was eight times the size of Boston and there was more of everything, women, bootleg liquor, money, and speakeasies. Put it this way: New York already had the biggest ballpark (the Polo Grounds) and tallest building in the world (the fifty-seven-story Woolworth Building). Fenway Park was in shambles and the Custom Tower, less than 500 feet in height, would remain Boston's tallest building until 1964. Culturally, economically, and in every other way imaginable, New York had surpassed Boston. Getting Ruth was just more evidence that was so.

Still, Ruth had his usual round of fun on the train ride down, and arrived in Jacksonville on March 1, one of twenty-two Yankees on hand for the start of spring training. The Yankees worked out at Barrs Field, a rather common spring training park, featuring a small grandstand and ringed by a low fence plastered with advertisements, the dimensions of which are not precisely known. Jacksonville itself, while not quite as torrid as Hot Springs, was not exactly a sleepy little town where they rolled up the sidewalks at dusk, either. In the last decade, it had emerged as a popular resort town, easy to reach by boat or train from the Northeast in only a few days. It even served as the winter home for what remained of the silent picture industry on the East Coast.

Ruth spent relatively little time at the Hotel Burbridge, where the team boarded while in town. Most of the time, his teammates saw him leave in the late afternoon and then didn't see him again until breakfast, although they usually figured out where he'd been pretty quick—the straw hat Ruth wore everywhere but the ballfield hardly rendered him anonymous, and made his more sophisticated teammates, wise to the ways of Manhattan, see him as something of a rube. Helen Ruth was back in Massachusetts and Ruth had yet to work out the same kind of ruse concerning his night hours with Huggins as he had with Barrow. Yet already he was going his own way, a member of the team, but not a part of it like the other guys, already a law unto himself. He just went out and stayed out and nobody bothered to tell him anything different. On the Red Sox, that had eventually caused trouble. On the Yankees, so far nobody said anything

Little wonder where he went. Jacksonville's Houston Street was notorious for its bordellos, which operated more or less openly from the 1880s into the 1960s—the poet and novelist Stephen Crane's wife, Cora, owned one. And Pablo Beach was where everyone went to catch the sun or spend time in the cabarets. In short, there was plenty of temptation for Ruth and the other Yankees in Jacksonville and the ball club had little trouble convincing them to show up on time. Most raced down as fast as possible.

Unfortunately—or fortunately, depending on your perspective—it was cold and damp that spring and except for their time on the field, most players found their pleasures indoors. Of course, by then, liquor was illegal, something the players soon learned just made everyone a little more eager to drink it, and as the really illegal stuff started making the rounds, it was increasingly difficult to tell exactly what you were drinking or how powerful it was.

On Ruth's first day, while most of his teammates went to the ballpark, Ruth ignored the cold winds and went golfing instead—why get off on the right foot? He was part of a threesome with teammates Bob Shawkey and Del Pratt, as a trio of pitchers, Ernie Shore, Hank Thormahlen, and George Mogridge, tagged along to keep score and carry the bags . . . as did a few members of the press. Ruth must have been surprised the next day to see his golf game so closely scrutinized, written about more in a single day with the Yankees than it had been over the course of his whole career in Boston. Bill Hanna of the *New York Tribune* noted that Ruth "has a long drive but is not the phenomenal driver he is in baseball" and added that "inaccuracy handicapped him." He even made mention of Ruth's attire—"white flannels and a thin silk shirt"—and added, "The Babe has a new silk shirt for every day of the week."

And that's who he was now in New York: the Babe. Not George, not "Babe" Ruth, but more often simply the Babe.

Later that night at the hotel and at the ballpark the next day, he officially met many of his teammates, garrulous outfielder Ping Bodie taking him around. Of course, he had played against most of them, and with guys like Shore and Mays, so it wasn't as if he was walking into alien territory. Besides, once he got to the ballpark, Ruth always felt at home.

He pulled on the Yankee pinstripes for the first time on the afternoon of March 2, skipping the optional morning workout so as not to set a dangerous precedent of being on time. Wrote Damon Runyon of the *New York American*, "the first official motion" of Huggins "was to flatwheel around the behemoth," and get a good look at his new prize. The same could be said of the press. Over the course of spring training, they, too, "flatwheeled" around Ruth. He was the main reason they were there; as Runyon later explained to readers, they wrote so much about Ruth because "all our life we have been so poor and Babe cost so much that even to talk about him gives us a wealthy feeling." Guys like Bugs Baer, assigned that spring to cover the Giants, who were training in Gainesville, felt left out. Being around Ruth meant a party was never far off.

He took batting practice, and everyone crowded around to watch. In fact, it can probably be said with some certainty that more people saw Babe Ruth bat in person during his career than any other ballplayer ever, for in Ruth's time batting practice usually took place in public before crowds with the gates already open, unlike today when more teams take batting practice out of the public eye. Anytime Ruth held a bat in his hand, almost everyone stopped to watch.

On this day, however, as one paper reported, "he hit them rather high than far," failing to reach the fence, or as Runyon put it, "There was no excessive Babe Ruthing during the afternoon." Then again, Ruth was using his spring training bat, all 54 ounces of it, preferring the workout provided by the extra weight. He then enthusiastically took fielding practice, yelling at Bodie, who was slapping him infield grounders to "Hit 'em harder, hit 'em harder!"

This was to be no repeat of spring in Tampa, where Ruth hit everything but the oranges on the trees. He began like it was the regular season and stopped hitting from the start. A lot of Yankees were finding the fences to their liking—even Carl Mays was knocking them out—and in 1920 everybody seemed to notice a difference in the ball. Old Cy Young, winner of 511 games and only retired a decade, made the rounds that spring and later noted, "When I had a chance to take a gander at that lively ball shortly before the '20 season began, my first thoughts were that I was sure glad I was retired." Of course, under the new rules the ball was also dry and pitchers were no longer allowed to scuff it, cut it, sand it, shine it, or do anything else that made it dart erratically over the plate.

They weren't doing much of that in batting practice, anyway, but it didn't matter much to Ruth. Regardless what they threw to him, he wasn't hitting it. In the first intra-squad game, the Yannigans vs. the Regulars, Ruth came up twice with men on base and Mogridge, a back-of-the-rotation starter hardly known for his strikeout ability, got Ruth both times on curveballs and he popped up in a third at bat. Not to worry, cautioned the press, "The Babe simply isn't in slugging trim."

Ruth started to press. Two days later, on March 12, in another contest against the Yannigans, only one day before their spring opener against Brooklyn, who also trained in Jacksonville, Ruth had another bad day. The ball club even brought out what one special correspondent termed "a bagful of Babe's own special fence wrecking brand of ordnance." Presumably, they were referring to a new bag of balls, but perhaps there actually were juiced balls made just for Ruth to crack home runs and entertain crowds. On this day, it didn't matter, as all Ruth could do was pop up.

He was getting frustrated and tossed his bat into the weeds. It showed in the field, too, as he threw to the wrong base. Sniffed the *Times*, "his fielding is decidedly good but his batting continues to be poor." When people were making more of Ruth's fielding rather than his hitting, something was wrong. Huggins, afraid of putting him in proximity to any kind of wall or fence, was trying him out in center field. Although Ruth ran well for his size, he hardly had the speed for the position.

Largely, however, the press held back. They weren't down there to rip Ruth before the season started. That wasn't going to do anyone any good. But the truth was that Ruth was terrible thus far. He hadn't even hit a home run in batting practice. A year earlier, against live pitching, he'd hit seven in 10 at bats.

His slump continued when the Yankees started playing exhibitions, first with Brooklyn, and then in Miami, where they met the Cincinnati Reds, the newly crowned champions of the baseball. The Yankees returned to Jacksonville feeling pretty good, rapping the Reds 9–0 on March 16 behind five innings of shutout ball from Bob Shawkey—one of those "10-cent" players Barrow wasn't interested in, then coming from behind to beat them again 7–4.

Well, everyone was feeling good but Ruth. He went hitless in the first game, "his swings cutting the air with a mighty swish," according to one report, and showed up for game two clearly under the weather, which meant under the lingering influence of some good Cuban rum currently flooding the city. He did manage a hit in the second game, his double starting the Yankee rally, but it was hardly the kind of hit the Colonels were playing $20,000 for, a hard ground ball that caromed off the shins of Reds first baseman Jake Daubert and then into no-man's-land in center field. Ruppert was none too pleased with Ruth's headache and promised the Yankees would never play another game in Miami.

It was seventeen long days, and hundreds and hundreds and hundreds of batting practice swings before Ruth finally broke through. Even then, it came not in a game, but in practice, against a pitcher, Mario De Vitalis, on a brief tryout with the Yankees, someone who not only never made the major leagues, but pitched only two seasons in the minors. And, oh yeah, the wind was blowing so hard that Huggins canceled an intra-squad game scheduled for the afternoon.

Nevertheless, the papers finally had something to trumpet, and Ruth's home run, hit to dead center field where it allegedly landed 50 feet beyond a fence 428 feet from home plate, led everybody's coverage. The *Times* even said, "Ruth figures it's the second hardest he ever hit," comparing it to his "550 foot" blast in Tampa.

Damon Runyon could hardly contain himself . . . or find the words, writing "What a swat it was. My! My! My! My! My! My! My! My! My! My! My! My! My! My! My! My! My! My! Plumb over." For the record, a blast worthy of 18 "Mys." Had it landed atop the fence in right field, wobbled a bit, and then dropped over due to a housefly giving it a push he'd have been no less enthusiastic. It's what the people wanted.

But Ruth still wasn't happy. He wasn't right and he knew it. One day later the Yankees played the Robins in an exhibition. Ruth managed a single and even stole a base, but he also struck out twice, this time against real pitching.

Out in the left field bleachers, a fan had been letting Ruth have it all afternoon, calling him, in the newspaper's delicate euphemism, "a big piece of cheese," likely referring to something with a more striking odor. He was particularly brutal after the last strikeout, and when the Yankees came in to bat in the ninth inning, Ruth decided he'd had enough.

He stalked down the line toward his tormentor, matching him word for word, and when the fan challenged Ruth to come into the stands, Ruth vaulted over the barricade and started after him. As he did, his nemesis pulled a knife.

Ernie Shore, sitting in street clothes in the stands nearby, jumped to Ruth's defense and quickly got between Ruth and the knife. The situation rapidly defused, but if not for Shore's quick thinking, Ruth could have gotten hurt.

It was just the kind of thing that had worried Frazee, that worried everyone invested in Ruth. Could he keep himself under control? Huston watched the whole thing, and after the game was none too pleased. "That kind of stuff has to be stopped right away," he said. "If criticism down here gets under Ruth's skin what will he do in the big league parks?"

Ruth left March just as he entered it, all lamb and no lion. So far, he had been a colossal bust. When the Yankees first arrived in town, every fence board and light pole was plastered with notices of Ruth's arrival, an invitation to come out to the park and see "the Home Run King." By April, those posters were tattered and no one was bothering to replace them. Jacksonville fans had turned out in droves for the first games, but with only a few days remaining before the Yankees broke camp to spend the better part of two weeks barnstorming north, enthusiasm had damped considerably.

It was April Fool's Day before Ruth hit another home run. Fans had to be reminded that it wasn't a joke, but had really happened, as the Yankees beat Brooklyn 6–2 in their seventh meeting of the spring.

They were still settling into their seats when Ruth came up in the first with a man on third. Al Mamaux threw a ball shoulder high and as William Macbeth described it, "he leaned against it. . . . There was the usual sharp crack of the bat, the usual hurtling of the ball, the usual craning of the necks." It was a home run, what the papers called the first in a game ever hit at Barrs Field.

Hi Myers, Brooklyn's center fielder, cooperated. When he reached the place at the fence where the ball passed over, he scratched a Big X in the wood, as Runyon noted, at "The approximate point of exodus of the pill," to commemorate Ruth's blast. As if inspired, Ruth played his best ball of the spring the rest of the game, making two fine running catches. The *New York Daily News* breathlessly announced, "all doubt as to whether batterin' behemoth Babe Ruth has lost his batting eye was dispelled today." Speculation immediately centered on whether the ball would have made the center field bleachers at the Polo Grounds, but no one at the time was certain exactly how far from home that was—the *Times* said 385 feet, and estimated Ruth's drive at 415.

You could almost hear the relief. The *Daily News*, only one year old and the latest arrival on the street in New York's newspaper wars, had bet heavily on Ruth. The tabloid didn't just want him to succeed; like Ruppert, they needed him to. In a first, and as a measure of the impact Ruth was expected to have on circulation, they had assigned a single reporter, Marshall Hunt, to cover Ruth. He was the beat, the ballplayer, and not his team. Hunt was to write about Ruth, and only Ruth, every day. That had never happened before, and hardly ever since, a situation more akin to the recent assignments of some Japanese reporters covering stars like Ichiro Suzuki and Hideki Matsui. There was the full expectation that more people would be interested in the Babe than they would be in the Yankees.

That was starting to appear to be the case. Although the Yankees were playing well, "the old hoodoo" had also taken hold. Baker was gone, and he was soon joined by infielder Chick Fewster, who was beaned and fractured his skull. Players were beginning to notice that not only did the new ball travel farther, but when it hit you now, it really stung. Bob Meusel was looking pretty good at third, and hitting better than any man on the team, including Ruth, but all was not well on the good ship Yankee. There was almost an insurrection.

Second baseman Del Pratt took offense at the distribution of third place money from the year before, which had finally been released by the National Commission and earned each veteran of 1919 another 450 some odd dollars. He had learned that several nonplayers and a few players he felt undeserving had been awarded shares, and Pratt got everyone all riled up about it. The Colonels eventually reached into their own pockets to make up the difference, each player getting an additional $37, but so much for team camaraderie. Ruth, once again, stayed out of it. He was new to the team, it wasn't his battle, and he stuck his neck out for no one but himself.

Everyone hoped the hit would prove to be the finger pulled from the dike that sparked the deluge; the press was getting a little tired of having to make things up about Ruth. Unfortunately, that wasn't the case. The home runs that had come so easily just a few months before, in 1919, were now somehow out of reach. When Ruth came to bat, it was as if all the fences had been moved back.

The Yankees broke camp on April 4, leaving Jacksonville by train with the Robins, as the two clubs planned to play their way north, with two dates in South Carolina, one each in North Carolina and Virginia, then spending a weekend in Brooklyn before the Yankees opened the season in Philadelphia against the A's. Perhaps Ruth would get hot on the way, just as he had in Baltimore the previous year.

He did and he didn't. By the time the games started, the tickets were already sold and what Ruth did didn't matter much to the Robins, who were likely a little tired of all the attention Ruth and the Yankees were getting, whether Ruth hit a home run or not, and they pitched around him when they could. But sometimes they missed.

In Winston-Salem, North Carolina, hometown of Ernie Shore, the two teams squared off on a temporary field tucked onto a fairgrounds, a racehorse track beyond the outfield, far in distance. Nearly 6,000 fans turned out for the game, and before it even started the umpires decided the overflow crowd required a special set of ground rules. Since there was no fence, any ball hit into the crowd strung behind the ropes would be a ground rule double. It wouldn't matter how far Ruth hit one; a ball hit half a mile would only count as a double.

He didn't do it all at once, but cumulatively, he came close. Amid a swirling wind kicking up dust devils in the infield, Ruth hit one the *Tribune* described as "so far over the heads of the people in left center it cleared both fences of the half-mile race track." Ernie Shore's cousin, K. E. Shore, promised to mark it off the next day, but the estimate was almost 600 feet. Later in the game Ruth hit another, shorter blast for another double that still would have made the stands at the Polo Grounds, and then in the ninth inning hit one even farther down the line in right, only to have the umpire call it foul, which sent the crowd howling. The press didn't hold back: "BABE RUTH ROBBED OF TRIO OF HOMERS," read the headline, although they wisely neglected to mention the wind. Why ruin a good story? Besides, both clubs would be in New York in a few days and there were still tickets to sell there.

After one more game, in Lynchburg, Virginia, accented by a Ruth triple, the teams made it to Brooklyn. There was a time when you could have made a lot of money on a bet that asked the question "Where in New York did Babe Ruth play his first game as a Yankee?" The answer isn't Yankee Stadium, which did not yet exist, or the Polo Grounds, but Brooklyn's Ebbets Field in the first of two exhibition games on April 11, 1920.

Now that Ruth was in New York, the struggles that the newspapers had done their best to bury were forgotten. In the *Tribune*, Bill McGeehan warned baseball that given the "war between the Yankees and Ban Johnson," the rumors of scandal percolating about the 1919 World Series, and the "spirit of Bolshevism" among the players, the health of the game was at stake.

The solution was already in town. No less an authority than the *New York Times* beat the drum for Ruth. In an un-bylined opinion piece entitled "Baseball Park, a Stronghold of Free Speech," the author concluded:

> The paper chronicles every move of Babe Ruth. The public reads that he is
> a big overgrown irresponsible boy. The sporting page tells us just what an

odd duck he is. He pokes the ball harder and further than any of the sluggers of bygone days. Naturally there are any number of men who would
willingly pass up an important business engagement to get a peek at an individual so important. What better excuse for taking the afternoon off?
That is what many a man is looking for on hot afternoons in Summer.

In Brooklyn, anyway, a capacity crowd decided "Why wait till summer?"
and a raucous 15,000 jammed the ballpark to see Ruth. No one else even
mattered.

From the start, Ruth had their full attention, first in the form of rasp-
berries and insults as they gave a Brooklyn welcome to the big star. He hit
fourth, played center field, and came up in the first with Roger Peckinpaugh
on second base, facing pitcher Sherry Smith. The crowd howled, half hoping to see Ruth bust one out, and lacking that, at least strike out. That's
the way it was with Ruth, all or nothing, and anything in between, be it a
ground ball, a single, or a triple, somehow seemed a disappointment.

This time he disappointed, lofting a routine fly ball to right field, only
this being Ruth, the routine often became something else again. Amid the
howling of the crowd, neither outfielder Hi Myers nor Bernie Neis could
hear the other calling for the ball. Both played spectator and watched the
ball drop for a single as Ruth laughed his way to first. Later in the game,
as the Yankees rolled to an 11–0 win, Ruth tripled off the wall in deep left
center, and walked twice. Nevertheless, he received the biggest cheer,
termed a "joyous moment" in one account, when he struck out.

But the big news came with two out in the ninth. Hi Myers rolled a slow
ground ball to Del Pratt at second base. He bent to field it, missed, and by
the time he looked up, half of Brooklyn was on the diamond.

Assuming the game was over, much of the crowd vaulted onto the field.
Most of them made their way toward Ruth.

He wasn't in any danger. They just wanted to see him up close, hear him
talk, slap his back, walk the same earth and breathe the same air he did.
For a moment, the umpires tried to clear the field, but it was impossible,
the fans weren't leaving until Ruth did. After a short consultation with Huggins and Brooklyn manager Will Robinson, they called the game.

They managed to finish the next one the following day—this time Ruth only
managed a single—and then the Yankees prepared to leave for Philadelphia.

Ruth had been a little overwhelmed by the move to New York, but not so much that he hadn't managed to improve his lodgings. In Boston, he kept a reasonably sized apartment on Commonwealth Avenue, close enough to Fenway he could walk. In New York, he secured an eight-room apartment at the luxurious residential Hotel Ansonia on the Upper West Side, on Broadway between 73rd and 74th Streets.

For Ruth, only a few years removed from the dormitory at St. Mary's, it was quite a step up. The Beaux Arts building featured a Parisian mansard roof, once had a rooftop farm, and was the first air-conditioned building in New York, turrets reaching to the sky on every corner. He wasn't the only ballplayer in the building, either. The White Sox' Chick Gandil kept a place there, as well. And it was only a quick drive to the Polo Grounds, although there were beginning to be so many cars in New York there was no such thing as a quick drive anymore, but Ruth couldn't risk the subway. In the daytime, he was impossible to miss. At night, he could move around more or less anonymously, but in the daylight it was already hard for him and getting harder.

He was only twenty-five years old, but it seemed as if he had been around almost forever. It was as if the entire sport, the entire nation had been waiting for him and hadn't even realized it until he'd shown up.

He was unmistakable. Like no one else. And he hadn't even played an official game yet as a Yankee.

11

A New Day

"You've probably heard the good news by now, but if you haven't here's
our lay: Babe Ruth went on a batting spree in Harlem Hollow."
—*Damon Runyon,* New York American

Ruth had little time to settle in to New York before boarding the
train with his teammates for Philadelphia. Once they arrived, things did
not quite go as planned.

It was cold in Philadelphia and chilly, but sunny. Still, 12,000 fans turned
out for Opening Day to watch their ball club, which had finished last in
1919 and was little better in 1920. Most of the crowd abandoned the grandstand for the bleachers before the game even if they paid for more expensive seats. Part of the reason was the sun, which made it warmer out there
than huddled in the shade of the stands, but the other reason was Ruth.
From the bleachers you could see him up close, and there was always the
chance he would hit one in your lap. It wasn't until Ruth and the lively ball,
after all, that it made any sense for young boys to bring their gloves to ballgames. Ruth debuted for the Yankees playing center field and hitting
fourth.

Everything started out swell. During batting practice, he dropped three
balls over the fence as if on command and fans looked forward to more of
the same once the game began.

They got it in the first inning, not off the bat of Ruth but the hitter that preceded him, Wally Pipp. If Ruth was having a hard time finding his range with the lively baseball, the same could not be said of many of his teammates and others in the league.

They had all noticed—it was hard not to. The ball jumped off the bat in ways it never had, or at least in ways they had not noticed until the second half of the 1919 season. Now everyone was starting to realize this was a permanent change, and not just due to the vagaries of manufacturing after the war. Once Ruth got going, there would be no turning back.

It wasn't just the home run that Ruth was popularizing. He was also taking the stigma out of the strikeout. Even before the pitching distance settled in at 60 feet, 6 inches and pitchers started throwing overhand, the strikeout had been considered the ultimate embarrassment, the batting equivalent of tripping over a base or throwing the ball over the backstop, something to be avoided at almost any cost. Guys like Joe Jackson, Ty Cobb, and others took pride on keeping their strikeouts down to only 20 or 30 a season. It was considered better to ground out, pop out, or fall prostrate over the plate and fake a heart attack than strike out.

Not anymore. Fans found Ruth's strikeouts exciting—and he didn't much care if he struck out, either. Ruth figured it was all part of the process, one that might result in a home run the next time. Every swing and miss resulted in a correction in the following at bat.

No one paid closer attention to that than Ruth's Yankee teammates. He was conducting a clinic in a new way of hitting every time he picked up the bat. Not worrying about strikeouts gave them license to swing and swing hard. And they did. As a team, even without Ruth's contribution, their strikeouts would skyrocket in 1920, but so would their power and number of long hits. The same would hold true for almost every other team.

The crowd buzzed as Pipp toured the bases, and it buzzed some more when Ruth stepped in, but he could only manage a sharp single. His next time up, he again drew the biggest cheer of the day with—what else?—a strikeout. Entering the eighth inning the score was tied 1–1 as Shawkey of the Yankees and the A's Scott Perry were each on their game.

Then Shawkey wobbled, giving up a couple of base hits. One runner was cut down at home, but with two outs Joe Dugan lifted a fly ball to center field.

"The situation," offered the *Daily News* the next day, "was much like the climax of a novel for school boys in which a college hero catches the ball and by a phenomenal heave chucks the pellet home and then by a series of clever plays the college nine is terribly defeated." But that didn't happen. Ruth circled under the ball . . . and dropped it. Both runners scored and Ruth cost the Yankees a win in his very first official appearance as the A's held on 3–1.

It didn't help when Ruth followed that performance by striking out three times the next day. "The crowd went wild," reported the *Tribune*. "To see the prince of all sluggers breeze three times is something hostile fans has hardly dared hope for." In Philadelphia, they knew they wouldn't have much more to cheer about. To top it off, before the game Ruth had been called to the plate and awarded a small brown derby hat before he then went out and completed the "hat trick." Some start.

So far, the Babe was hardly worth the ballyhoo, but largely the poison pens in the press held their tongues. It rained the next two days, giving Ruth a reprieve, and he may have been heartened to return to Boston, where the Red Sox, according to tradition, celebrated Patriots' Day, a local holiday commemorating the battles of Lexington and Concord, with a doubleheader and the Boston Marathon. Frazee made it a split admission affair, one in the morning before the marathoners ran through nearby Governor's Square, and another in the afternoon. Frazee wasn't about to miss the opportunity to take advantage of two potentially big crowds.

So far, the Red Sox were feeling pretty good about themselves, having opened the season with two wins over Washington, even hanging a loss on Walter Johnson. And Frazee was feeling pretty good, too. Ruth's rough spring had changed some minds in the local press, Johnson appeared defeated, and so far all the financial arrangements he hoped to make were moving along nicely. *My Lady Friends* was nearing the end of its run but had grossed several hundred thousand dollars and earned Frazee a profit of at least $25,000—the exact figure is only known because the playwright later sued Frazee, charging he hadn't received his fair share. Frazee was moving forward on the purchase of the Harris Theatre, and on March 8, he and Lannin had settled their suits against each other. Before that, Lannin had slapped a lien on Frazee's holdings, which for a time even prevented him from making trades, but they'd now come to an agreement, allowing

Frazee to move forward with his plans to take title to Fenway and then take out the mortgage from Ruppert. In turn, Frazee had dropped his counterclaim over the indebtedness stemming from the Federal League suit. Everything was rosy. If Ruth came close to fulfilling his expectations for Ruppert, everyone would be happy.

A huge crowd was expected for Ruth's return. It was a holiday, and after all the hand-wringing over how much Ruth would be missed, there was every reason to expect the park to fill up twice. The Marathon, of course, was an attraction, but it would still be possible to watch the morning game, dash out to watch the leaders plod and wheeze their way to the finish, and go back to Fenway and see Ruth a second time.

That's why it was a surprise when the morning crowd was so sparse. By game time, only 6,000 or so fans filled the stands. Some might have been put off by the early hours or the prospect of double admission, but the limits of the Boston market were also made clear: there just were not enough fans in Boston, and that was something even Ruth's popularity could not completely counteract.

Then the game started and the Red Sox, as best described by Macbeth, "took the Yankees—Babe Ruth and all—by the scruff of the neck and the seat of the trousers and tossed them right overboard like so many English tea chests." In the *Globe*, Mel Webb took another view, noting that the Yankees, including ex-Sox Mays, Ruth, Lewis, and Shore, "neither conquered nor celebrated." Ruth received a nice hand from the crowd, but Waite Hoyt shut down the Yankees almost entirely.

Ruth knocked out two inconsequential hits, both of which would have been outs for any other player. In the past, outfielders had stubbornly played Ruth too shallow. Now they did the opposite. Harry Hooper, in right field for Boston, stood almost with his back to the fence and caught each ball on the first bounce. Had another player been at bat, Hooper would have been closer in and caught each for a fly ball out.

That's part of the reason Ruth's batting average soared. Given the gloves outfielders used at the time, running catches almost always required the use of two hands. It was almost impossible to make a one-handed catch over your head. So when Ruth came to bat, outfielders were beginning to play him deep, far enough back if he hit one over their heads it would leave the park. That left plenty of room in front for short flies and liners to find the ground for base hits. No other player in baseball at the time had so much open space to work with, and Ruth took advantage of every square inch.

The crowd was bigger in the afternoon, as a near sellout variously described as between 22,000 and 28,000, fresh off watching Peter Trivoulides cross the finish line in Copley Square seconds under two and half hours, spun through the turnstiles. Still, total turnout for the day was 20,000 or so below expectations. The Yankees played as if anxious to leave and dropped game two as well, highlighted by the reception the Fenway crowd gave Carl Mays. He was hissed and booed as a turncoat and quitter in what was described as the roughest reception an opposing player had ever received. When he left the mound, he derisively tipped his cap.

They treated Ruth much better. Each time he came to bat, fans allowed to stand up against the fence in center field scrambled back into the stands in fear of being struck by a batted ball. They need not have bothered, as all he collected was another pointless hit.

It got no better for the Yankees the next day. They dropped their third in a row to their Boston cousins, as this time Pennock kept them down. Once again the crowd was small, only 5,800. So much for Ruth as a drawing card in his old hometown. He went hitless and failed to make solid contact, breaking his back, wrote Webb, "chasing Pennock's slow rounders." As if to rub it in, Ruth's replacement in left field for Boston, Mike Menosky, acquired in the Harper deal, collected three hits and knocked in the game-winner in the ninth. The final game of the set was rained out, and the Yankees left for their home opener at the Polo Grounds in seventh place, 1–4, while the Red Sox led the American League. Frazee might have been disappointed in the crowds—only about 40,000 for the three games—but the on-field results, at least, delivered a measure of joy.

Back in New York, everyone acted as if the Yankees had simply been playing an extended exhibition schedule and now the real season was about to begin. The papers expressed some concern over the Yankees, who just weren't playing well. While noting that Ruth had yet to homer, there was no real concern over the slugger—yet.

It was a fine, sunny, warm day in New York on the morning of April 22, the sky a cloudless blue for Ruth's official debut in New York as a Yankee. Expecting a big crowd, the gates at the Polo Grounds were unlocked at

12:30 for the 3:30 start, all the better to give the fans as much time as possible to gawk at Ruth and munch on overpriced peanuts.

There was perhaps no ballpark more beautiful on Opening Day than the Polo Grounds, at the time the largest, most spacious, and most ornate ballpark on the country. The immense, double-decked concrete and steel grandstand, rebuilt after a fire burned down the original in 1911, stood before the rocky outcrop of Coogan's Bluff, the double-decked grandstand beginning halfway between the left field fence and the infield, wrapping around the playing area all the way to the right field corner. In the outfield, expansive stands of bleachers enclosed the field entirely. At intervals atop the grandstand were flags, and the second deck hung almost directly over the lower deck, giving the entire place something of a Globe Theatre feel and allowing fans to look nearly straight down upon the field. It was 279 feet to the fence down the left field line and only 258 feet in right, but unless one hit the ball directly down the line, there were few cheap home runs at the Polo Grounds, for the fence angled sharply back and it was some 455 feet to the asymmetrical barrier in the deepest part of center field.

The facade of the upper deck was decorated in an ornate, bas relief, decorative frieze, and topped by carved eagles, while the lower deck facade featured eight shields, each one different from the other, representing the eight teams in the National League. The field boxes were even modeled after the royal boxes at the Roman Colosseum. With seating capacity of nearly 40,000, it was potentially the most lucrative ballpark in the world.

It also made a place like Fenway Park look like a dump. On this day, it was even more magnificent, as bunting draped the stands, the sky overhead was a rich blue, and the entire field was bathed in sunshine, the grass an electric spring green. For the opposition, it could be an intimidating place to play, but it had never bothered Ruth. Now it was his home and all he needed to do to be installed as emperor was to hit some home runs. He shone in the sun as he stood in the outfield warming up before the game, impossible to miss, every eye riveted on him.

His long hits while barnstorming through the Carolinas had quelled any rampant anxiety over his bat, but everybody would clearly feel better if he started knocking a few out, even in batting practice. Because if anyone had been paying close attention, since the start of spring training Ruth had seen thousands of pitches in batting practice and hundreds in game situations.

He had hit a few home runs, and hit a few balls long, but with nothing like the frequency he had shown the last half of the 1919 season.

So what was it? Well, with Ruth one can never be too certain, since whatever took place off the field usually stayed buried beneath bromides and other obfuscations, but it may have been as simple as he might have been feeling some pressure. After all, he did have to move and had to take care of all the myriad changes in his life that required, while at the same time adjusting to new teammates and a level of scrutiny he had never before experienced. Don't forget, until this point, his offensive performance had been an unexpected bonus. Now, for the first time, he was expected to produce, expected to hit home runs, a very different situation. There's a tendency to treat Ruth, as a person, as either a complete simpleton or someone utterly blind to his situation, and there are certainly elements of each in his character. But he was also human.

And let's not forget one thing more. Ruth was playing a new position, center field, one that required more of him than either left field or first base ever had. He was not a natural outfielder. At St. Mary's he usually caught while not pitching—and as a professional, to this point, he had played only about a hundred games in the outfield. Center field, given the ballparks of the era, presented a real challenge. Play too deep, and balls dropped in; play too shallow, and if they went over your head they rolled forever. It was easy to look bad and Ruth had struggled. He wouldn't have been the first ballplayer to let his fielding concerns trouble him at the plate, or vice versa. It may not have been any one thing that caused him to struggle, but a combination.

Ruth was a major investment—and a risk—and the Yankees were not stupid. They hedged their bets and as soon as he was acquired had taken out a $150,000 insurance policy, payable if he was injured off the field and unable to play. The only things that could mess that up was if Ruth broke a leg running the bases, got beaned, or ran into a fence.

The crowd started arriving early, and for a time it appeared as if the park would fill, but it was a weekday, after all, and despite Ruth, the Yankees were playing the A's, nearly the worst team in the game. At full capacity, nearly 40,000 fans could squeeze inside, but on this day the crowd was closer to 25,000, still a good turnout, but not every seat was filled.

Most wanted to see one thing, and one thing only, and that was a home run off the bat of Ruth, something of which he was surely aware, and probably feeling some pressure to produce, particularly after the debacle in Boston. The press wouldn't play patty-cake with him forever. Although Ruth's success was in everyone's self-interest, that could turn rather quickly. If one writer got out the needle the others were certain to take a few stabs themselves.

Ruth stepped in for batting practice against pitcher Rip Collins and tried his best to please the crowd. They cheered wildly as he waved his bat at the pitcher, screaming for Ruth to kill the ball, to murder one, making as loud a racket as they ever had in a game.

Collins threw and Ruth took a big swing, missing, grunting out loud and twisting completely around. Then he dropped the bat and grabbed at his right side. He gingerly walked behind the batting screen, and the pain brought him to one knee. His teammates rushed to his side and lifted him up, holding the big man and helping him walk to the bench. Doc Woods, the Yankee trainer, dashed over and worked on Ruth's side for a few minutes, trying to massage away whatever ailment bothered him. After a time, Ruth stood, grabbed his bat, and slowly walked back to the batting cage.

He took one swing, missed, then turned around and slowly walked back to the bench.

As the *Times* noted, "the old hoodoo that has pursued the Yankees for ever so many years was again on deck and picked out the shining mark, Babe Ruth, for a target." Something had pulled loose in his rib cage, affecting his follow-through, and as it did Ruth had also wrenched his troublesome left knee.

He insisted he could play, and as game time approached, Woods wrapped him in tape as best he could. The Yankees didn't try to stop him from taking the field, even as he limped and grimaced around the dugout. In fact, they may well have asked him to play in spite of the pain. After all, if it was a serious injury, they couldn't file an insurance claim on anything that happened on the field. Better to have him play through and then take a convenient tumble down a set of stairs.

He made it out to center field and through an uneventful top half of the first, but in the bottom half of the inning, shortstop Roger Peckinpaugh walked, and Wally Pipp, taking advantage of the better pitches he saw hitting in front of Ruth, doubled him home. Up stepped Ruth with one out.

Most of the crowd was still oblivious to what taken place, or if they were not, had been heartened by his appearance in the field. An enormous roar surged through the stands.

It wasn't quite fair. The A's Rollie Naylor could have rolled the ball to the plate and Ruth would have been just as helpless. He swung hard at the first pitch, apparently figuring that if he had only one swing he night as well get as much out if it as possible, but he went down to one knee after taking the cut, and then had to hobble out of the batter's box, bent at the waist for a moment, before stepping in again.

What followed was another swing, this time far more feeble, but one that once again caused him to step from the box as a wave of pain swept over his body. One more swing sent him back to the bench with a strikeout in his first official home at bat for the Yankees.

This time the crowd cheered only in sympathy, for it was clear something was wrong. In between innings, he trudged off the field to the club-house as the announcement "Gleich takes Ruth's place" echoed through the ballpark, the highlight of a very brief career for the new center fielder Frank Gleich. New York went on to win 8–6, but the only news that mattered was Ruth.

It soon got worse. While the Yankees and the "Apathetics," as some members of the press called them, were rained out the following day, the Yankees sent Ruth to see the club physician. He examined Ruth, X-rayed him, and the club announced that he had strained a muscle near the eleventh rib on his right side. He would, said the doctor, be out of the lineup for as many as ten days. "In this regard," wrote Bill McGeehan, "it will not only be painful but serious to the gate receipts." Ruth would recover, but with the Yankees scheduled to be at home another ten days for one of only eight home stands of the season, that had the potential of taking quite a hit out of the bottom line.

But this was 1920. Medical treatment options were limited, but not non-existent, and not completely ineffective. Team trainers were reasonably adept in the use of liniments and rubdowns, and one can imagine that Doc Woods soon got to work on him. They knew how to tape joints and muscles as well as to help prevent against sprains or aggravating existing injuries.

And there were always drugs. Not until the enforcement of the Harrison Act in the 1920s was there any real regulation of what drugs could be administered by doctors. All sorts of medications now banned were still widely available, including most narcotics, and there was little concern about either the long- or the short-term impact of their use. A surprising number of ballplayers before 1920 ended up addicted to opiates, most due to treatment of chronic pain from arm and leg injuries.

Whatever the miracle was, a drug, a massage, a piece of tape, or something else altogether, Ruth surprised everyone when he returned to service only two days later against Washington, pinch-hitting and smacking a long flyout to center field. New York won, and afterward Ruth reported happily, "I swung as hard as I ever swung in my life and didn't feel the least twinge of pain." Perhaps some old scar tissue had just broken loose. Regardless, the Yankees were happy to have him back. Without Ruth in the lineup you could sit wherever you wanted in the Polo Grounds—there were more than 30,000 empty seats.

He returned to the starting lineup on April 29, collecting single hits in the last two games of the month. But in his absence, Miller Huggins made a subtle change. To this point of the season, Ruth—when he was healthy— had played center, Duffy Lewis left, and Sammy Vick right field. When Ruth returned from the pulled muscle, Huggins installed Ping Bodie in center and shifted Ruth to right. Whether it was done to save his legs and keep pressure off his knee, or just because he was more comfortable in right (with the least amount of ground to cover in the Polo Grounds) is uncertain. Huggins didn't reveal his thinking. Whatever the reason, Ruth would primarily remain a right fielder for the rest of his career.

The switch would coincide with a deluge. The Red Sox were coming to New York for five games. By the time they left, it would be a different season, and a different game.

12

Making the Sale

"Was there ever a guy like Ruth? As a matter of fact, there was never even a good imitation . . . he came to New York and took the cover off the siege gun."

—Sportswriter John Kieran

Entering May, Ruth's season and that of the Yankees was at a crossroads. Ruth was hitting .226 in nine games with only a single extra base hit and one walk. The only record he was pursuing was the strikeout mark. With eight in 32 plate appearances, he was on pace to strike out more than 130 times for the season. To date, no one had ever approached 100. In nearly 600 appearances in 1919, Joe Jackson had struck out only 10 times and only 234 times for his entire career. Strikeouts were okay only if they were countered by home runs.

It was even worse than that. The Yankees were only 4–6, still in sixth place. Boston? Minus Ruth, they were a stellar 9–2. The press was referring to them as the "Ruthless" Red Sox, fully aware of the irony the name entailed. If there was truly a "Ruthless" team thus far, it had been the Yankees. So far, Ruth had been a hit only at the box office, but if he didn't start banging the ball soon, one had to wonder how long that would last.

For Ruth, the 1920 season was shaping up as a repeat of 1919, only this time he was wearing pinstripes. Once more, his slow start threatened to bury his team in the pennant race early, risking that whatever he did later in the season, no matter how spectacular, might be diminished. He had been given a pass on that in 1919, but if the same thing happened in 1920 it was unlikely to go unnoticed a second time. That was the problem with all the press in New York. When they were on your side, it was grand, but they could also gang up on you. More than one Yankee manager had felt their wrath.

Although the Yankee–Red Sox rivalry was not as pronounced as it would later become, each team already considered the other its main rival. The Ruth sale put an accent on that, at least in the minds of the fans. For Boston, coming into New York in first place was a familiar feeling. Since the founding of the American League the Red Sox, despite lacking the resources of New York City, had been the team the Yankees one day hoped to be, a champion and near annual contender. So far, nothing had much seemed to change.

In game one, on April 30, it appeared as if that would hold. Before a sizable weekday crowd of 8,000 who turned out despite intermittent showers, the Red Sox tried their best to put their foot on the Yankees' neck. After all, a five-game sweep would virtually ruin New York, and put them in the same position the Red Sox had been a year ago, likely too far back to climb into the race.

Ruth did his best to prevent that in the first inning, cracking a single to knock in a run and give the Yankees the lead, but that was to be his only hit of the day. Waite Hoyt settled down and Boston went to 10–2 for the season with a 4–2 win, as the Yankees fell to 4–7.

The only other notable occurrence came every time Ruth ran out to right field, and every time he ran back in. In only his third appearance in the position at the Polo Grounds, fans packed the right field bleachers to get as close as possible, a disproportionate number compared to the rest of the stands. Every time Ruth ran out to take his position, they cheered and applauded madly. And every time he left them, they cheered again. The same thing happened when he stepped out of the dugout, or into the batter's box, or scratched his nose. He hadn't even done anything yet and was getting twenty or more standing ovations a day. One writer termed it "The Babe Ruth roar. . . . Down as far as 125th Street [in] Harlem folks can now tell when Ruth comes to bat. The roar shakes the whole vicinity. The fans roar

for Babe to hit 'em and when he misses fire they roar because he didn't."
In this game, it was more the latter than the former.

Shawkey, the Yankees' ace, took the mound the next day, May Day. Thus far, although he'd pitched well, he was 0–3—the Yanks had scored more than three runs only once all season. Offense was up everywhere, it seemed, other than in the Polo Grounds. Those Ruthless Red Sox, in contrast, were scoring runs at a frightening rate. So far, they had been held to three runs or under only three times. The rest of the time, they were clubbing teams to death like defenseless rabbits, and giving ammunition to those who still favored the scientific approach.

This, time, however, Shawkey was sharp from the start. The only question was whether the Yankees could take advantage. They scored one in the first—Ruth reached on a force-out, moved around to third, and then, on a ground ball to Everett Scott, Ruth deked his old shortstop into thinking he was staying at third, then timed Scott's throw to first perfectly, taking off for home and beating Stuffy McInnis's throw to the plate. Although Ruth was never quite the ballplayer who "never made a mistake on the field" as the hyperbole later suggested, he was a smart player, surprisingly quick for his size—particularly before he ate his way through half of Manhattan—and he knew baseball. Hundreds of games played at St. Mary's had developed his instincts beyond his years. If anything, Ruth was sometimes too aggressive on the bases, overestimating both his speed and his ability to surprise.

He did it again in the fourth. Ruth rapped a hard liner between McInnis and first base, the ball passing the bag fair, then it hit the ground, then skipped to the wall, where it caromed off the concrete base and sent Harry Hooper racing after as Ruth pulled into second for a double. He wisely moved to third on an infield out and then, after Pratt grounded to second, Ruth timed a dash home again. It was closer this time, but he made a splendid fall-away slide, his foot sweeping across the plate as the catcher spun and reached out to make the tag. The Yankees led 2–0, and so far it was all due to Ruth.

Something was building, you could tell. If he had been bothered by any lingering discomfort from the pulled muscle, the slides proved either he was healed, or the injury taped, or somehow masked over. Ruth was feeling no pain.

Pipp struck out Pennock to lead off the sixth, bringing up Ruth, who was greeted with the now customary histrionics, this time even a little louder due to his performance in the first half of the game.

Pennock threw one pitch and a sound like no other rocketed through the park. The ball went up and up and toward right field.

What happened next released a deluge of adjectives and adverbs from the New York press, verbiage they'd been sitting on since the first week of January. Now that they had a chance to use it, they didn't stop.

The embellishment prize went to George Daley, writing under the pseudonym "Monitor" in the *New York World*:

> Ruth strolled to the plate, decided it was time to OPEN THE SEASON and sunk his war club into the first ball Pennock tried to pass over the plate.
>
> There came a burst of thunder sound: that ball, oh, where was it? Why clear OVER the right field roof of Brush Stadium [the Polo Grounds] and dropping into the greensward of old Manhattan Field around the junction of Eighth Avenue and 156th Street—the longest drive they say EVER seen on the P.G. and longer even that the tremendous wallop that gave Babe his twenty-ninth homer last September.
>
> Eyes were strained in the watching of the spheroid's flight; throats were strained in acclaiming its all-fired bigness, and hands were strained in a riot of applause to the hitter thereof as he ambled around the bases and, lifting his cap, disappeared into the dugout.

Whew. What he meant was it left the field between the third and fourth flagpole atop the roof in right field and landed in the park next door, only the third ball ever to leave the yard, as Ruth joined himself and Joe Jackson as the only prior practitioners. To be fair, the ball was driven about 400 feet when it left the field, although no one could say with any certainty whether it struck the top of the roof or sailed cleanly over it. The grandstand roof was some sixty feet above the field, but its front edge, where the ball passed over, only a bit more than 300 feet from home. Regardless, it was still, in the parlance of the day, "a prodigious blast" and "fierce clout," absolutely "lambasted," one that "flitted out of the park," "a bomb."

It also gave the Yankees a 3–0 lead. A moment later, while the fans were still cheering, Duffy Lewis, up next, duplicated the feat, although in much more mortal fashion, smacking a home run into the left field bleachers.

That occurrence, back-to-back home runs, was so rare no one could recall it happening before. Two consecutive home runs? Both OVER the fence? The lively ball needed no more proof.

Ruth's home run, his first as a Yankee, was the one he needed most. Now the dam was broken, now everything he was supposed to be, he suddenly was, now the pressure was off and the game was fun again. Now he was, unquestionably and everlastingly, the Babe. The remainder of his career fell beneath the shadow of what was to come.

After the game, a 6–0 Yankee win, the press noted that it was Ruth's 50th career home run. Heck, Ty Cobb, who had been playing since 1905, only had 67 career home runs. Home Run Baker had just 80. Ruth already had 50. He had hit only one home run as a Yankee and the press was already setting goals and targets. They would do so for most of the next fifteen years. Hardly anyone even mentioned that the victory might prove a turnaround for the team. The Babe was all and everything.

In case no one had noticed, the next day Ruth did it again, as the *Times* noted, "At what was known in the old days as an opportune time." In his first two times up, he collected a "mighty" strikeout (they all were "mighty" now) and then lofted a "near home run" (just about any deep fly ball) before coming up in the sixth with two on and the Yankees trailing 1–0.

After a swinging strike and a foul tip off Sam Jones, his former teammate tried to sneak one past . . . and failed. This was no blast over the roof but a drive down the line. But even that wasn't special enough. It was described as "the lowest and fastest home run drive uncoiled in the Harlem park in years," maybe the shortest of Ruth's career, sneaking over the fence and into the upper deck just fair of the iron foul pole, 258 feet away.

It didn't matter to the fans, 25,000 of whom filled the park, the second home Sunday date of the year, bringing the Sabbath total to more than 50,000. As Ruth rounded the bases, they climbed on the dugout roof and tossed papers and hats onto the field. There were even reports of celebrations emanating from the apartment windows of buildings on Coogan's Bluff. Even the Polo Grounds stage wasn't big enough for Ruth.

The countdown began the next day. The *Times* noted, "Babe needs only twenty-eight more homers to beat the big record he set last season. At the rate of one a day that mark won't last long." They weren't trying to be funny. And oh yeah, the Yankees won again, 7–1.

As if exhausted, Ruth went hitless the next two days, but then again, Boston pitchers were getting wise. The two clubs split the last two games of the series, and New York stayed out of the cemetery by taking three of five from Boston and pulling into fourth place.

Ruth's struggles weren't quite over, however, as the Yankees went on the road and Ruth, perhaps a little homer happy, seemed to press. After doubling twice off Walter Johnson in Washington to start the road trip, he went hitless in his next four games and his batting average dropped to .210. But it was only a temporary lull. When the Yankees returned to the Polo Grounds on May 11, so did the Babe. It was September 1919 all over again, not only for Ruth, but increasingly for a lot of other guys, too.

On May 11 against Chicago, Ruth came up in the first and belted the ball into the right field bleachers at the Polo Grounds, only the second ball ever hit there. In the third, he banged one off the center field fence, 430 some feet away, and only the fact that Chicago center fielder Happy Felsch was playing halfway to the Bronx kept Ruth from circling the bases—he settled for a triple. In the fifth, he smacked a second home run into the upper grandstand in right. Ruth accounted for five of New York's six runs in the 6–5 win.

Roger Peckinpaugh, who hit a home run into the left field bleachers, accounted for the other and Chicago scored when Happy Felsch did the same thing. Although neither hit was as far as any of Ruth's shots, they were each more than 300 feet. For the day, Ruth and his other home run companions accounted for more than a quarter mile of hits and four home runs.

That was the kind of thing that just didn't happen—or at least, hadn't happened, except by some fluke in some bandbox. These were all legitimate home runs. If there was any question that baseball had entered a new, lively ball era, that question was answered.

It wasn't just the ball either, or that pitchers were no longer allowed to scuff it. In the Polo Grounds, in particular, the large crowds made it increasingly difficult to retrieve foul balls hit into the stands, still a common practice in some parks, and with fewer players just trying to make contact, but swinging freely, more and more balls were being fouled off and lost. That meant a new ball had to be put in play ten, fifteen, even twenty times a game. Only a few years before, games sometimes went from beginning to end with only a couple of balls. Not anymore.

The baseballs were not just harder and livelier. Now that they weren't being spit on with tobacco juice and rubbed into the ground, they were brighter, whiter, and easier to see. The age-old practice of selecting a pitcher due to lighting conditions passed without notice. Hitters for the first time could actually see the seams on the ball, and get that split-second tipoff whether the pitch was a breaking ball or a fastball.

Pitchers hated using the new balls. They were often slick, and hard to grip. With the dead ball, savvy pitchers knew how to raise the seams and/or scuff the surface to help their breaking pitches. Forced to use a brand-new or nearly new baseball all the time, a lot of pitchers discovered their breaking ball wasn't as good as they thought it was. The hitters found that out, too. They saw a lot more hanging curveballs and a lot more straight fastballs. Speed, rather than movement, was suddenly at a premium. A lot of pitchers didn't have enough on the ball.

The runs came in bunches, and so did the home runs and other long hits. The next day the Yankees pounded Chicago 14–8, the kind of score that used to happen to a team only a couple times a year, but now seemed to take place every week. Asked one paper after the game, "Naturally the question arises 'was Ruth at bat all the time?'" He wasn't, but his style of play was, and he still hit a home run—into the second deck in right field again. Ho-hum. So did the Yankees' Aaron Ward. A new promotion gave Ruth a new pair of socks after every homer. Before long, he'd be wearing a new pair after every game.

After Ruth singled later in the game a reporter offered that "it is a good thing there is no home run hitters union for if there was Ruth would probably be heavily fined for such a puny hit." But the fans seemed little bored. After Ruth's last hit, with the Yankees leading 14–5, the crowd started to clear out. If Ruth wasn't going to bat again, why stay?

Ruth was thrown out of the next contest for arguing a call, but the Yankee pitcher, Jack Quinn, picked up the cudgel and hit a home run before 25,000 fans. The 2–0 win—the players must have been exhausted from running the bases the day before—lifted the Yankee record to 12–11. They'd never fall under .500 for the rest of the year. Unlike the 1919 Red Sox, there would be no burying this team.

Even when they lost, they won, or at least Ruppert and Huston did. The first place Indians came into town on Sunday, and the fine weather, Babe Ruth, a four-game Yankees winning streak, and the novelty of Sunday baseball brought out nearly every fan in the five boroughs and even a few more than that. But really, it was mostly Ruth. Apart from Sunday baseball, all those other things had happened before and there had never been a crowd like this.

The first game drew what was then the largest crowd in the history of the Polo Grounds, and the largest in the history of New York, which meant the largest in the history of baseball, or pretty close to it, the tenant Yankees far outdrawing their landlord. By 2:30 there were more than 38,000 fans inside the ballpark and the game was still an hour off. They locked the gates and in the next hour between 10,000 and 15,000 blocked the streets, looking for a way in. Late-arriving sportswriters showed their credentials and were then told to scale a fence to get inside. Worried club officials feared that if they opened a gate to let them in they might never get it closed again.

Had Ruth blasted a home run, the ballpark might have fallen apart. He didn't, contributing only a ninth inning double, but by then the Indians, who scored five first inning runs, had the game in hand. That actually worked out pretty well for the Yankee coffers. After the Indians jumped out to the big lead, enough fans left the park early that the Yanks were able to reopen the gates and let several thousand more fans pay for the privilege of wedging themselves inside. Official attendance may have only been 38,500, but the club sold well over 40,000 tickets.

Although Ruth only had five home runs, the newspapers breathlessly reported that he was ahead of his record pace in 1919, when to this point in that season he had hit only one. But Ruth wasn't doing himself any favors. He pulled something over the weekend and had to sit out the next four ballgames. Or maybe he was sick. The papers couldn't decide and the sportswriters either didn't ask or didn't care. He could have been in a car wreck, been punched in the nose, or lost in a suburban bedroom. Whatever. He didn't play again until the following Sunday against the Browns, when another huge crowd of almost 30,000 turned out. Never before in the history of baseball had a team seen such crowds. It was as if every day was the World Series and it was only mid-May.

"Babe Ruth Makes Sick Ball Game Well" read one headline later. He returned with "violent health" and in the sixth inning, with the Yankees trailing 2–1, Ruth ended it with yet another blast onto the grandstand roof, causing a storm of straw hats to rain down on the field. Then the Browns' Baby Doll Jacobson hit a long home run as well, giving headline writers some fun fitting Babe and Baby Doll into the same head. Ruth inspired everyone.

Scientific baseball was starting to disappear, the Great Plains bison of baseball. In the last full season, 1917, American League teams had combined for 1,268 stolen bases and 1,731 sacrifice hits as they scratched out an average of 3.6 runs a game per team, while hitting only 133 home runs. In 1920, they would steal only 751 bases and complete 1,624 sacrifices while averaging an additional run per game and hitting 369 home runs. Ever so slowly, teams were learning to wait for the home run. In this, the Yankees were several years ahead of their competition.

Ruth finished the month in a flourish. After collecting the Yankees' only two hits in a loss to the Tigers on May 24, he homered in the final two games of the home stand, first putting the Tigers under with a first inning home run, then adding an exclamation point with an eighth inning blast in game two, both Yankee victories.

With the team scheduled to embark on a short, four-game road trip to Boston, the crowd at the Polo Grounds acted as if they might die of longing before Ruth returned. Everything he did solicited cheers, and everyone was running out of ways to say it, but Ruth was the most amazing thing that had ever happened in the game. One paper offered that the opposition needed three extra outfielders, one in the stands, another on the roof, and a third parked outside, just to have a chance. When Ruth hit his second home run, he doffed his cap at least a dozen times between home plate and the dugout. In the papers Ty Cobb, heretofore the greatest player in the game, got nary a mention. It was as if he didn't exist. Ruth eclipsed everyone else.

There was never any love lost between the two men, each emblematic of a different age and style, as Ruth's earlier statement to *The Sporting*

News indicated. But Ruth recognized both Cobb's talent and his personality. Of the Tiger outfielder, Ruth reportedly once said "Cobb is a prick. But he sure can hit. God Almighty, that man can hit." Cobb was less forgiving. He thought Ruth was black, a rather common belief both among Southerners (as well as in the African American community, which claimed him as their own), and as a result Cobb generally dismissed his talents. He couldn't stand it that Ruth was now considered the game's greatest. That had long been Cobb's place, but no more.

Ruth and the Yankees capped off the month with the trip to Boston, but Ruppert and Huston must have already been over the moon. In 22 home dates at the Polo Grounds, the Yankees had already drawn nearly a quarter of a million fans, what the Philadelphia A's would draw all season. In ticket sales alone, conservatively, the ball club had grossed somewhere above $300,000. That was already enough to cover their payroll, to pay Ruth, to pay their rent to the Giants, and put some money in the bank. In addition, they still had another 50 home games to play. Baseball was suddenly more lucrative than beer had ever been.

The triple bank shot had worked. Everything fell into place. Johnson had been all but defeated. Ruth had made the Yankees a financial success. On March 31, Frazee purchased the Harris Theatre. On May 3, he signed a purchase and sale agreement to acquire Fenway Park and simultaneously settled his debt with Lannin. On May 22, just as the mortgage with Ruppert was being executed, the Giants, outmaneuvered, suddenly decided to extend the Yankees' lease another year. On May 25, at long last, the mortgage on Fenway from the Yankees closed. The only residual effect of the war would be a continuing chill between the Insurrectos and the Loyal Five. Over the next three years, the Insurrectos would be frozen out by the rest of the league, forced to trade almost exclusively with one another. The Sox and Yankees would complete seven trades during that time, and although some would use the deals as evidence that Frazee was giving the Yankees a gift, when one considers the deals in context, and compares the players' values and WAR at the time of the deals, most were equitable.

The Red Sox, unfortunately, would soon take on the Yankees' hoodoo. The Yankees went into Boston on Thursday, May 27, for four games, culminating in a doubleheader on Saturday. Babe Ruth was not just the biggest name in baseball, but just about the biggest name in the country. Although Boston had cooled after their quick start, at 21–9 the Ruthless Red Sox still led the American League, with the Yankees five games back, in fourth place, 17–15. Maybe the Red Sox really didn't need Ruth.

Their fans didn't. If Frazee had thought Ruth's return to Boston would mean a sellout crowd every time he played, he was disappointed, as Fenway wasn't even half full for the Thursday contest. They missed a gem.

Ruth was magnificent, cracking two home runs. One, a no-doubter to deep right field left Harry Hooper frozen, still as a statue, hands on his knees as the ball carried over his head. The second went to deep left center, where it struck the top of the left field wall out toward the flagpole and then bounced over Lansdowne Street. The crowd cheered Boston—except when Ruth came to bat, and New York knocked the Red Sox out of first place with a 6–1 win.

They hit them on their way down the next day, too, before another 10,000 fans, as Ruth remained silent with only a single to show for his effort. It was another cheap hit, as the papers noted that had the outfield not been playing so deep, the ball would have easily been caught.

Finally, on Saturday, Fenway Park was full, so full that the crowd stood behind ropes in the outfield as nearly 30,000 fans turned out for the doubleheader. Although the crowds to see Ruth were somewhat disappointing, for the season they would still account for about 130,000, or nearly one third of Boston's gate.

Ruth did not disappoint. Now, it seemed he never did. The Yankees swept both games and Ruth knocked another home run, this one to left, 20 feet above the clock atop the wall.

And if that were not enough, another record crowd followed Ruth to the ballpark on Memorial Day back at the Polo Grounds. The Colonels did not mess around, turning the doubleheader against Washington into a split admission, one game in the morning and the other in the afternoon. Ruth went hitless in the first contest before 11,000 fans as the Yankees won anyway. Instead, Ruth waited until the stands were packed with nearly another 40,000 in the afternoon contest before he provided an exclamation point to the most amazing month a home run hitter had ever had to that point in the entire history of baseball.

The Senators took a lead, then called on the great Walter Johnson to hold it. He couldn't and New York tied the game in the sixth. The game entered the eighth with the score still knotted 7–7.

Perhaps the greatest pitcher in the game, Johnson was finding it hard to adjust to the new ball, and he was scuffling for the first time since he had been a teenager. Although only thirty-two, he had already thrown more than 4,000 innings and some 50,000 pitches in the major leagues. What-ever the reason, for the first time in more than a decade he was almost human.

Peck led off the inning with a triple. Then Meusel rattled one around the outfield for another three-bagger to put the Yankees up by a run. That brought up Ruth.

The past and future of the game stood 60 feet, 6 inches from one an-other, the game's two greatest stars, one on the way up and the other one just beginning a slow descent down. The crowd fell silent, knowing they were seeing something they might never see again.

The man who had already given them a season's worth of memories in only two short months came through again. Ruth ripped the pitch, which rode a wave of cheers, deep to right, where it crashed off the facade atop the upper deck, his 12th home run of the season, and 12th of the month, another new record falling before him. The Polo Grounds almost came apart, the 50,000 fans to watch baseball there in one day a record, too.

My God, it was only MAY. Summer had yet to come. What might Ruth do then?

13

⚾

The Babe

*"A Modern Goliath of the bludgeon is Ruth. . . . He has become a na-
tional curiosity and the sight-seeing pilgrims who daily flock into Manhattan are as anxious to rest eyes upon him as they are to peek at the
Woolworth building or the bungalows of the impressively rich on Fifth
Avenue."*

—New York Times

By the time the calendar turned to June, it had all changed. Ruth
had fulfilled all expectations and then some. Whatever questions or
hesitations about his talents, they had been answered by a month-long performance that saw his batting average soar above .300, and his profile
challenge that of any statue or monument in the nation's capital. This time
his offensive explosion coincided with victory for his team. The Yankees
went 19–8 in May, rising from sixth place to second, as Ruth hit .329 for
the month with 12 home runs and 26 RBI, all of which resulted in an OPS
of 1.384. He wasn't striking out as much anymore either, whiffing only 12
times while walking 18. It was already one of the greatest offensive months
by any player in baseball history, but Ruth wasn't even warmed up yet.

True to form, he was already cashing in, but he wasn't so much seeking
out a fortune as simply reaching out and grabbing cash as opportunities
came his way like batting practice fastballs. Whatever he was selling, America was buying.

He hadn't been in New York a month before the United News Service
gave Ruth his own ghostwritten column, likely penned by Marshall Hunt,

in the *Daily News*. And by the end of May, as record after record began to fall before him, Ruth began to receive invites and entreaties from New York's upper crust, all curious and eager to see just what this Ruth fellow was about, the ultimate drawing card of drawing cards. They invited him to parties and viewed him like a specimen from another planet. Even other celebrities, movie stars and singers and dancers and actors, wanted to meet him. Politicians wanted to be seen with him, and everyone wanted an autograph: enterprising fans figured out that if they sent Ruth a check for any amount, he would cash it. Upon return, the endorsed checks for 50 cents or a dollar became family heirlooms.

Ruth didn't mind, the food was good, the liquor top-notch, and the women better dressed but just as accommodating as ever. It was different than it was in Boston, where the Brahmins, ever so class-conscious, rarely deigned to look his way or even acknowledge the existence of life beyond the Back Bay and west of Massachusetts Avenue. Ruth would soon learn, just as Harry Frazee had in reverse fashion, that unlike Boston, New York was a meritocracy. What you could do was more important than who you were. Money and fame mattered more than breeding and upbringing and where you went to school.

In New York, the upper crust didn't just invite Ruth out, they often came to him. Many evenings he didn't even bother to go out at all but held court in his suite at the Ansonia as dozens of newfound friends and admirers drank his liquor, ate his sandwiches, and fought for his attention. Even the press was welcome inside, a measure of the ease he felt being himself in their presence. The only one not enjoying everything was Mrs. Ruth, who was often left alone in a corner. The Babe was on an elevator going up fast and there just wasn't room for her on the car.

It helped that Ruth could, to a degree, play and look the part. In Boston, he had favored straw hats; in New York he wore a stylish driving cap, a camel hair coat, a brand-new silk shirt every day of the week, had his shoes polished, drove a sleek Packard, and smoked expensive cigars. Among the high and mighty Ruth's crude manner and off-color way of speaking were considered deliciously scandalous, something one had to witness in person, an experience to collect like a rare orchid.

With fame, came fortune and opportunity. His longtime advisor, Johnny

Igoe, now way over his head, began to lose his grip on Ruth. He didn't belong to anyone anymore: he belonged to the world.

From the start, Ruth began to separate himself from his teammates. On the field, he was a central part, a key figure, the first straw that stirred the drink, but that ended outside the lines. Before summer began, he stopped taking a roommate on the road, and although the Yankees paid for the players' food and hotel at the rate of $7 a day, Ruth already had higher standards, greater needs, and special dispensation. He took care of himself, usually paying for and staying in suites alone rather than splitting a room with another player. Eventually, he even had a private phone line installed next to his locker at the Polo Grounds. He was special, different.

Of course, the public knew little of this. He was presented to them as a big, guileless, overgrown kid. In Boston, where Ruth ran with the rabble, his exploits, for better or worse, were also better known; if he was drunk in an alley the night before, everybody knew it by noon the next day. In New York, it was different. In New York, a celebrity could still have privacy, protected by a cooperative press and culture built around discretion.

No one could get enough of him, and on June 1, after four games in three days and another doubleheader scheduled the next day, the pitching staff was stressed so the Yankees pressed Ruth into service on the mound against Washington.

He didn't tell the Yankees no. The day was all Ruth, his full game on display. Despite some rust—apart from fooling around on the sidelines Ruth hadn't pitched since September—after giving up two first inning runs Ruth settled down and followed with three innings of shutout ball. By then, the Yankees led 12–2. At the plate, in the first inning Ruth, batting cleanup, hit what was described as "a ball so high it broke all the altitude records in baseball," that fell just shy of the fence. He later legged out a base hit and cracked a double in the eventual 14–7 Yankee win.

The growing cacophony for all things Ruth only increased the next day, when Ruth followed with what might have been his greatest day in the major leagues to date, something that now seemed to be happening once or twice a week. In a doubleheader versus Washington, he slammed three home runs, giving him 15 for the season, and as the *Times* noted, "He is hitting them harder and sending them farther every day." That was probably true, for as spring gave way to summer increases in temperature and humidity combine to make the ball carry, the warm air and moisture increasing lift. There was open speculation that it was only a matter of time until he homered to dead center field in the Polo Grounds, where no one had gone before, or even come close, except for Ruth.

The Yankees split the doubleheader, but first place now seemed only a matter of time, a collateral outcome of Ruth's prodigious slugging. But he wasn't the only one getting the job done. Ruth's home runs were only three of eight struck that day, including three by the Senators. The press called it a "home run epidemic." Over a seven-game stretch in late May and early June, the Yankees as a team collected 92 hits, 39 for extra bases, and averaged 13 hits and nine runs a game. A few years before that would have been almost a month's work.

The offensive explosion was even the subject of a column by Grantland Rice, who did not often take much of an analytical view. He concluded that "the amazing growth of home runs this season is due to a brace of combinations," citing a "ball made up of better ammunition" due to "better wool," and a late spring that he believed left pitchers behind the hitters. The acerbic and cynical Ring Lardner provided an alternate view, writing, "the masterminds that control baseball say to themselves that if it is the home run the public wants to see, give them home runs. So they fixed up a ball that if you don't miss it entirely it will clear the fence, and the result is that the ballplayer that used to specialize in humpback liners to the pitcher is now amongst our leading sluggers."

Whatever the reason, the results were undeniable and Lardner's comments telling. Baseball's old guard may have looked at the power surge with suspicion, but they also realized there was no stopping it. The public—a different public from what filled the ballparks before the war, much younger and enamored with all things new—had already voted with their feet and spun through the turnstiles at a dizzying rate. Although baseball would go through some pains to get the Reach company to claim the ball had not been purposely doctored, at the same time they also never asked the company to go back to their old way of doing things. Reach wouldn't have done so anyway—they were in the business of selling baseballs, after all, and Ruth was helping them sell more than ever before. Baseball was expanding again. There were already seven new minor leagues in 1920, and from the sandlots through the schools everybody was playing baseball. Ruth and the home run were the reason. The game was not going to turn the clock back—or the ball—under any circumstance. Even old fans like Lardner, who found the new game crude and lacking the managerial strategy of scientific ball, recognized that. Going back to the old ball would be like abandoning the automobile for the horse and buggy, or giving up electric lights for coal oil lamps.

The Yankees kept up their impressive performance at the plate even as Ruth took a brief break from hitting home runs, going homerless in seven straight games, but it hardly mattered as he hit almost .500 and the Yankees scored more than 10 runs four different times. The only thing that seemed able to slow Ruth down were the New York police—he picked up his second speeding ticket, and the press took some delight in delivering a mild scold that just made Ruth seem like even more of a scamp.

Although he still got his hits, Ruth might have been bothered by something else. At nearly every at bat now, a newsreel film photographer risked death from foul balls by setting up just off the plate to record Ruth's swings.

At least Ruth thought it was for the newsreels. A few months later, a film would be released called *Babe Ruth "Over the Fence,"* a collection of his greatest swings spliced together with shots of the Polo Grounds crowd going apoplectic and Ruth touring the bases. Ruth knew nothing about it, and the Babe ended up suing on the grounds that the film violated his civil rights. What he was really mad about was that filmmaker Raoul Walsh had already offered him $10,000 to cooperate in a documentary on hitting, and the guerrilla film stole their thunder. Ruth eventually lost the suit, *Over the Fence* was lost to history, and the other film, unfortunately, never made. But this would hardly be Ruth's only experience with a movie camera.

The business of Babe Ruth was already in full swing and expanding. Although no one used the term at the time, Babe Ruth was a brand unlike any other. The whole business of celebrity endorsements, at least the way we look at celebrity endorsements today, was in its infancy, but the growth of popular culture, making movie stars and athletes famous beyond their business, was just taking hold. Ballplayers had long endorsed tobacco products and the like, but this was different. Babe Ruth's name on just about anything sold. All you needed was a photo of Ruth, some ad-agency-produced copy, a facsimile autograph, and voilà, instant sales.

It wasn't like Ruth had an army of lawyers vetting his offers. They usually weren't called in until after the fact. He sometimes signed away his rights for relatively nothing, and at other times, companies just used his name and image without permission, leaving it to Ruth to track them down and file a complaint. It was impossible to keep up.

Ruth also became an author—at least gullible young boys would believe he had. The A. L. Burt Company signed Ruth up and then hired some long-forgotten scribe to put words to Ruth's pen, the result being a children's novel, *The Home Run Kid: or How Pep Pindar Won His Title.* It wasn't Ruth's first foray into the literary arts. Ghostwritten copy was already being produced under his name in the papers, and over the years Ruth would "write" hundreds of articles and dozens of books, including no fewer than four autobiographies. No player of his era was more prolific.

Or more frustrating for biographers, for Ruth never even read much of the material, much less write it or vet it for accuracy. That was all done by sportswriters, produced under a filter to turn out a good "yarn," and virtually useless in terms of history. Ruth wasn't a journal keeper or much of a letter writer, either. Most of the statements attributed to him are as spurious as the fake Ruth signatures that still flood the memorabilia market. Truth is, no one much knows what Ruth believed or thought or said about much of anything, and what little we do know has filtered down through anecdotes and a scant few oral histories. But there is no denying what he did on the field.

There, his life could be quantified and measured. Now that Ruth was on his way, the daily watch became all about numbers. He was halfway to a new home run record, and every subsequent home run Ruth hit in 1920 came with a number attached to it. Even though the Yankees were challenging for their first pennant, their place in the standings usually took second billing to Ruth's home runs. That's just the way it was.

As the Yankees danced around first place, even taking possession of it all by themselves for a few hours on June 6, Ruth finally hit home run number 16 against the Tigers on June 11. But a few days later the team suffered a blow when Duffy Lewis went down with a knee injury. Yankee pennant hopes took a hit as they lost three of four to Cleveland, Ruth keying the lone win in a 14–0 victory with home run 17. The press wondered if it was the old hoodoo coming back again.

Now it was already showing in Boston and affecting the Red Sox. The Red Sox, after being the class of the league for two months, were collapsing. The reason, primarily, was injuries. Outfielder Tim Hendryx had been leading the league in hitting for much of the first two months, but went down with a leg injury and the Sox didn't have the depth to adjust. Waite Hoyt tore a groin muscle so badly he needed surgery, Allen Russell suffered an aneurysm, and Harry Hooper was hospitalized with an abscess in his leg. The Ruthless Red Sox were suddenly less a whole lot more often, and it showed. They would not challenge for the pennant in 1920, and over the next several seasons would follow a similar pattern, a quick start leading to optimism in the local press, then injuries, accidents, and collapse.

A few days later, it almost looked as if the Yankees might suffer the same fate and become "Ruthless" themselves. The Babe was on first base in Chicago when Bob Meusel ripped one to Buck Weaver, playing shortstop. Weaver raced to second to force Ruth and threw to first in one motion.

The Babe didn't get down, and first the ball and then Weaver's fist hit him above the left eye. Ruth went down, falling over the bag, losing consciousness for a moment before he came to, clearly dazed, the swelling already starting to show. He tried to continue but left the game an inning later. He was back in the lineup the next afternoon, but Ruth had been lucky. Another half inch lower and the ball would have struck him flush in the eye. He wouldn't have been the first promising hitter to lose his career to being struck by a ball.

For all the power he displayed at the plate, Ruth was rarely targeted by opposing pitchers. For one, he had good instincts and was adept at avoiding being struck, but he also pulled off the plate as he swung. He was also respected. Every player in baseball knew that Ruth made them money, and no one went head-hunting with Ruth at the plate. Over the course of his career, he would only be struck by a pitch 43 times. In 1927, when he set the home run record with 60, he was not hit by a single pitch.

The club returned to New York at the end of the 15-game road trip, which the papers called the most successful of all time, by any team, ever, in terms of attendance. More than 200,000 fans had turned out to see Ruth, and a couple of thousand more to actually see their own home team. That's just the way it was. On the way back to New York, the Yankees even got off the train and played an exhibition in Columbus, Ohio, that drew 7,000 more. For such contests, Ruppert and the Yankees demanded—and received—85 percent of the gate, of which the players received not a single dime. All Ruth did was hit six out during batting practice, one more in the game, steal two bases, double, and walk twice.

Back in the Polo Grounds, Boston came to town, and Ruth seemed to save some of his best for his old team, diminished as they were. As the Yankees took three of four, Ruth added a triple and two more home runs, bringing his total for the season up to an astounding 23. He was already approaching his 1919 standard, and the season was only half over.

Earlier, Grantland Rice had speculated that Ruth might hit 40 for the season. Now speculation increased to 50, an overwhelming amount as shocking then to think about as 100 home runs is today. Bookmakers loved it. The only time they had been able to take bets on individual achievements before were when pitchers like Walter Johnson, Joe Wood, or Rube Marquard had long winning streaks, but this was different. How many home runs Ruth would hit was a question it would take the rest of the year to answer. The bookies set 50 as a target for Ruth, one they believed was just a bit higher than he was likely to reach and started laying odds. Every fan in the game put a couple dollars down, and some put down five figures.

Ruth was surprising everyone. Never in his wildest dreams had Ruppert imagined this. He would have been happy if Ruth had hit 25 home runs and hit .300—that still would have been spectacular. Now, it was almost as if he had bought two players instead of one.

With only his own record for Ruth to chase, the writers scurried back to the record books and now came up with another mark for Ruth to take aim at, the professional baseball record of 45 home runs set by Perry Worden of Minneapolis in the Western League in 1895, assisted by another little bandbox of a park. It wasn't much of a record, but it served its purpose, and they soon uncovered several other minor leaguers who had struck more than 30 home runs as well. However, this year Ruth did not need anyone else to set a goal. He was taking care of that all by himself.

Ruth's home run bat took a rest when the team went back on the road, but he kept hitting, the fence being his only impediment. The Yankees kept winning, running a winning streak to nine games and taking over first place as Ruth's batting average climbed above .380 behind only Joe Jackson and tied for second with the Browns' George Sisler.

Increasingly, Ruth went his own way. The Yankees, figuring if it wasn't broken, it didn't need to be fixed, put few restrictions on his behavior. On the East Coast, Ruth usually didn't even bother traveling with his teammates anymore. Instead, he drove his Packard, taking great delight in racing from town to town faster than the team, usually smoking a cigar and talking a mile a minute with whomever he decided to bring along.

Early one morning in July, just after midnight, Ruth, the Mrs.—or at least someone the press said was the Mrs.—outfielder Frank Gleich, and Yankee coach Charlie O'Leary were in rural Pennsylvania, just outside Wawa, on their way back to New York. Ruth later claimed that another car cut in front of them, causing him to run off the road, his car flipping over in a ditch. Everyone was banged up—Mrs. Ruth in particular, apparently—and O'Leary temporarily knocked out. Ruth was fine, but at least one newspaper reported that he had been killed. The Colonels drew a deep breath and requested that Ruth travel by train the rest of the year. By this time, the $150,000 insurance policy was woefully inadequate, Ruth was already worth a great deal more. With every home run, his value kept going up.

Back in New York, Ruth found his home run swing again. Whatever had once caused it to evaporate for weeks or months at a time was no longer an issue. Now, his droughts rarely lasted a week, and he homered in three straight games against the Tigers in mid-month to lift his season total to 27. The *Times* noted he showed no favorites and had struck nearly the same number off lefties as he had righties. The last against Detroit, in a 5–4 loss, was notable because it was Ruth's first home run of the year in the Polo Grounds to land in the lower deck. Every other home run had either been into the second deck or onto and over the roof, or into the more distant bleachers. W. O. McGeehan couldn't resist, and wryly noted, "There was some speculation as to whether or not the Infant Swatigy is starting to lose his sock. It might be that they have taken some of the kangaroo wool out of the league baseball, or that there is a falling off in the quality of the thoroughbred horsehide . . . or it might be that The Babe stuck one in the lower stands by way of variety."

With Ruth only three home runs away from a new major league record, crowds over the next few days were immense. Everyone knew that three home runs in a game for Ruth was not impossible. The way things were going, it almost seemed inevitable.

On July 13, a Tuesday, the Yankees scheduled a doubleheader with the Browns to account for an earlier rainout. The crowd started arriving at noon "lured by the prospect of seeing The Babe equal his home run record," according to the *Tribune*. They kept coming until an official record of 38,823 had paid admission. Those were holiday numbers. This was a weekday, at a time when workmen still worked ten- or twelve-hour days and even bankers rarely got off before 3:00 p.m. Suffice to say there was not much work accomplished in Manhattan that day, except in the counting room at the Polo Grounds. Ruth didn't hit any home runs, but he did provide all the entertainment in the sweep, striking out five times and giving all 38,823 fans another record to talk about—no one had ever struck out five times in one day before. He couldn't even fail like anyone else.

He made up for it the following day, hitting a home run before "only" 15,000 fans on a Wednesday, as those who'd played hooky the day before returned to work. He tied the record the next day, hitting a game winner off the facade in the 11th to send another 10,000 fans home happy on a damp and rainy day that led many to think the game would be rained out.

Now that a new record was on deck, the big crowds turned even larger, and the Colonels didn't much care how quickly Ruth broke the mark. He had another 60 games to try, about half in New York. Ruth accommodated them as best as he could by waiting four days, long enough to draw another 100,000 fans into the Polo Grounds, but by now he hit home runs like others found pennies on the sidewalk, by accident. He could hardly help himself.

Ruth went homerless in the first game of the doubleheader against the White Sox on July 20, but ended the drama in the fourth inning of game two off Dickey Kerr. With the count 2–2, Kerr tried a curve and Ruth tried his usual strategy. He swung hard, and knocked the ball just into the stands in deep right field, not his longest of the year by any measure, but longer than anyone else's knock. "Idols are made of Clay," wrote Arthur Robinson in the *New York American*, "and heroes of dust, but the huge bulk of Babe Ruth was covered with the mud of a rain-soaked field . . . [when] he put his massive shoulder behind a terrific swing."

As fans fought for the ball in the bleachers, the crowd did what it could to rise to the occasion and out-cheer every other cheer Ruth had received in 1920, what Marshall Hunt in the *Daily News* termed "an ovation befitting a King." Ruth responded by trying to out-doff himself. After doffing his cap as he wound his way round the bases, and doffing his cap after crossing the plate, Ruth, running out of responses, bowed down to the crowd, sending them into even more hysterics. And just in case anyone had blinked on the first one, in the ninth he dropped number 31 into the stands. After the game, a black youngster allegedly appeared in the clubhouse with the ball, asking only for the privilege of shaking Ruth's hand in return. Ruth not only accommodated but according to Robinson in the *American*, "The Babe smiled, shook the little fellow's hand, patted him on the back and gave him a season pass for the rest of the Yankee games."

The record was his, and henceforth so was history, because that, as much as anything else, is what Ruth and the home runs gave to baseball in 1920: its history. As the professional game evolved over the better part of four decades through the last half of the nineteenth century, the game, the rules, and the conditions under which it was played changed so much and so often that statistical records, beyond who finished first, had little meaning. But as the twentieth century dawned, and the major leagues came to be represented by two stable leagues, the basic rules remaining intact, that had changed. Ruth, by his remarkable performance, caused everyone to look back and realize, perhaps for the first time, that baseball had a history, that it was possible to compare earlier apples with today's oranges. The numbers of the game became a way for games past to live again, and for players not to disappear into history, but emerge from it, to remain significant and valued long after they last appeared on the field. To a degree, this had never happened before. Ruth just wasn't the game's present and its future, but he was also the bearer of its past.

There was talk afterward that the home run had earned Ruth a movie deal worth $100,000. It may not have been tied to the record, and it wasn't worth $100,000, but in the wake of the new mark Ruth did agree to appear in a silent feature. He would soon start filming his dramatic debut, *Headin' Home*.

Directed by Lawrence Windom, the "screenplay" was penned by the *Daily News*'s Bugs Baer, and, ironically, the movie may have been partially financed by the notorious gambler Abe Atell, who would soon be implicated in the Black Sox scandal. The film was a vaguely biographical treatment of Ruth's own life, depicting the slugger as a country boy with a home run bat who can't get a spot on his local team until he hits a towering home run and then finds fame, fortune, and a girl playing in New York. If ever anyone needed evidence of the emerging Ruth myth, *Headin' Home* is it, Ruth's personal biography scrubbed and polished. Filming was scheduled to get under way in August.

Now it was all easy pickings for Ruth, gravy ladled on more gravy, every subsequent home run a record. And now, for the first time, really, they started to lose a little of their shine, what had once seemed so spectacular now a little commonplace, at least in the way the newspapermen reacted. Ruth added four more home runs over the remainder of the home stand the next week to lift his total to 35, as fans kept turning out in record numbers, nearly 65,000 for a split doubleheader on another Tuesday, then 25,000 for games on Wednesday and Thursday and Friday before culminating in two more full houses over the weekend. It didn't hurt that the Yankees were playing mostly winning ball, and that every win or loss seemed to dance them in or out of first place. The Giants were playing well, too, and although they weren't drawing as well as the Yankees, with emerging stars like George "High Pockets" Kelly and Frankie Frisch, they were having a pretty good season, battling Brooklyn for first place. New York was the center of the baseball universe.

Still, the crowds that came out for Ruth were stupefying. For the Saturday game against Cleveland, it wasn't just the 40,000 fans who made it inside the Polo Grounds, there were reported to be another 40,000 who poured out of the subways and failed to get in. And that didn't include the thousands more who wanted to be there who probably figured they'd have no chance of getting a ticket and stayed home. You either had to be there, hear about in the tavern later that night, or read about it in papers. There was, as yet, no radio.

In his column in the *Tribune*, Bill McGeehan took note, writing, "It looks very much like a baseball park with a capacity of 100,000 will have to be built in the near future, for New York, at any rate." He also noted that Ruppert and Huston "displayed considerable acumen," buying the Yankees when they were "a joke," then taking the "biggest gamble" of all on Ruth. It had all paid off.

Ruth went on the team's next western road trip like a conquering hero, greeted with glee everywhere, drawing enormous crowds and sending them home happy in St. Louis, Chicago, and Detroit, hitting home runs in all three cities, failing only in Cleveland. He returned to New York with 41 home runs.

The only notable change had come in Detroit. After batting fourth for the entire year in Detroit, Huggins moved Ruth up a spot in the batting order. Part of the reason was because Bob Meusel, the rookie who was developing into a fearsome hitter in his own right, was in the midst of a slump. Lewis had been batting fifth behind Ruth, but now that he was hurt, the opposition had taken to walking Ruth rather than pitch to him. In one game against Boston, Sam Jones walked him four times. Ruth hated the intentional walk, and there was more than one call for the practice to be banned, although just how that could be enforced was never quite clear. Batting Ruth third allowed Del Pratt, a dangerous hitter, to bat behind the Babe.

Huggins indicated it was just a temporary move, but it became permanent. Ruth would primarily hit third for the remainder of his Yankee career—even when paired with Lou Gehrig, Ruth hit third and Gehrig batted cleanup. Not only did it place Ruth in the most productive spot in the lineup, it also meant the one player in the majors most likely to hit a home run batted in the first inning of every game, giving the Yankees a fair chance at an early lead. It also kept the other team from pitching around him quite as much. When they did, they were more likely to pay a price.

The Yankees retuned to New York and opened a home stand against Cleveland on August 16. Trailing the Indians by only half a game, the three-game series was perhaps the most important the Yankees had played since facing Boston at the tail end of the 1904 season with the pennant on the line. A sweep could give the Yankees both first place and some margin for error in the race. If they were swept, however, their pennant hopes would likely pass.

New York lost the first game 4–3, Ruth contributing only a single hit. But the game would go down in baseball history as the most tragic ever played. Leading off the fifth inning against Carl Mays, Cleveland shortstop Ray Chapman crouched over the plate. Mays threw, the pitch sailed up and in, he heard a crack, saw the ball bouncing back, and thinking it had struck Chapman's bat, fielded the ball and threw to first. Only then did he and everyone else realize that the sound had not come from the ball hitting the bat, but from striking Chapman's skull. The pitch had hit him on the left side of the head and the batter now lay half conscious in the batter's box.

Although Chapman managed to stand, he had to be helped from the field and then collapsed again and was rushed to the hospital. The pitch had caused a three-and-a-half-inch depressed fracture of his skull. Chapman underwent emergency surgery, but died the next day, the only death caused by an on-field injury in the history of major league baseball.

Mays, roundly hated by the baseball community, would take the brunt of the blame, as players charged that he both beaned Chapman on purpose, threw an illegal pitch, or both. Despite some calls to have him banned for the game—Ban Johnson blurted that he couldn't see how Mays could possibly pitch again—others came to the pitcher's defense. His catcher, Muddy Ruel, said he thought Chapman lost the pitch and that he never moved to get out of the way.

The Yankees backed their pitcher—this was a pennant race, after all. And Mays, while not unaffected, pitched a week later. Ruth, however, was apparently not indifferent. He never made a public comment about the tragedy or about whether he thought the pitch was intentional. Every batter knew they were taking a chance stepping in the box. That's just the way the game was played. But the incident would still have a major impact on Ruth's career.

It is somewhat surprising that Chapman's death did not spark a debate about the baseball. After all, no one had ever been killed by the old, dead ball. But at this point, the lively ball—or whatever it was—was too well established, and the home run game too lucrative, to change. And it was impossible to gauge how much impact the ball had on the injury.

In the wake of Chapman's death, baseball became even more generous with the use of new baseballs. Over time, any ball that was discolored or scuffed in any way would be removed and a new clean baseball, presumably easier to see and less prone to taking an erratic break on the way to the plate, put into play. Ruth would be the greatest beneficiary of anyone taking a swing at a ball that was easier to see.

The Yankees, perhaps distracted by Chapman's death, scuffled for the next week. In the meantime, however, the show went on. Ruth spent his mornings traveling to a movie studio in Haverstraw, New Jersey, shooting scenes for *Headin' Home*, often arriving at the ballpark sporting pancake makeup and eyeliner. He'd been paid $15,000 up front and promised another $35,000 and the filmmaker was trying to rush the seventy-one-minute film to completion before the end of the season. Ruth played okay during filming, but he managed only two home runs for the home stand. On the morning of August 22, the crew took over the ballpark, filming the penultimate passage, Ruth at bat cracking the game-winning home run, and then being swarmed by the fans, the staged scene the only one in the whole movie with a shred of truth to it.

After homering on August 26 for number 44, however, Ruth was out of the lineup. The official story was that he'd been stung by something during filming, and that his wrist had become infected. But the *Tribune* implied something a bit less innocent, calling the malady the "Jersey Jiggers," which they termed a form of "dry hydrophobia," which may have been a veiled reference to something alcohol-related. Ruth was hospitalized, and supposedly had tissue removed. That sent local gamblers into a panic. A lot of money had been put down betting that Ruth would break the home run barrier of 50.

While Ruth sat out, his legal battles over the earlier film headed to the courts, a series of injunctions and countersuits and counter-injunctions. Ruth eventually lost on all counts, the attorneys for both parties the only individuals making any real money out of it.

It was a bad time for Ruth to be out of the lineup. By the time he returned, although the Yankees had slipped back into first place, they hadn't really been playing well. With Ruth, they might have opened up a lead over Cleveland, but they didn't. The Indians then began playing inspired baseball and the White Sox weren't giving up, either. There was some grousing among Ruth's teammates who thought he should have been in the lineup, but where the Yankees finished was now third on the club's list of priorities, behind Ruth's home run count and the attendance. Still, the World Series held out the promise of even more money for everyone.

Or did it? In the National League, the Robins were the surprise of the league and had opened up ground on the Giants. As lucrative as a World Series between the Yankees and Robins might have been, Ebbets Field lacked the capacity of the Polo Grounds, and the Yankees' real rival was the Giants, and always had been. If Brooklyn took the pennant, and the

Yankees finished behind either Cleveland or Chicago, that would leave both the Yanks and the Giants available for a city series, a once common post-season exhibition between two teams from the same city. They often charged World Series prices, and on the local level were often bigger than the World Series, particularly among gamblers. Ruth was already a bigger attraction than the Robins, World Series or not, and a city series between the Giants and Yankees, with every game played in the Polo Grounds before 40,000 fans, could draw nearly 300,000, far more lucrative for either club than the World Series, where the take had to be split among the National Commission and the second, third, and fourth place teams. It was almost as if the Yankees didn't need to win—there would be a big payday anyway.

Ruth returned to duty two days before Labor Day in Boston, guaranteeing Frazee a big crowd for the Saturday doubleheader. He homered twice, calming the gamblers worried about losing their rolls, and the Yankees took two of three. Although Ruth was pitched around for much of the next ten days, walking 20 times, the Yankees won 10 of 12 to not only stay in the race, but pull ahead, as they took two of three from the Indians in Cleveland and swept Detroit, Ruth chipping in three more home runs to bring his season total to 49, then hitting two more in an exhibition in Toledo on September 15. The Yankees might well have done better to rest, however, because they went into Chicago on September 16 with the pennant on the line.

The first game came down to Ruth, or at least that is how everyone saw it afterward. The White Sox jumped out to a 4–0 lead, but in the sixth the Yankees pushed across two, bringing Ruth to the plate with two out, two on, and Dickey Kerr on the mound. He worked the count to 2-2. A home run would put the Yankees up by a run.

They weren't so easy to hit when they really mattered. Ruth took a called third strike. The White Sox rolled to an 8–3 win and dropped the Yankees out of first place as Cleveland won to take first.

The Yankees never made it back to the top. Ruth went hitless the next day in a 6–4 loss and then New York made it three in a row, being blown out 15–9 after falling behind 8–0 in the first two innings. The White Sox passed the Yankees, now in third place, trailing by three games with only 10 left to play, and Ruth homerless since striking number 49.

Nevertheless, he was still attracting a crowd in New York. *Headin' Home* was finished, and promoter Tex Rickard, owner of Madison Square Garden, paid $35,000 for exclusive rights to debut the film. The Garden wasn't meant to be a movie theater, but Rickard figured Ruth was worth it. He had to overhaul and redecorate to accommodate the picture, draping thousands of yards of fabric over the windows, and due to the size of the room, had to have a special movie screen made, 35 feet by 27 feet, then the biggest in the world, to show the film. With a seating capacity of almost 10,000, and the appetite for Ruth ravenous, he thought he would print money.

Unfortunately, *Headin' Home* was no *Intolerance*. It was a predictable, wooden set piece. Ruth was serviceable but hardly a Valentino, who in another year would make the ladies swoon. As one critic put it, "The story is ridiculous. . . . He [Ruth] and he alone makes it worth five minutes of anybody's time." Ouch. Today, the main interest in the film is the brief footage it shows of Ruth batting in the Polo Grounds, swinging his bat. It's thrilling to see.

The Yankees weren't going to win the pennant and Ruth was never going to become a film star. That was obvious. Now it was all about the numbers.

Without the pressure of the pennant race, Ruth seemed able to relax again. The Yankees returned home on September 24 for a doubleheader versus Washington and Ruth still proved a draw, pulling nearly 30,000 fans to see the real thing. He didn't disappoint, cracking home run number 50 in game one and 51 in game two. The *Times* called him "the greatest pickler the world has ever known."

The gamblers called him something else. As the *New York Sun* reported, "more money than Babe Ruth's salary, a good deal more . . . changed hands yesterday. The bet for Ruth to hit 50 was one of the liveliest betting propositions of the year." The paper reported that although "a majority of baseball fans" had not thought Ruth would make the mark, many gamblers did, and some cleared as much as $50,000. And for those keeping track, it was also Ruth's 100th career home run.

The season wasn't quite over yet, but everybody was already in the counting house. The Colonels announced they were ready to throw off the yoke of the Polo Grounds and would soon build their own ballpark. They claimed to be looking at three different sites. Ruth had made it possible. Although construction on Yankee Stadium would not start until 1922, and not be complete until 1923, it would not just be the House that Ruth Built but also the House Built for Ruth, not only bigger than the Polo Grounds but with dimensions that suited the Yankee slugger, not quite as close down the line in right, but much closer and more forgiving in the power alley. It would be his private stage, and a place he would rule even long after he played his last game there.

Fans poured into the Polo Grounds the last week of the season as if paying tribute, but Ruth played his final game at the Polo Grounds in 1920 on September 26, still stuck at 51 home runs. This time, however, he would not jump his team at the finish. The Yankees went to Philadelphia to end the season, and Ruth played all three games, not that the A's provided much competition or played very hard. He hit home runs 52 and 53 on September 27 in a game that took all of 66 minutes to play, and then finished his slugging in the final inning of the first game of a doubleheader two days later, homering in the ninth to settle on number 54 for the season, 25 more than he or any other human being had hit in 1919.

The Yankees finished third, behind pennant-winning Cleveland and Chicago. In addition to his 54 home runs, Ruth scored a record 158 runs, knocked in 135, and walked 150 times while striking out 80. He hit .376, with a .532 on base percentage, .847 slugging percentage, and modern day OPS of a gaudy 1.379, the last three figures the best single season marks of his career. The Yankees drew a stunning 1,289,422 fans to the Polo Grounds, 300,000 more than the Giants and nearly twice the number of fans any team had ever drawn in a previous season. The Red Sox drew just over 400,000. Five million fans spun through the turnstiles in the American League, almost a million and half more than ever before, about half of the total at games featuring Ruth, as he was clearly the biggest road draw in history.

The Yankees earned a pretax profit of $666,000, as home ticket receipts increased by a half million dollars to $864,830 and road receipts tripled to $273,000. League-wide, the men who owned baseball probably grossed at least an extra $2 million in 1920, all because of Ruth. For that, Ruth was paid $20,000.

And that wasn't the half of it.

The sale of the Babe to the Yankees not only resulted in selling an entire city on Ruth, but an entire nation, as fans of the sport embraced an entirely new game, played a new way, for a new reason. Just as the Babe would take the title as the King of All Sluggers (or depending on your taste, the Bambino, the Big Bam, the Sultan of Swat, Behemoth of Bust, Maharajah of Mash, Wazir of Wham, Rajah of Rap, or the Caliph of Clout), his signature accomplishment, the home run, was now the one single play that brought fans out to the ballpark. It was what kept them talking about the game and reading the papers afterward, and that lit the fires of the Hot Stove League all winter long.

Moreover, he fired the imagination, and expanded the capacity of dreams, of possibilities. After seeing Ruth, all things seemed possible.

Babe Ruth had delivered in every possible way.

The Yankees and Giants still wanted to play a city series, salivating at the financial returns, but Ban Johnson still had some pull. And he had not forgotten.

While Ruth was distracting most of the baseball public, the festering rumors over the 1919 World Series came to a head. A grand jury was convened in Chicago to investigate. One day before the end of the season, on September 28, Joe Jackson and Eddie Cicotte confessed. In another month, indictments would be handed down.

Baseball was already nervous. Rumors of scandal were everywhere. National League president John Heydler, speaking for the National Commission, let it be known that the three-man group, including Johnson, would not authorize any plans for a city series between the Yankees and Giants, even one that featured Babe Ruth. They would, he said, block any attempt to hold such a "money-making scheme."

Epilogue:
Closing the Sale

In every possible way but a pennant, Ruth's first season had been a resounding success. It was already hard to imagine George Ruth before Babe Ruth, Babe Ruth before the Babe, the Yankees, and even New York or the game of baseball before the Babe. He and the sport were now synonymous, the game's history cleaved in two, the Dead Ball Era and the present.

Ruth was also synonymous with one more thing—money. And since organized baseball would not authorize a city series, Ruth did the next best thing and went barnstorming, putting a team together with his old Boston teammate Wally Schang and Carl Mays, the inclusion of the pitcher a macabre attraction in the wake of Chapman's death. At the same time, while he toured the Northeast and New England, he was "writing" an account of the World Series between the Indians and Brooklyn for the newspapers. A minor scandal broke out when one reporter had the audacity to reveal that Ruth, in fact, was nowhere near the World Series, hadn't seen an inning, and was barely following it at all. "Babe is apparently as good a long distance reporter as he is a long distance hitter," wrote the *Times*.

Then Ruth ended up back in court—over money. He hadn't received the $35,000 he was still due for *Headin' Home* and was ticked off. He went to court and sued for the remaining amount. However, he also got some bad advice and had a restraining order taken out prohibiting the showing of the film, which had long since left Madison Square Garden for much more modest theaters.

Ruth would eventually become a victim of both Hollywood accounting and his own naïveté. Shutting down the picture cut off any possible source of income from the film. Prohibited from showing the film, the company that produced the picture folded, leaving Ruth only a bounced check and a fat legal fee. Outside the batter's box, he was still a rube. Bad advice was proving ever more costly.

He hurt his wrist sliding during a game in Oneonta, New York, and reports suggested he'd broken a small bone, but he still hit a home run. He probably should have sat out the rest of the off-season but the lure of the sun, and the dollar bill, proved too strong. He finished the barnstorming tour, laughed off the story about the broken wrist, and went into business with Giants manager John McGraw, money bringing the rivals together.

Only a year before, McGraw had said that Ruth would hit into "a hundred double plays." That hadn't happened, but he had drawn millions of fans to the ballpark, and that's all McGraw cared about now. He had put together a team to go to Cuba for a month and Ruth came along, the number one draw. He didn't play very well or make much money—well, he did earn $20,000, but he lost it all gambling.

In the meantime, the Black Sox scandal blew wide open. In mid-October eight members of the Chicago White Sox, pitchers Eddie Cicotte and Lefty Williams, third baseman Buck Weaver, infielders Fred McMullin and Swede Risberg, outfielders Joe Jackson and Happy Felsch, and Ruth's neighbor at the Ansonia, Chick Gandil, were indicted by a grand jury for their role in fixing the 1919 World Series. If one included Sport Sullivan, Ruth had more than a passing relationship with at least three of the men, and while no one has ever suggested Ruth had any involvement in the scandal, that had to be of some concern, not only to him, but to Jacob Ruppert and the National Commission. He needed to be careful who he hung around with.

While it would later become a cliché to say that Ruth saved baseball after the scandal, the truth is he already had. The Black Sox could have been indicted for murder and it wouldn't have made any difference to the future of the game. Fans would have continued to pour into the stands. The game as it had been played in 1919 was already dead. Nobody outside the newspapers and Chicago much cared.

However, it proved to be the final blow for Ban Johnson. After the season, the owners of the National League and the Insurrectos all met in Chicago to discuss the so-called Lasker plan, floated by Cubs owner Albert Lasker, a proposal to have major league baseball administered by a single, impartial commissioner, or at least one not so obviously and inextricably bound up in the petty politics of the club owners. The plan much resembled the same idea earlier put forth by Harry Frazee, and one that he had long advocated.

Another bitter, tempestuous meeting ensued, followed by backroom arm-twisting, virtual bribery and threats, as Johnson and the Loyal Five resisted as long as possible, but in the end, faced with a threat from the National League and the Insurrectos to break off and form their own league—significantly, taking Ruth with them—they capitulated. The notion of a major league existing apart from Ruth was no longer tenable— that's how big he was. In the end, baseball scrapped the old National Agreement that had governed baseball for decades, and adopted the commissioner system. On November 12, Judge Kenesaw Mountain Landis, familiar with the sport through his work on both the Federal League case and the Black Sox scandal, agreed to become the first commissioner of baseball.

Ban Johnson was finished, a figurehead from here forward, but his league would continue on, in part due to his initial genius at its creation, but moving forward, fueled by the engine of Ruth, the home run, and the game he created. Johnson, totally by chance, had played a major role in that, but not in any way he ever intended or planned. It remains a lasting yet thoroughly accidental legacy. Johnson stayed on as AL president another six years, the bulk of his power gone, resigning because of ill health in 1927 before passing away on March 28, 1931.

Frazee had kept his team, and over the next few seasons the Red Sox would repeat their familiar pattern of getting off to a good start, then fading. Frozen out by the Loyal Five, Frazee stubbornly held on and tried to rebuild his ball club, but he simply could not compete with the juggernaut in New York. No one could, at least in the box office or the bank account. The Red Sox, after finishing fifth in 1920 and 1921, then fell to last place. Still, on Frazee's terms, the Ruth sale had been a success and done exactly what he needed it to; he had saved his team, and protected its value. Midway through the 1923 season, he finally sold out, getting $1.2 million— twice what he had paid for the club, from a syndicate led by Bob Quinn. Frazee turned his full attention back to the theater. Opening first in Chicago in 1924, *No, No, Nanette* became a hit, made it to Broadway in 1925 and then overseas, earning Frazee millions. Unfortunately, he would have only five years to enjoy his success, dying of Bright's disease on June 4, 1929. When he died, no one blamed him for anything.

Under Bob Quinn, the Red Sox sank to the very bottom as their main investor, Palmer Winslow, died, leaving the team underfinanced. In 1933, they were purchased by Tom Yawkey, who spent millions of the team, but under Yawkey and those who ran the franchise in the Yawkey tradition, saddled by mismanagement and institutional racism, the Red Sox failed to win another world championship until 2004. The spurious "Curse of the Bambino" would be invented out of whole cloth years later, a way to excuse the continuing failure of the Red Sox under Yawkey, who despite his wallet never won anything apart from a reputation as a bigot. Not until the Yawkey legacy was finally erased did the team manage to accomplish what it had last done in 1918, when Frazee owned the team and Ruth was a pitcher.

The deal worked for Joseph Lannin, too. He got his money from Frazee, made his real estate deal, and continued to find some success as a real estate developer. But on May 15, 1928, he fell—or jumped, or was pushed, no one was ever certain—from a narrow window of the Hotel Granada in Brooklyn, and died at age sixty-two.

It also worked for Jacob Ruppert. His big gamble paid off in every way possible, as Ruth outperformed even the most generous and optimistic expectations. Under Ruppert, the Yankees became a dynasty and Ruppert's legacy became one not built from beer and politics, but baseball. By the time he passed on January 13, 1939, his Yankees had won seven world championships and the Yankees, who Ruppert and Huston purchased for less than a half million dollars, were valued at more than $3 million. And in 2014, he was finally inducted into the National Baseball Hall of Fame.

The game Ruth created reigned. Season by season, more and more players adopted his style of hitting, and in only a few years the old scientific style of baseball became an utter anachronism. New, younger sluggers, who grew up swinging the bat the way Ruth did, and not the way Cobb had, soon began entering the game. Lou Gehrig, Ruth's teammate, a native New Yorker and Columbia graduate, was one of the first and perhaps the best of this new breed. Their success in tandem in the Yankee lineup fully relegated the old style of play to the history books, proof that Ruth was not singularly superhuman—not quite—but that his method and approach could be learned and put into practice by others. As result, major league attendance would maintain the lofty levels it reached in 1920, and never look back, surviving even the Depression and another world war. Everybody would make money off Ruth and his game. By the 1940s, there were no players left who had been active in the Dead Ball Era.

And Ruth himself? Fifty-four home runs in 1920 would be followed by 59 in 1921, and 60 in 1927. He would play at the highest level for the next decade, setting records too numerous to count. The Yankees would make the World Series for the first time in 1921, win it for the first time in 1923, and win three more titles with Ruth on the roster, becoming baseball's dominant team and most enduring dynasty.

Off the field, Ruth remained much the same problematic, self-absorbed, guileless yet occasionally troublesome player he had been in Boston. While making records in New York he'd also suffered from venereal disease, alcoholism, gain a tremendous amount of weight, and suffer from a host of other physical maladies, be suspended by his team several times, reportedly be stabbed and shot at by angry husbands and jilted women, wreck any number of cars, leave his wife, and do all sorts of things that would have brought down any other man in the game . . . and be celebrated for it.

Ruth's inherent, candid good nature was part of the reason, but so was the way his talent was inoculated by those around him. Ruth was too big to fail, too important to the game, and as Ruth's career continued, his protectors became more adept. Home runs, it seemed, covered all sins large and small, and Ruth had a great time seeing just how true that was. So did sportswriters, and no one would have a greater influence on Ruth—or, in the end, cover more of his sins with boyish boosterish and often bamboozling goodwill—than a young writer named Christy Walsh. Late in 1920, Walsh met Ruth, and closed the sale for good.

An attorney by trade, Walsh first dabbled in the newspaper business before joining an auto company in advertising. After being fired, he returned to words and had his first big success in 1919, ghostwriting an account of the Indianapolis 500 for world war flying ace Eddie Rickenbacker, splitting the $800 fee. This gave Walsh the germ of an idea; he envisioned his own syndicate of athlete-authors, all backed by a stable of ghostwriters he would pluck from the pages of American newspapers.

There was nothing new about the idea itself—newspapers had featured such stories for years, but putting it all together under a single, organized umbrella, managed by one man, was. Walsh envisioned not just doing a single story with an athlete and then moving on, but—for lack of a better phrase—building a brand.

Who better to start with than Ruth? Walsh had briefly met the Babe in 1919, but by the end of the 1920 season, even as it became more and more obvious that Ruth needed some kind of financial help and advisor, Ruth was beginning to use a bit more caution with whom he met and invited to his apartment. Walsh used to wait outside and Ruth repeatedly brushed him off. At the same time, Ruth was besieged by offers for endorsements and investments and business deals of all kinds. He was ill equipped to sort them out and after the debacle with the film, and now the Black Sox scandal, increasingly untrusting.

Walsh finally worked a ruse to get an audience with Ruth, making a delivery of beer. Once inside, he got Ruth's ear and peppered him with questions about his business deals. When he discovered Ruth was putting his name to a small, syndicated series of stories for only $5 an article, Walsh told Ruth he could get him at least 500 bucks to put his name on anything.

That got Ruth's attention. Walsh went off with Ruth's tacit permission to act as his agent, and came back the next day with a contract, pushing it through the gated door. Ruth signed it and Walsh left, promising to return with cash. When he did, he produced a more formal document. It promised that Walsh would solicit "syndicated baseball columns" ghostwritten "by qualified sporting writers" and signed "By Babe Ruth." In return, Walsh indicated "I agree to pay you Fifty (50) Percent of the gross receipts, a special consideration. My profit and all office and syndicating expenses, including printing, postage etc. will come from the balance." Ruth scrawled his name to the contract.

With that signature, the Babe became the first baseball player to sign with an agent. Walsh eventually became his closest friend and most trusted advisor, protecting both his reputation and his bank account.

From that moment on, the selling of the Babe was a full-fledged business. The modern game—the Babe's game—was now fully in place.

Notes

Introduction

2. There are thousands upon thousands of words credited to Ruth's lips: A particularly good discussion of Ruth and the role his ghostwriters played in his life appears in Kal Wagenheim, *Babe Ruth: His Life and Legend* (New York: Henry Holt, 1974).

Prologue: September 11, 1918

5. In the eighth inning of the sixth and final game: Composite details of Game 6 of the 1918 World Series were re-created from several sources, namely game reports dated September 12, 1918, from the following newspapers: *Boston Globe, Boston Post, Boston Herald and Journal, Boston American, New York Times,* and *Chicago Tribune.* Also useful were the author's previous accounts of the 1918 World Series: "1918," *Boston Magazine,* October 1987, pp. 141–47; and "The Last Champions," *New England Sport,* Summer 1993, pp. 23–31; and in Richard Johnson and Glenn Stout, *Red Sox Century* (Boston: Houghton Mifflin, 1999), pp. 133–34.

5. Boston's left fielder: George Whiteman's role in the series is discussed in detail in F. C. Lane, "Hero of the Series," *Baseball Magazine,* November 1918.

1. George Herman Ruth

11. "I saw a man": Harry Hooper as quoted by Lawrence Ritter in his oral history, *The Glory of Their Times* (New York: Macmillan, 1984), p. 137.

11. When George Ruth arrived: As explained in the head notes to the Bibliography, in addition to newspaper accounts, three books were of particular help in re-creating the events of 1918 in this and subsequent chapters: Allan Wood's *1918: Babe Ruth and the World Champion Boston Red Sox* (New York: Writers Club, 2000); Kerry Keene, Ray Sinibaldi, and David Hickey's *The Babe in Red Stockings* (Champaign, Ill.: Sagamore, 1997); and Ty Waterman and Mel Springer's *The Year the Red Sox Won the World Series* (Boston: Northeastern University Press, 1999).

11. spring training in Hot Springs, Arkansas: Boston's trip to Hot Springs is described from the following: "Red Sox Take Ozark Trail Today," *Boston Daily Globe,* March 9, 1918; and "Eibel Fails to Join Red Sox in Albany," *Boston Daily Globe,* March 10, 1918. Other events of spring training are primarily built from press reports in the *Boston Globe*

and *Boston Post*, March 1918. Useful background on Hot Springs as a spring training site can be found in Tim Gay, *Tris Speaker* (Guilford, Conn.: Lyons/University of Nebraska, 2007); Paul Zingg, *Harry Hooper* (Urbana: University of Illinois Press, 1993); and Richard A. Johnson and Glenn Stout, *Red Sox Century* (Boston: Houghton Mifflin, 1999).

12. Ruth's performance finally earned him a big contract: According to Ruth's contract, his initial salary in 1918 was $5,000. A facsimile appears here: http://news.yahoo .com/babe-ruth-s-1919-contract-sells-for—1-02-million-at-auction-140200668.html.

12. He just wasn't like other players: Average size of war recruits is discussed here: http://www.tommy1418.com/wwi-facts—figures—myths.html. Ruth's height and address in Boston appear on his draft card, available here: http://www.archives.gov/atlanta/wwi -draft/ruth.html.

13. "he bends things of metal": *Boston Post*, January 12, 1918.

13. He didn't even use the same bat as other players: Depending on the source, the weight of the bat used by Ruth is usually described as anywhere between 37 ounces and 54 ounces, the 54-ounce bat usually cited as the bat Ruth used in 1918 but only in spring training thereafter. Records held by Louisville Slugger indicate that after 1920 Ruth generally ordered bats between 40 and 47 ounces. See http://www.ask.com/sports -active-lifestyle/weight-babe-ruth-s-bat-44377e44b466a6d9#.

15. Batavia Street became so notorious the city later renamed it: Nation's Cities v. 16–17, National League of Cities; American Municipal Association. n.d. p. 17.

16. With the average yearly household income: Average American income in 1918 is provided by the National Bureau of Labor Statistics: http://www.bls.gov/opub/uscs/1918 -19.pdf.

16. The basics of his biography: For basic biographical details in regard to Ruth's early life, see Robert Creamer, *Babe: The Legend Comes to Life* (New York: Simon & Schuster, 1992); and Wagenheim, *Babe Ruth*.

17. "Ruth's power": *Boston Post*, January 11, 1918.

20. After studying law and working for a newspaper, the young Johnson: Basic background on Ban Johnson, as well as some information in regard to Johnson's war with Frazee, can be found in Eugene Murdock, *Ban Johnson: Czar of Baseball* (Westport, Conn.: Greenwood, 1982).

20. Still, no one was quite sure how the war would affect the game: Basic background information on the impact of World War I on major league baseball can be found in Harold Seymour, *Baseball—The Golden Age* (New York: Oxford University Press, 1971).

21. Who was Harry Frazee?: Harry Frazee's basic biography appears in F. C. Lane, "The Fire Brand of the American League," *Baseball Magazine*, March 1919, p. 676; and "H. H. Frazee," *New York Clipper*, June 8, 1912, p. 3.

25. "essentially show business": Lane, "The Fire Brand of the American League," p. 676.

26. Why, he even employed *black actors*: In regard to Frazee's relationship with African Americans, in addition to backing black boxers and hiring black actors, documents

in his archive indicate he made substantial donations to Fisk University, the historically black college in Nashville, Tennessee. One letter from Fisk asks for $100,000.

27. "never forgets an enemy": Murdock, *Ban Johnson.*

28. "the heaviest financial deal": *Boston Herald and Journal*, January 11, 1918.

29. "Well, Ed": *Boston American*, February 16, 1918.

2. This Means War

31. "I'd be the laughingstock": Creamer, *Babe*, p. 152.

33. "'Hal Chase' Ruth": *Boston Globe*, March 18, 1918.

33. Although it was about 360 feet to the fence: Background on Whittington Park and Hot Springs baseball can be found at http://www.hotspringsbaseballtrail.com/.

34. "He could experiment at the plate": Creamer, *Babe*, p. 109.

34. "This is getting painful": *Boston Globe,* March 21, 1918.

34. "the colossus": Keene, Sinibaldi, and Hickey, *The Babe in Red Stockings*, p. 156.

35. "the right field pavilion": *Boston Post,* March 24, 1918.

37. "disappointed when they don't read": Keene, Sinibaldi, and Hickey, *The Babe in Red Stockings,* p. 159.

37. "There is every reason": *Boston Herald and Journal*, April 14, 1918.

3. 1918

39. "He was like a damn animal": Martin Smelser, *The Life That Ruth Built* (New York: Quadrangle/New York Times, 1975), p. 76.

40. In less than a decade, the number of minor leagues: Information on attendance and minor leagues in regard to baseball's popularity appears in *Total Baseball* (third edition).

41. "formed by yarn": David Nemec, *The Official Rules of Baseball Illustrated* (Boston: Lyons, 2006).

42. He arrived early: Ruth's usual pregame routine in Boston is discussed in Wood, *1918.*

43. "with a sort of conservation of appreciation apparent": *Boston Globe*, April 16, 1918.

44. so-called blue laws were in place: For a discussion of baseball and the blue laws, see http://www.thebaseballzealot.com/baseball-history/sunday-baseball-the-history-of -blue-laws. Although Sunday baseball was legalized in New York in 1918 it was not put into effect in the major leagues until the 1920 season.

45. "colossal southpaw pitcher": *Boston Herald and Journal*, April 30, 1918.

45. The New York Yankees were the most intriguing destination: For background on Yankees history pre-Ruppert, see Richard Johnson and Glenn Stout, *Yankees Century* (Boston: Houghton Mifflin, 2003).

48. "the fear of the Lord": *New York Tribune*, May 5, 1918, in Waterman and Springer, *The Year the Red Sox Won the World Series*, p. 62.

48. "Babe Ruth Is Hero, Wields Vicious Cudgel": *New York Times*, May 5, 1918.

49. horsehide the leather of choice: Information on the use of horsehide by the U.S. government during World War I can be found in Bernard M. Baruch, *American Industry in the War: A Report of the War Industries Board* (Washington, D.C.: U.S. Government Printing Office, 1921).

49. Almost overnight, the quality of materials: A good discussion of the changing quality of wool used in baseballs during this period appears in William F. McNeil, *The Evolution of Pitching in Major League Baseball* (Jefferson, N.C.: McFarland, 2006), pp. 59, 60. A terrific discussion of the topic appears here: http://www.baseball-fever.com /showthread.php?31016-Discussion-on-Baseballs-through-the-years. See also Seymour, *Baseball: The Golden Age*, p. 423; and http://www.baseball-reference.com/bullpen /Deadball_Era. For a discussion of knitting and World War I see http://www.historylink .org/index.cfm?DisplayPage=output.cfm&File_Id=5721.

51. "Ruth Starts Rally, but Red Sox Lose": *Boston Globe*, May 7, 1918.

51. "knocked the back out of the seat": *New York Tribune*, May 7, 1918.

52. "Babe Ruth remains the hitting idol": *Boston Post*, May 7, 1918.

52. "it sailed on and on": *Boston Herald and Journal*, May 8, 1918, in Waterman and Springer, *The Year the Red Sox Won the World Series*, p. 65.

55. "Ruth is the large rumble": *The Sporting News,* May 16, 1918.

55. "It's lonesome out there": *Boston Herald and Journal*, May 11, 1918, in Waterman and Springer, *The Year the Red Sox Won the World Series*, p. 67.

56. "There is a world of speculation": Nick Flately, *Boston Record*, May 11, 1918, in ibid.

56. "the most valuable player": *Boston Record*, May 13, 1918.

57. For the next week, baseball stomped its feet and whined: The machinations between major league baseball and the United States War Department in regard to the eligibility of ballplayers for the draft and their possible exemption from the "work or fight" order could easily be the subject of a book itself. The author has previously discussed this in detail in Johnson and Stout, *Red Sox Century*. It also receives a full explication in Seymour, *Baseball: The Golden Age. The Sporting News* during this period also published dozens of articles on baseball's reactions to the war.

57. "No ruling as to whether baseball players": *Boston Globe,* May 24, 1918, p. 1.

57. "Certainly we want to win the war": Ibid.

57. "all forms of amusements" Ibid.

58. "It is a wonder": *Boston Herald and Journal*, May 17, 1918.

60. "the hardest hit ball of the year": *Boston Post*, June 3, 1918.

60. "it's almost impossible to keep him out of the game": *Detroit News*, June 1, 1918, in Waterman and Springer, *The Year the Red Sox Won the World Series*, p. 91.

60. "I get sleepy out there in the field": *Cleveland Press*, June 6, 1918, in ibid., p. 96.

63. "tornadic thumps": *Boston Herald and Journal*, June 26, 1918.

63. "Babe can hit telegraph poles": Ibid.

63. "his collection of four-play slams": *Boston American*, July 1, 1918, in Waterman and Springer, *The Year the Red Sox Won the World Series*, p. 120.

64. "That was a bum play": Creamer, *Babe*, p. 162.

65. "for heavy damages": *Boston Herald and Journal*, July 4, 1918, in Waterman and Springer, *The Year the Red Sox Won the World Series*, p. 122.

65. "Not a single player": *Boston Post,* July 4, 1918.

66. "only a big boy": *The Sporting News*, July 25, 1918.

66. "my wing was a little off": Wood, *1918*, p. 182.

67. "will absolutely crush a business": *Wilmington* (Delaware) *Morning Star*, June 22, 1918.

67. "the work-or-fight regulations include baseball": Wood, *1918*, p. 186.

67. "use of persons not available": Johnson and Stout, *Red Sox Century*, p. 125.

68. "not right and not necessary": Wood, *1918*, p. 188.

68. "BASEBALL GIVEN REPRIEVE": *Boston Globe*, July 27, 1918.

69. "From now on the club owners": Wood, *1918*, p. 201.

4. Hijinks and Heroes

71. "Babe Ruth tried to win the bat": *Boston Record*, September 15, 1918, in Waterman and Springer, *The Year the Red Sox Won the World Series*, p. 64.

73. First, the owners figured out a way to screw the players: The release of the players as a cost-cutting measure is discussed in detail in Wood, *1918*, p. 220.

73. "a Johnsonian slap at Frazee": *Boston Globe*, August 26, 1918.

73. "an insult to Boston fans": Michael T. Lynch Jr., *Harry Frazee, Ban Johnson and the Feud That Nearly Destroyed the American League* (Jefferson, N.C.: McFarland, 2008), p. 52.

73. "Someday Frazee will learn": *Chicago Tribune,* August 27, 1918.

74. Had the Series taken place a month or so before: For a more detailed discussion of the 1918 World Series, see Glenn Stout, "1918," *Boston Magazine*, October 1987, pp. 141–47; Glenn Stout, "The Last Champions," *New England Sport*, Summer 1993, pp. 23–31; and Johnson and Stout, *Red Sox Century*, pp. 133–134.

76. "was to keep the Battering Babe Ruth": Johnson and Stout, *Red Sox Century*, p. 126.

76. "I hope I don't have to sit": *Boston Herald and Journal*, September 4, 1918.

77. The situation was both tawdry and sad: A more complete explanation of the fight that resulted in the death of Ruth's father appears in Leigh Montville, *The Big Bam: The Life and Times of Babe Ruth* (New York: Broadway, 2006), pp. 75–76.

78. "Three times this afternoon": Johnson and Stout, *Red Sox Century*, p. 128.

78. "the effect of the war": *Boston Globe*, September 10, 1918.

86. "big Babe Ruth's mighty bat": Ibid.

88. "if they concede anything": *Boston American*, September 11, 1918.

88. "I made it possible Harry": Ibid.

89. "have agreed to play": Johnson and Stout, *Red Sox Century*, p. 133.

89. "a lot of other names": *Boston Globe*, September 11, 1918.

90. "baseball is dead": *Boston Post*, September 12, 1918.

91. "Hooper, Ruth, Mays, Shean, Schang, Scott": *Boston Globe*, September 12, 1918.

92. "I have never asked for anything in my life": Glenn Stout, "The Last Champions," *New England Sport,* Summer 1993, p. 36.

93. "the whole gang of them": William Ecenbarger, "A Field Where the Babe Was No Hero," *Chicago Tribune*, September 21, 1987.

5. Out of Left Field

95. "Ruth made a grave mistake": Robert Redmount, *Red Sox Encyclopedia* (Darby, Penn.: Diane Publishing, 2002), p. 268.

97. William Howard Taft about becoming the first commissioner of baseball: Johnson and Stout, *Red Sox Century*, p. 138.

97. "Looks Like He's Playing Lone Hand": Ibid.

98. "The players can sign": Ibid.

98. "eliminate the evil of playing double-headers": Lynch, *Harry Frazee, Ban Johnson and the Feud That Nearly Destroyed the American League*, p. 66.

98. "foolish piece of legislation": Ibid.

99. "Certified information": Johnson and Stout, *Red Sox Century*, p. 138.

99. "a war of extermination": Ibid., p. 139.

101. And there was yet one more ugly little factor to consider: For a detailed discussion of the belief in baseball that Frazee was Jewish, the anti-Semitic roots of the so-called Curse of the Bambino, and the impact it has since played on the way Frazee is perceived, see Glenn Stout, "A 'Curse' Born of Hate," ESPN.com, October 3, 2004; originally appeared in *Boston Baseball*, September 2004, reprinted in the *Elysian Fields Quarterly*, vol. 22, no. 4, 2005.

101. "A few years ago": "How the Jews Degraded Baseball," *Dearborn Independent*, September 10, 1921.

For a more complete discussion on the impact of the ballpark issue in regard to Fenway Park and the Polo Grounds and on the relationship between Ruppert and Frazee and their two ball clubs, see Glenn Stout, "When the Yankees Nearly Moved to Boston," ESPN.com, July 18, 2002, http://espn.go.com/mlb/s/2002/0718/1407265.html.

104. "I'll win more games playing in the outfield": Creamer, *Babe*, p. 187.

104. he cavorted with local schoolgirls: "School Girls Take Babe Ruth Coasting," *Boston Globe*, February 4, 1919.

104. broke up a fight between rowdies: "Babe Ruth Rebukes Rowdies at Dance," *Boston Globe,* February 9, 1919.

105. putting his money and his talents into "roller polo": "Ruth Now Wants to Buy a Polo Team," *Boston Globe*, March 1, 1919.

107. By showing up coated in a nice layer of fat: Spring training accounts are a composite made up primarily from daily reports in the *Boston Globe* and *Boston Post*, as are descriptions over the course of the season.

108. Plant Field: Information on Plant Field is gleaned primarily from http://www.tampapix.com/plantfield.htm; a close examination of period pictures; and author's visit to Tampa in February 2015.

109. "leaned on it": *Boston Post,* April 4, 1918.

110. "Ruth Drives Giants to Defeat": *Tampa Tribune*, April 4, 1919.

110. "After the game, Youngs marked": Edward Grant Barrow with James M. Kahn, *My Fifty Years in Baseball* (New York: Coward-McCann, 1951), p. 101.

113. "Babe doesn't feel right yet": *Boston Globe*, April 14, 1919.

114. "The Red Sox are a great ball team": *Boston Post*, April 19, 1919.

114. "next longest wallop": *Boston Globe*, April 20, 1919.

115. "hit into a hundred double plays": Creamer, *Babe*, p. 190.

6. Rebellion and Revolution

116. "As a batter, Ruth is an accident": John E. Dreifort, *Baseball History from Outside the Lines: A Reader* (Lincoln: University of Nebraska Press, 2001), p. 133.

118. "struck a hard spot on the turf": *Boston Post*, April 24, 1919.

119. When he saw Ruth at the park the next day: The description of Ruth's confrontation with Barrow is a composite created from the accounts that appear in Barrow, *My Fifty Years in Baseball*; Creamer, *Babe*; and Wagenheim, *Babe Ruth*.

125. "the longest fly ever caught": *Boston Globe*, July 1, 1919.

127. Carl Mays became unglued: The Carl Mays controversy gets a thorough retelling in Johnson and Stout, *Red Sox Century*; and Lynch, *Harry Frazee, Ban Johnson and the Feud That Nearly Destroyed the American League*.

127. "permanent toothache": Carl Mays vignette by Allan Wood, http://sabr.org/bioproj/person/99ca7c89.

128. "I'll never pitch another ball": Lynch, *Harry Frazee, Ban Johnson and the Feud That Nearly Destroyed the American League*, p. 75.

128. "Mays Refuses": *Boston Post,* July 20, 1919.

130. "Barrow Responsible for Red Sox Downward Slide," *Boston Post*, July 21, 1919.

131. "Fritz apparently forgot": *Boston Globe*, July 19, 1919. The story was written by an anonymous Cleveland stringer.

132. And Lee Fohl lost his job: Untitled story, *Boston Globe*, July 20, 1919, p. 10.

133. there were shows in production and contracts to be filled: The Internet Broadway Database, imbd.com, contains detailed information on all of Harry Frazee's Broadway shows, including length of run, dates, theaters, number of performances, and so forth. Even a cursory search for Frazee on the Web site provides ample evidence of his success as a theatrical entrepreneur over nearly three decades.

135. "This action of Johnson's is a joke": Johnson and Stout, *Red Sox Century*, p. 142.

135. "war to the knife": *New York Tribune*, August 1, 1919.

140. "Babe Ruth Act": *Boston Globe,* August 27, 1919.

140. "lured by the reputation": *Boston Post*, September 2, 1919.

143. Although later held up as an example of the "rape" of the Red Sox: Most of the

misinformation and framing of Harry Frazee as a financial failure who purposely "raped" the Red Sox for his financial gain can be attributed to the influence of Frederick Lieb's *The Boston Red Sox* (New York: G. P. Putnam's, 1947). Lieb credits Mel Webb for coining the phrase "the rape of the Red Sox" and presents an incomplete and thoroughly one-sided portrait of Frazee that may be colored by Lieb's belief in a variety of fringe, spiritualist religions with anti-Semitic leanings (Lieb authored several books on spiritualism). A more complete version appears on the author's Web site, www.glennstout.net. Interestingly, Frazee's archive incudes a letter from Lieb asking for free tickets for he and his wife to attend a show. Lieb miscasts many of the trades between the Red Sox and Yankees. As demonstrated by subsequent research, including Steve Steinberg's "The Curse of the . . . Hurlers?," *Baseball Research Journal* 35, at the time of the trades, most were equitable. Most of the mistruths regarding the Ruth sale received wide distribution in Dan Shaughnessy's discredited *The Curse of the Bambino* (New York: Dutton, 1990). Later reduced to shorthand by a generation of journalists and self-confessed Red Sox fans eager to preserve franchise myths, an even more misleading account of baseball history emerged.

143. "the ball never got by": *Boston Globe*, September 2, 1919.

144. "It is not often": Ibid.

145. "Babe Ruth Equals Home Run Record": *Boston Globe*, September 6, 1919.

145. "I could never hit like Ruth": *Boston Globe*, September 9, 1919.

146. "put out of baseball": Lynch, *Harry Frazee, Ban Johnson and the Feud That Nearly Destroyed the American League*, p. 94.

148. "Rome may have been": *Boston Globe*, September 21, 1919.

149. Then came the ceremonies: Details of the between-game ceremonies for Ruth are described here: "Detail for Ruth Ceremonies," *Boston Globe*, September 20, 1919.

150. "attend to your police duties": Ibid.

7. The Insurrectos

155. "A rabbit didn't have to think": Smelser, *The Life That Ruth Built*, p. 172.

156. "barrels of shekels": *Boston Globe*, October 7, 1919.

157. "many of the present seats": *Boston Globe*, October 24, 1919.

159. the race driver Barney Oldfield: Lynch, *Harry Frazee, Ban Johnson and the Feud That Nearly Destroyed the American League*, p. 88.

160. "did not evince": Johnson and Stout, *Red Sox Century*, p. 144.

160. "a blow from which": Ibid.

161. a dinner sponsored by the Knights of Columbus: *Boston Globe*, October 15, 1919.

162. "was played up like a movie actor" and other quotes and descriptions from Ruth's California trip: "No Excuse for Not Knowing Babe's IT," *The Sporting News*, November 13, 1919.

162. "I feel I made a bad move": *Boston Globe*, October 25, 1919.

162. "Frazee knows what I want": *Boston Globe*, November 4, 1919.

164. "Then presumably there will be another lawsuit": Johnson and Stout, *Red Sox Century*, p. 211.

164. "the Pipe Dream League": *The Sporting News*, November 13, 1919.

165. Frazee, however, likely had the money: The Harry H. Frazee Collection contains a letter from the theatrical firm Sanger and Jordan dated in January of 1920 asking the price to take *My Lady Friends* to Europe. Another letter dated November 11, 1919, offers $8,000 for the world motion picture rights to Frazee's production *A Good Bad Woman*.

166. "Big Baseball Trades Due": *Boston Globe*, December 7, 1919.

166. "had been analyzing the celebrated Mays case": *The Sporting News*, November 27, 1919.

8. For Sale

171. the Giants were in pursuit of St. Louis Cardinals infielder Rogers Hornsby: In regard to McGraw's $70,000 bid for Rogers Hornsby, see Jonathan Damore, *Hornsby: A Biography*, (Westport, Conn.: Greenwood, 2004).

173. Ruppert had already indicated he'd pay as much as $150,000.00 for Ruth: Lynch, *Harry Frazee, Ban Johnson and the Feud That Nearly Destroyed the American League*, p. 112.

176. "losing Ruth is bad enough": Barrow, *My Fifty Years in Baseball*, p. 108.

178. "I had in mind that if you did not take": Letter dated January 12, 1920, from Thomas J. Barry, Frazee's attorney, to Frazee in the Harry H. Frazee Collection.

179. "BABE RUTH IN MARKET FOR TRADE": *Boston Post,* December 20, 1919.

180. The five-page contract transferring Ruth to the Yankees: The original sale document detailing the transfer of Ruth from Boston to New York has been widely reproduced. The bulk of the contract is a standard agreement governing such transactions.

181. The agreement to secure a first mortgage on Fenway Park: The author acquired a copy of the original mortgage document from the Frazee family and is dated May 25, 1920. The Purchase and Sale document for Frazee's acquisition of Fenway Park is in the Harry H. Frazee Collection and is dated May 3, 1920.

182. While it is true that *Nanette* was based on an earlier show, *My Lady Friends*: First print mention of Frazee's intention to turn *My Lady Friends* into a musical appears in the *New York Clipper* on October 25, 1922.

183. The subsequent meeting: Standard retelling of Ruth's first meeting with Huggins appears in Creamer, *Babe*, pp. 211–13.

183. "I am not surprised": *New York Tribune*, January 5, 1920.

9. Welcome to New York

185. "I told you Boston was some town": *The Annotated Stories of Ring Lardner* (Palo Alto, Calif.: Stanford University Press, 1997), p. 81.

186. reaction to the sale: For more detailed reaction to the trade of Ruth, see Johnson and Stout, *Red Sox Century*; and Johnson and Stout, *Yankees Century*.

187. "For Sale" cartoon: *Boston Herald*, January 7, 1920.

187. "The Bull in Frazee's China Shop": Cartoon, *Boston Post*, January 7, 1920.

243. "We can't manage him": Cartoon, "Officer Call a Cop," *Boston Herald*, January 8, 1920.

187. "I figure the Red Sox is now practically ruined": *Boston American,* January 5, 1920.

188. "this is not the first time": *Boston Post*, January 6, 1920.

188. "it is believed": Ibid.

189. "Ruth had become simply impossible": Ibid.

190. Although Frazee would later release: Harry Frazee, "The Reasons That Led Me to Sell the 'Babe,'" *Baseball Magazine*, April 1920, p. 626.

191. In fact, they even had a name for it, the old "hoodoo": The Yankees' long history of jinxes over their first fifteen years known as the "hoodoo" is discussed in Johnson and Stout, *Yankees Century.*

191. "But how that gorilla glanded baby": *New York American*, January 6, 1920.

192. One in the *New York Evening Journal* showed him as a Colossus: Cartoon, "The Catch of the Season," *New York Evening Journal,* January 5, 1920.

192. "We'll sure make life miserable": *New York Tribune*, January 7, 1920.

193. "Just what homerless germ": *New York Tribune,* January 13, 1920.

193. "Babe is willing": *New York Tribune*, January 13, 1920.

194. "Frazee is not good enough": *New York Times*, January 16, 1920.

195. "bosh": *New York Times*, January 23, 1920.

10. The "Infant Swatigy"

197. "Everybody interested or connected": "An Awful Thing if Ruth Should Fail," *The Sporting News*, January 12, 1920.

198. "After we got away for the spring training": Babe Ruth and William R. Cobb, *Playing the Game: My Early Years in Baseball,* edited by Paul Dickson, p. 60.

199. Jacksonville itself: For background on life in Jacksonville circa 1920, see Ennis Davis and Robert Mann, *"Reclaiming Jacksonville: Stories Behind the River City's Historic Landmarks* (Charleston, S.C.: History Press, 2012).

200. "has a long drive": *New York Herald*, March 2, 1920.

200. "the first official motion": *New York American,* March 2, 1920.

200. "all our life we have been so poor": *New York American,* March 3, 1920.

201. "When I had a chance to take a gander": McNeil, *The Evolution of Pitching in Major League Baseball*, p. 60.

201. "a bagful of Babe's own": *New York Times*, March 13, 1920.

202. "his swings cutting the air": *New York Times*, March 17, 1920.

203. "Ruth figures it's the second hardest": *New York Times*, March 20, 1920.

203. "What a swat it was": *New York American,* March 20, 1920.

203. "a big piece of cheese": *New York Times*, March 21, 1920.

204. "he leaned against it": *New York Tribune*, April 2, 1920.

204. "The approximate point of exodus": *New York American*, April 2, 1920.

204. "all doubt as to whether": *New York Daily News*, April 2, 1920.

204. they had assigned a single reporter, Marshall Hunt, to cover Ruth: Wagenheim, *Babe Ruth*, includes interviews with Marshall Hunt that shed light on the reporting on Ruth in the era. For more on sportswriting during this period, see Jerome Holtzman, ed., *No Cheering in the Press Box* (New York: Henry Holt, 1973).

206. "so far over the heads": *New York Tribune*, April 9, 1920.

206. "BABE RUTH ROBBED OF TRIO OF HOMERS": *New York Times*, April 9, 1920.

206. "war between the Yankees and Ban Johnson": *New York Tribune*, April 12, 1920.

206. "Baseball Park, a Stronghold of Free Speech": *New York Times*, April 11, 1920.

207. "joyous moment": *New York Tribune*, April 12, 1920.

11. A New Day

209. "You've probably heard the good news": *New York American,* April 14, 1920.

209. Still, 12,000 fans turned out for Opening Day: Game events of the 1920 season are composites re-created primarily through game reports in the *New York Times* and the *New York Tribune*. In general, they are also the most authoritative—reporters James Harrison of the *Times* and W. O. "Bill" McGeehan of the *Tribune* were two of the most respected beat writers of their era. Reports in other New York papers of this period, while certainly colorful, are sometimes lacking in detail.

211. "The situation": *New York Daily News*, April 15, 1920.

211. "The crowd went wild": *New York Tribune*, April 16, 1920.

212. "neither conquered nor celebrated": *Boston Globe*, April 20, 1920.

213. "chasing Pennock's slow rounders": *Boston Globe,* April 21, 1920.

216. "the old hoodoo": *New York Times,* April 23, 1920.

217. "In this regard": *New York Tribune*, April 24, 1920.

218. "I swung as hard as I ever swung": *New York Tribune*, April 29, 1920.

12. Making the Sale

220. "The Babe Ruth roar": *New York Times*, May 1, 1920.

222. "Ruth strolled to the plate": *New York World*, May 2, 1920.

223. "At what was known in the old days": *New York Times*, May 3, 1920.

223. "Babe needs only twenty-eight more": *New York Times*, May 4, 1920.

225. "Naturally the question arises": *New York Times*, May 13, 1920.

227. "Babe Ruth Makes Sick Ball Game Well": *New York Tribune*, May 24, 1920.

227. "violent health": *New York Times,* May 24, 1920.

228. "Cobb is a prick": The earliest reference I could find for this quote cites a "New York sportswriter," in William Curran, *Big Sticks: The Phenomenal Decade of Ruth, Gehrig, Cobb, and Hornsby* (New York: HarperPerennial, 1991). This underscores the

problem with the veracity of Ruth's quotes, for the language would never have been used in a New York newspaper.

13. The Babe

231. "A Modern Goliath of the bludgeon": *New York Times*, June 3, 1920.

233. "a ball so high": *New York Times*, June 2, 1920.

233. "He is hitting them harder": *New York Times,* June 3, 1920.

234. "the amazing growth of home runs": *New York Tribune*, June 4, 1920.

234. "the masterminds that control baseball": Richard Bak, *Peach: Ty Cobb in His Time and Ours* (Sports Media Group, 2005), p. 121.

239. "There was some speculation": *New York Tribune*, July 12, 1920.

240. "lured by the prospect": *New York Tribune,* July 13, 1920.

240. "Idols are made of Clay": *New York American,* July 21, 1920.

240. "an ovation befitting a King": *New York Daily News*, July 21, 1920.

241. There was talk afterward that the home run had earned Ruth a movie deal: Background information on Ruth's film career and litigation in 1920 is from *Reel Baseball: Essays and Interviews on the National Pastime and Hollywood* (Jefferson, N.C.: McFarland, 2003).

242. "It looks very much": *New York Tribune*, July 26, 1920.

243. But the game would go down in baseball history: Mike Sowell's *The Pitch That Killed* (New York: Macmillan, 1989) remains the definitive work on the death of Ray Chapman.

245. *Headin' Home*: Several versions of Ruth's film are on YouTube, and the film is also commercially available for purchase. The shots filmed inside the Polo Grounds justify watching the film.

245. "Jersey Jiggers": *New York Tribune*, August 28, 1920.

247. "the greatest pickler": *New York Times*, September 25, 1920.

248. The Yankees earned a pretax profit: Figures regarding the Yankees' profitability are from Michael Haupert and Kenneth Winter, "Pay Ball, Estimating the Profitability of the New York Yankees, 1915–1937," in *Essays in Economic and Business History*, 2003.

249. "money-making scheme": Lyle Spatz and Steve Steinberg, *1921: The Yankees, the Giants, and the Battle for Baseball Supremacy in New York* (Lincoln: University of Nebraska Press, 2012), p. 71.

Epilogue: Closing the Sale

254. Late in 1920, Walsh met Ruth: For details of Christy Walsh's meeting with Ruth, see Creamer, *Babe*; Montville, *The Big Bam*; and Christy Walsh, *Adios to Ghosts* (Self-published, 1937).

255. It promised that Walsh: The quotations from the contract appear from a document described as "1921 First Partnership Between Babe Ruth & Christy Walsh Signed Document," that was made available for auction in 2010.

Bibliography

Notes on Sources

Although Babe Ruth may be the best known figure in the history of baseball, that does not mean that the details of his biography have been fully explored, or even that what we do know does not still contain questions, gaps, and uncertainties. In fact, Ruth's own outsized personality and accomplishments have, in some areas, served to obscure his biography. Certain aspects of his life—his upbringing, his performance in 1927, his "called shot," and other notable events—have been fully explored, yet others have been almost ignored or overlooked.

The years covered in this book, 1918 through 1920, have nearly been skipped over in many treatments of Ruth as biographers have rushed into the Yankee years at the expense of his final seasons in Boston. For that reason—as well as the author's preference and desire to produce original work—this book is built far more from period newspaper accounts that it is from previous biographies, which were generally only consulted in regard to basic information and time frames.

In most significant instances I have noted important newspaper sources in the text itself, although for variety and ease of reading I have occasionally simply referred to "a newspaper account" or "a reporter," but all such direct quotes from previously published sources, including newspapers, are referenced by date and source in these notes. Please note that events of individual games are in many cases composites, re-created with bits of information from a number of sources. Researchers should keep in mind that game reports are generally dated one day after the game in question took place. Due to the vagaries of reporting and the fallibility of game reports at the time, some accounts are often contradictory in specific detail, e.g., one report may refer to a hit as a "fly ball," and another may refer to it as a "line drive." In these instances, I have tried to discern the most trustworthy report and have used my judgment.

I have previously written about many of the events in baseball during the 1918, 1919, and 1920 seasons in several other books, namely *Red Sox Century*, *Yankees Century*, *The Dodgers*, and *The Cubs*, and numerous articles. I have also written extensively about the cultural life of Boston in *Fenway 1912* and New York in *Young Woman and the Sea* (see below for complete citations of these books and others during the research of this volume). I refer the reader to these earlier works when a particular point is more fully explicated there. In instances where the facts and conclusions of this book differ from those of my earlier published work, the reader should depend upon my most recent conclusions. History is cumulative, and this retelling takes advantage of not only my earlier research, but material not available in these earlier works.

Major newspapers consulted for this project, virtually on a daily basis, included the *Boston Globe, Boston Post, New York Tribune* (the *Herald Tribune* beginning in 1924), and *New York Times.* Other newspapers that were the subject of more targeted research include the *Boston Herald* (in 1918 known as *Boston Herald and Journal*), *Boston American, New York World, New York Daily News, New York Mirror, New York Sun, New York American* and *New York Evening Journal.* I also consulted the weekly *Sporting News* during this period and the monthly *Baseball Magazine.* The *Boston Globe, New York Tribune, New York Times,* and *Boston Post* are available online, although much of my earlier research from these sources was conducted from microfilm. The other significant newspaper sources cited can only be accessed through microfilm. I generally used files available at the Boston Public Library, New York Public Library, and my own extensive clip files accumulated over the past thirty years during which time I have been writing and publishing sports history, during which I have also made trips to the library at the National Baseball Hall of Fame in Cooperstown, New York. On occasion, other newspaper sources were consulted on newpaperarchives.com and newslibrary.com.

There is also no substantive, comprehensive archival collection in regard to Babe Ruth consisting of personal letters, journals, etc., that allow us to know, definitively, what Ruth thought or believed about many aspects of his career. Generally speaking, Babe Ruth "collections" consist primarily of memorabilia. As stated elsewhere, Ruth made very few public statements in regard to the period of his life covered by this volume, and most statements of any kind assigned to Ruth were almost always penned by ghostwriters, often with no input from Ruth whatsoever. The writer of history is left to write about Ruth primarily through his on-field acts and in reflection, through the impressions of others. Fortunately, nearly everyone whose life intersected with Ruth formed an impression. The basic details of Ruth's biography were gleaned from the standard Ruth biographies, most prominently Robert Creamer's *Babe: The Legend Comes to Life* and Kal Wagenheim's *Babe Ruth: His Life and Legend.* I found them superior and more useful than either of the other two other substantive Ruth biographies, Martin Smelser's *The Life That Ruth Built* and Leigh Montville's *The Big Bam.*

In combination, three books cover the 1918 season rather completely, Allan Wood's *1918*, Kerry Keene, Ray Sinibaldi, and David Hickey's *The Babe in Red Stockings,* and Ty Waterman and Mel Springer's *The Year the Red Sox Won the World Series,* which is more or less a scrapbook of newspaper clippings. All three were useful. The war between Harry Frazee and Ban Johnson is described in detail in Michael T. Lynch Jr.'s *Harry Frazee, Ban Johnson and the Feud That Nearly Destroyed the American League.* Previously published literature on the New York Yankees that was particularly helpful includes *The Colonel and Hug: The Partnership That Transformed the New York Yankees* by Steve

Steinberg and Lyle Spatz. Oddly enough, no previous books have been written that take as their direct subject the 1918, 1919, and 1920 seasons, when the Dead Ball Era ended and the Lively Ball Era began. The author also accumulated an extensive clip file on Jacob Ruppert and many principal figures with both the Yankees and the Red Sox while researching *Red Sox Century, Yankees Century,* and other historical baseball books.

The Harry H. Frazee Collection is part of the Performing Arts Collection held at the Harry Ransom Center at the University of Texas in Austin. The massive collection consists of more than forty linear feet of material—forty-five document boxes, forty-three oversized boxes, and two oversized folders, containing hundreds of thousands, if not millions, of pages of documents. Apparently sold to the university by the family of a Frazee employee (the university considers its provenance confidential), the collection is both critical to an understanding of Frazee and frustrating. As described in the finding aid, the collection "contains typescript and manuscript plays; actors' sides; scripts and lyric sheets for *No, No, Nanette* and *Yes, Yes, Yvette*; telegrams, letters, cards and other correspondence; orchestra parts, orchestrations, and printed music for *No No Nanette* and *Yes Yes Yvette*; scrapbooks, booking registers, checkbooks, clippings; financial records of productions; real estate papers, bills, financial and theatrical correspondence, taxes, legal documents, contracts for productions, Longacre Theater construction, etc.; checkbooks; accounts, ledgers, photographs, and other papers relating to Frazee's ownership of the American League Boston Red Sox baseball team, 1916–1923; and miscellaneous oversize materials." Baseball-related material is confined primarily to one document box. Since the provenance of the collection is uncertain, there is no way to determine if what exists is complete or if it was culled or stripped. For that reason, there is no real way to judge the meaning of the incomplete material that remains. For instance, the collection includes Frazee's income tax "worksheets," but not the returns themselves, ledgers of plays, but not for every production, stock certificates for nearly a dozen corporations created by Frazee, but little information about them. There is hardly any information of a personal nature. Thus it is extremely difficult to reach a definitive conclusion about anything based on the material in the collection, in particular an accurate picture of Frazee's finances, which were never static. For this reason, I have not based my conclusions, particularly in regards to Frazee's finances, solely upon the records found in this collection. Rather, I have used them in context, to inform the circumstantial evidence of Frazee's lifestyle and activities as reported in newspapers, magazines, and other sources over the course of his career.

While researching this book, I spent four complete days in the Ransom Center and personally viewed the contents of every box apart from those that according to the finding aid included only sheet music and theatrical manuscripts. My conclusions are based on this research, the written evidence in period newspaper accounts, and my own thirty years doing historical sports research. It is particularly frustrating that so little of Frazee's corporate records appear to exist, which would provide a fuller dimension of his business career, but even more so that his baseball records are so incomplete. Frazee owned the Red Sox from 1917 to 1923, and it is extremely difficult to come to any definitive conclusion on that time period based on the contents of one single box consisting of perhaps five hundred assorted pages of documents.

The Eugene C. Murdock Baseball Collection at the Cleveland Public Library contains three scrapbooks apparently maintained by Frazee. Unfortunately, two only contain clippings subsequent to the sale of Ruth and a third was apparently stolen and is now listed as missing. In all likelihood, the bulk of Frazee's other financial records were lost or destroyed after his death and the bulk of his records with the Red Sox, like most of the other early historical records of the team, were apparently discarded during the Fenway Park renovation of 1933 and 1934 after the team was purchased by Thomas A. Yawkey. At the time, corporate records of baseball as a business were little valued, and the memorabilia market had yet to exist.

Although the Frazee family and heirs retain little original material pertaining to Frazee, the author did have the opportunity to interview Frazee's grandson Harry a number of years ago, and the family has shared a handful of useful documents, among them the sale agreement detailing Harry Frazee's ultimate purchase of Fenway Park in May of 1920.

Unless noted otherwise, statistics used throughout have been gleaned from baseball -reference.com. Yearly and league attendance figures are from *Total Baseball* (third edition). Ballpark information, particularly in terms of dimensions of the major league ballparks mentioned, is from Philip Lowry's *Green Cathedrals* and ballpark data and drawings maintained at www.andrewclem.com.

All dialogue in this book is taken from a previously published source, and anything that appears in quotation marks is from a written document. Absolutely no dialogue has been created or invented or surmised, but the reader and research should be aware that in regard to Ruth, particularly in the period covered by this book and before, all statements by Ruth himself should be taken with a grain of salt. At this juncture, it is virtually impossible to determine with any certainty whether Ruth actually spoke any of the words now credited to him. Newspaper reporting at the time rarely quoted players directly, and ghostwriters have always found Ruth a tempting subject to embellish.

The author would like to extend special thanks to the research staffs at the Boston Public Library and Harry Ransom Center at the University of Texas and researcher Zach Ripple.

Selected Books

Alexander, Charles. *John McGraw*. New York: Viking, 1988.

———. *Our Game: An American Baseball History*. New York: MJF Books, 1991.

Antonucci, Thomas J., and Eric Caren. *Newspaper Reports About Big League Baseball in the Big Apple: New York Yankees from 1901 to 1964*. Verplanck, N.Y.: Historical Briefs, 1995.

Barrow, Edward Grant, with James M. Kahn. *My Fifty Years in Baseball*. New York: Coward-McCann, 1951.

Benson, Michael. *Ballparks of North America: A Comprehensive Historical Reference to Baseball Grounds, Yards, and Stadiums, 1845 to Present.* Jefferson, N.C.: McFarland, 1989.

Caren, Eric. *New York Extra.* Edison, N.J.: Castle, 2000.

Creamer, Robert W. *Babe: The Legend Comes to Life.* New York: Simon & Schuster, 1992.

Damore, Jonathan. *Hornsby: A Biography,* Westport, Conn.: Greenwood, 2004.

Gay, Tim. *Tris Speaker: The Rough-and-Tumble Life of a Baseball Legend.* Guilford, Conn.: Lyons/University of Nebraska Press, 2007.

Ginsburg, Daniel E. *The Fix Is In: A History of Baseball Gambling and Game Fixing Scandals.* Jefferson, N.C.: McFarland, 1995.

Gutlon, Jerry. *It Was Never About The Babe*: New York, Skyhorse, 2009

Johnson, Richard, ed., text by Glenn Stout. *The Cubs.* Boston: Houghton Mifflin, 2007.

———. *The Dodgers.* Boston: Houghton Mifflin, 2004.

———. *Red Sox Century.* Boston: Houghton Mifflin, 1999.

———. *Yankees Century.* Boston: Houghton Mifflin, 2002.

Jones, David, ed. *Deadball Stars of the American League.* Dulles, Va.: Potomac, 2006.

Keene, Kerry, et al. *The Babe in Red Stockings.* Champaign, Ill.: Sagamore, 1997.

Levitt, Daniel R. *Ed Barrow.* Lincoln, Neb.: University of Nebraska Press, 2008

Lieb, Frederick. *Baseball As I Have Known It.* New York: Coward, McCann & Geoghegan, 1977.

———. *The Boston Red Sox.* New York: G. P. Putnam's, 1947.

———. *Connie Mack: Grand Old Man of Baseball.* New York: G. P. Putnam's, 1945.

Lowry, Philip. *Green Cathedrals.* Reading, Mass.: Addison-Wesley, 1992.

Lynch, Michael T., Jr. *Harry Frazee, Ban Johnson and the Feud That Nearly Destroyed the American League.* Jefferson, N.C.: McFarland, 2008.

Macht, Norman L. *Connie Mack and the Early Years of Baseball.* Lincoln: University of Nebraska Press, 2007.

Mack, Connie. *My 66 Years in the Big Leagues.* Philadelphia: John C. Winston, 1950.

McNeil, William F. *The Evolution of Pitching in Major League Baseball.* Jefferson, N.C.: McFarland, 2006.

Montville, Leigh *The Big Bam: The Life and Times of Babe Ruth.* New York: Broadway, 2006.

Murdock, Eugene. *Ban Johnson: Czar of Baseball.* Westport, Conn.: Greenwood, 1982.

Nash, Peter J. *Boston's Royal Rooters.* Charleston, S.C.: Arcadia, 2005.

Neft, David S., and Richard Cohen. *The Sports Encyclopedia: Baseball.* New York: St. Martin's, 1997.

Nowlin, Bill, ed. *When Boston Still Had the Babe.* Burlington, Mass.: Rounder, 2008.

Ritter, Lawrence. *The Glory of Their Times.* New York: Macmillan, 1984.

Seymour, Harold. *Baseball—The Early Years.* New York: Oxford University Press, 1960.

———. *Baseball—The Golden Age.* New York: Oxford University Press, 1971.

Smelser, Martin. *The Life That Ruth Built.* New York: Quadrangle/New York Times, 1975.

Steinberg, Steven, and Lyle Spatz. *The Colonel and Hug: The Partnership That Transformed the New York Yankees.* Lincoln: University of Nebraska Press, 2015.

Stout, Glenn. *Fenway 1912.* Boston: Houghton Mifflin Harcourt, 2011.

Stout, Glenn, ed. *Impossible Dreams: A Red Sox Collection.* Boston: Houghton Mifflin, 2003.

Stout, Glenn, *Young Woman and the Sea.* Boston: Houghton Mifflin, 2009.

Thomas, Henry W. *Walter Johnson: Baseball's Big Train.* Bison, 1998.

Thorn, John, and Pete Palmer, eds. *Total Baseball.* New York: Harper/Perennial; third ed., 1993.

Voigt, David Q. *American Baseball, Volumes I, II, and III.* Norman: University of Oklahoma Press, 1983.

Wagenheim, Kal. *Babe Ruth: His Life and Legend.* New York: Henry Holt, 1974.

Waterman, Ty, and Mel Springer. *The Year the Red Sox Won the World Series.* Boston: Northeastern University Press, 1999.

Wood, Allan. *1918: Babe Ruth and the World Champion Red Sox.* New York: Writers Club, 2000.

Zingg, Paul. *Harry Hooper: An American Baseball Life.* Urbana: University of Illinois Press, 1993.

Notable Articles

Lane, F. C. "Fire Brand of the American League." *Baseball Magazine*, March 1918.

———. "Hero of the Series." *Baseball Magazine,* November 1918.

Steinberg, Steve. "The Curse of the . . . Hurlers?" *Baseball Research Journal*, Vol. 35.

Stout, Glenn. "1918." *Boston Magazine*, October 1987.

———. "A 'Curse' Born of Hate." ESPN.com, October 3, 2004. Originally appeared in *Boston Baseball*, September 2004. Reprinted in *Elysian Fields Quarterly*, Vol. 22, No. 4, 2005, http://sports.espn.go.com/mlb/playoffs2004/news/story?page =Curse041005.

———. The Last Champions." *New England Sports*, Summer 1993.

———. "When the Yankees Nearly Moved to Boston." ESPN.com, July 18, 2002, http:// espn.go.com/mlb/s/2002/0718/1407265.html.

Special Collections

George Edward "Duffy" Lewis Collection. A scrapbook of items on Red Sox left fielder Lewis. Microtext Department, the Boston Tradition in Sports Collection, Boston Public Library.

Harry H. Frazee Collection, Performing Arts Collection held at the Harry Ransom Center at the University of Texas in Austin, Texas.

Michael T. "Nuf Ced" McGreevey Collection. Donated by this owner of a Columbus Avenue saloon, this collection consists of more than 170 photographs of professional baseball in Boston and personal scrapbooks from the 1890s to 1912. Originally displayed at McGreevey's tavern, Third Base, the photographs form the largest collection of its kind. The scrapbooks have been microfilmed and are on call number: GV865. M29A3, the Boston Tradition in Sports Collection, Boston Public Library.

Online Resources

Baseballalmanac.com
Baseballfever.com. Researcher Bill Burgess maintains a remarkable archive of biographical information on American baseball and sportswriters on this Web site.
Baseball-reference.com
Bioproj.sabr.org
RedSox.com
Yankees.com

Babe Ruth Home Run Log

1915 through 1920

HR #	DATE	TEAM	PITCHER (L/R)	OPPONENT	BALLPARK
1	05/06/1915	BOS	Jack Warhop (R)	at New York Yankees	Polo Grounds
2	06/02/1915	BOS	Jack Warhop (R)	at New York Yankees	Polo Grounds
3	06/25/1915	BOS	Ray Caldwell (R)	vs . New York Yankees	Fenway Park
4	07/21/1915	BOS	Bill H. James (R)	at St. Louis Browns	Sportsman's Park
5	06/09/1916	BOS	Jean Dubuc (R)	at Detroit Tigers	Navin Field
6	06/12/1916	BOS	Jim Park (R)	at St. Louis Browns	Sportsman's Park
7	06/13/1916	BOS	Dave Davenport (R)	at St. Louis Browns	Sportsman's Park
8	08/10/1917	BOS	Bill H. James (R)	vs . Detroit Tigers	Fenway Park
9	09/15/1917	BOS	Ed Monroe (R)	at New York Yankees	Polo Grounds
10	05/04/1918	BOS	Allan Russell (R)	at New York Yankees	Polo Grounds
11	05/06/1918	BOS	George Mogridge (L)	at New York Yankees	Polo Grounds
12	05/07/1918	BOS	Walter Johnson (R)	at Washington Senators	National Park
13	06/02/1918	BOS	Eric Erickson (R)	at Detroit Tigers	Navin Field
14	06/03/1918	BOS	Hooks Dauss (R)	at Detroit Tigers	Navin Field
15	06/04/1918	BOS	Bill H. James (R)	at Detroit Tigers	Navin Field
16	06/05/1918	BOS	Johnny Enzmann (R)	at Cleveland Indians	League Park
17	06/15/1918	BOS	Tom Rogers (R)	at St. Louis Browns	Sportsman's Park
18	06/25/1918	BOS	Allan Russell (R)	at New York Yankees	Polo Grounds
19	06/28/1918	BOS	Harry Harper (L)	at Washington Senators	National Park
20	06/30/1918	BOS	Walter Johnson (R)	at Washington Senators	National Park
21	04/23/1919	BOS	George Mogridge (L)	at New York Yankees	Polo Grounds
22	05/20/1919	BOS	Dave Davenport (R)	at St. Louis Browns	Sportsman's Park
23	05/30/1919	BOS	Scott Perry (R)	at Philadelphia Athletics	Shibe Park
24	06/07/1919	BOS	Hooks Dauss (R)	vs . Detroit Tigers	Fenway Park
25	06/17/1919	BOS	Guy Morton Sr. (R)	vs . Cleveland Indians	Fenway Park
26	06/24/1919	BOS	Dick Robertson (R)	vs . Washington Senators	Fenway Park
27	06/30/1919	BOS	Bob Shawkey (R)	at New York Yankees	Polo Grounds
28	07/05/1919	BOS	Jing Johnson (R)	vs . Philadelphia Athletics	Fenway Park

HR #	DATE	TEAM	PITCHER (L/R)	OPPONENT	BALLPARK
29	07/05/1919	BOS	Jing Johnson (R)	vs . Philadelphia Athletics	Fenway Park
30	07/10/1919	BOS	Urban Shocker (R)	at St. Louis Browns	Sportsman's Park
31	07/12/1919	BOS	Dave Danforth (L)	at Chicago White Sox	Comiskey Park
32	07/18/1919	BOS	Hi Jasper (R)	at Cleveland Indians	League Park
33	07/18/1919	BOS	Fritz Coumbe (L)	at Cleveland Indians	League Park
34	07/21/1919	BOS	Howard Ehmke (R)	at Detroit Tigers	Navin Field
35	07/24/1919	BOS	Bob Shawkey (R)	vs . New York Yankees	Fenway Park
36	07/29/1919	BOS	Dutch Leonard (L)	vs . Detroit Tigers	Fenway Park
37	08/14/1919	BOS	Dickie Kerr (L)	at Chicago White Sox	Comiskey Park
38	08/16/1919	BOS	Erskine Mayer (R)	at Chicago White Sox	Comiskey Park
39	08/17/1919	BOS	Urban Shocker (R)	at St. Louis Browns	Sportsman's Park
40	08/23/1919	BOS	Hooks Dauss (R)	at Detroit Tigers	Navin Field
41	08/24/1919	BOS	Doc Ayers (R)	at Detroit Tigers	Navin Field
42	08/24/1919	BOS	Slim Love (L)	at Detroit Tigers	Navin Field
43	08/25/1919	BOS	Dutch Leonard (L)	at Detroit Tigers	Navin Field
44	09/01/1919	BOS	Jim Shaw (R)	vs . Washington Senators	Fenway Park
45	09/05/1919	BOS	Wynn Noyes (R)	at Philadelphia Athletics	Shibe Park
46	09/08/1919	BOS	Hank Thormahlen (L)	at New York Yankees	Polo Grounds
47	09/20/1919	BOS	Lefty Williams (L)	vs . Chicago White Sox	Fenway Park
48	09/24/1919	BOS	Bob Shawkey (R)	at New York Yankees	Polo Grounds
49	09/27/1919	BOS	Rip Jordan (R)	at Washington Senators	National Park
50	05/01/1920	NYY	Herb Pennock (L)	vs . Boston Red Sox	Polo Grounds
51	05/02/1920	NYY	Sad Sam Jones (R)	vs . Boston Red Sox	Polo Grounds
52	05/11/1920	NYY	Roy Wilkinson (R)	vs . Chicago White Sox	Polo Grounds
53	05/11/1920	NYY	Dickie Kerr (L)	vs . Chicago White Sox	Polo Grounds
54	05/12/1920	NYY	Lefty Williams (L)	vs . Chicago White Sox	Polo Grounds
55	05/23/1920	NYY	Carl Weilman (L)	vs . St. Louis Browns	Polo Grounds
56	05/25/1920	NYY	Dutch Leonard (L)	vs . Detroit Tigers	Polo Grounds
57	05/26/1920	NYY	Hooks Dauss (R)	vs . Detroit Tigers	Polo Grounds
58	05/27/1920	NYY	Harry Harper (L)	at Boston Red Sox	Fenway Park
59	05/27/1920	NYY	Benn Karr (R)	at Boston Red Sox	Fenway Park
60	05/29/1920	NYY	Joe Bush (R)	at Boston Red Sox	Fenway Park
61	05/31/1920	NYY	Walter Johnson (R)	vs . Washington Senators	Polo Grounds
62	06/02/1920	NYY	Tom Zachary (L)	vs . Washington Senators	Polo Grounds
63	06/02/1920	NYY	Leon Carlson (R)	vs . Washington Senators	Polo Grounds
64	06/02/1920	NYY	Bill Snyder (R)	s . Washington Senators	Polo Grounds
65	06/10/1920	NYY	Frank Okrie (L)	at Detroit Tigers	Navin Field
66	06/13/1920	NYY	Elmer Myers (R)	at Cleveland Indians	League Park
67	06/16/1920	NYY	Red Faber (R)	at Chicago White Sox	Comiskey Park
68	06/17/1920	NYY	Lefty Williams (L)	at Chicago White Sox	Comiskey Park
69	06/23/1920	NYY	Urban Shocker (R)	at St. Louis Browns	Sportsman's Park

HR #	DATE	TEAM	PITCHER (L/R)	OPPONENT	BALLPARK
70	06/25/1920	NYY	Herb Pennock (L)	vs . Boston Red Sox	Polo Grounds
71	06/25/1920	NYY	Herb Pennock (L)	vs . Boston Red Sox	Polo Grounds
72	06/30/1920	NYY	Lyle Bigbee (R)	at Philadelphia Athletics	Shibe Park
73	06/30/1920	NYY	Scott Perry (R)	at Philadelphia Athletics	Shibe Park
74	07/09/1920	NYY	Red Oldham (L)	vs . Detroit Tigers	Polo Grounds
75	07/10/1920	NYY	Hooks Dauss (R)	vs . Detroit Tigers	Polo Grounds
76	07/11/1920	NYY	Howard Ehmke (R)	vs . Detroit Tigers	Polo Grounds
77	07/14/1920	NYY	Dixie Davis (R)	vs . St. Louis Browns	Polo Grounds
78	07/15/1920	NYY	Bill Burwell (R)	vs . St. Louis Browns	Polo Grounds
79	07/19/1920	NYY	Dickie Kerr (L)	vs . Chicago White Sox	Polo Grounds
80	07/19/1920	NYY	Dickie Kerr (L)	vs . Chicago White Sox	Polo Grounds
81	07/20/1920	NYY	Red Faber (R)	vs . Chicago White Sox	Polo Grounds
82	07/23/1920	NYY	Guy Morton Sr. (R)	vs . Cleveland Indians	Polo Grounds
83	07/24/1920	NYY	Jim Bagby (R)	vs . Cleveland Indians	Polo Grounds
84	07/25/1920	NYY	Waite Hoyt (R)	vs . Boston Red Sox	Polo Grounds
85	07/30/1920	NYY	Elam Vangilder (R)	at St. Louis Browns	Sportsman's Park
86	07/31/1920	NYY	Urban Shocker (R)	at St. Louis Browns	Sportsman's Park
87	08/02/1920	NYY	Lefty Williams (L)	at Chicago White Sox	Comiskey Park
88	08/05/1920	NYY	Howard Ehmke (R)	at Detroit Tigers	Navin Field
89	08/06/1920	NYY	Hooks Dauss (R)	at Detroit Tigers	Navin Field
90	08/06/1920	NYY	Hooks Dauss (R)	at Detroit Tigers	Navin Field
91	08/14/1920	NYY	Jim Shaw (R)	at Washington Senators	Griffith Stadium
92	08/19/1920	NYY	Ray Caldwell (R)	vs . Cleveland Indians	Polo Grounds
93	08/26/1920	NYY	Dickie Kerr (L)	vs . Chicago White Sox	Polo Grounds
94	09/04/1920	NYY	Sad Sam Jones (R)	at Boston Red Sox	Fenway Park
95	09/04/1920	NYY	Joe Bush (R)	at Boston Red Sox	Fenway Park
96	09/09/1920	NYY	Stan Coveleski (R)	at Cleveland Indians	League Park
97	09/10/1920	NYY	Ray Caldwell (R)	at Cleveland Indians	League Park
98	09/13/1920	NYY	Howard Ehmke (R)	at Detroit Tigers	Navin Field
99	09/24/1920	NYY	Jose Acosta (R)	vs . Washington Senators	Polo Grounds
100	09/24/1920	NYY	Jim Shaw (R)	vs . Washington Senators	Polo Grounds
101	09/27/1920	NYY	Eddie Rommel (R)	at Philadelphia Athletics	Shibe Park
102	09/27/1920	NYY	Eddie Rommel (R)	at Philadelphia Athletics	Shibe Park
103	09/29/1920	NYY	Dave Keefe (R)	at Philadelphia Athletics	Shibe Park

Index